Interdisciplinary App
to Pedagogy and Place-Based
Education

Deric Shannon • Jeffery Galle
Editors

Interdisciplinary Approaches to Pedagogy and Place-Based Education

From Abstract to the Quotidian

Editors
Deric Shannon
Emory University
Oxford, Georgia, USA

Jeffery Galle
Emory University
Oxford, Georgia, USA

ISBN 978-3-319-84445-9   ISBN 978-3-319-50621-0 (eBook)
DOI 10.1007/978-3-319-50621-0

Cover image © Westend61 GmbH/Alamy Stock Photo

Printed on acid-free paper

This Palgrave Macmillan imprint is published by Springer Nature
The registered company is Springer International Publishing AG
The registered company address is: Gewerbestrasse 11, 6330 Cham, Switzerland

ACKNOWLEDGEMENTS

Deric Shannon: I would like to thank all of my students, past, present, and future. Your patience and generosity have taught me more than any books.

Jeffery Galle: I would like to first thank my colleagues at Oxford College of Emory University for their insights into the ways students learn and their devotion to our teaching and learning culture. They have made projects like this one a truly collaborative effort.

I also want to thank the students I have taught (and learned from) both inside and outside of the classroom. Our students possess a hunger for learning that connects the liberal arts to the many places within and beyond the college.

Finally, I thank my spouse Jo Galle for inspiring me daily and enriching each part of the journey.

CONTENTS

Notes on Contributors

Jill Petersen Adams is Director of Experiential Learning and Adjunct Assistant Professor in the Humanities Division at Oxford College of Emory University. She specializes in Asian and Continental philosophy of religion with emphases on Japan and Germany. Her current work explores alternative conceptions of mourning and memory, focusing on postwar issues in Hiroshima and Berlin specifically. She also works with a Japanese Buddhist group that pursues socially engaged religious practice with a view toward cultivating global peace and compassion, and her pedagogical interests center on global learning and experiential learning.

William Armaline is the director of the Human Rights Institute and an associate professor in the Department of Sociology and Interdisciplinary Social Sciences at San Jose State University. His areas of interest include political economy, critical race theory and anti-racism, critical pedagogy and transformative education, critical ethnography, inequality and youth, prison abolition, and drug policy reform. His recent publications include: (1) The Human Rights Enterprise: Political sociology, state power, and social movements (2015, Polity Press); (2) "The biggest gang in Oakland: Rethinking police legitimacy" (2014, Contemporary Justice Review, 17(3): 375–399).

Jasmine Brown has a B.S. in Natural Resources with a focus in Sustainable Forest Resources from UCONN and is currently working with the U.S. Forest Service. In the Fall she will begin a M.S in Forest

Ecosystems and Society at Oregon State University. She is also a spoken word poet who recently competed at a collegiate national competition.

Shane Burley has been working on housing issues—particularly through film and narrative—for years through Take Back the Land, Occupy Our Homes, and the Metro Justice Housing Committee. He is currently an independent scholar and film maker, and his most recent documentary, Expect Resistance, looks at contemporary housing struggles.

Jeffrey Scott Coker is the director of the Elon Core Curriculum and associate professor of biology at Elon University. He has published and presented widely on experiential learning and other high-impact educational practices. His research on experiential learning began 15 years ago while doing surveys on student research practices for state and national scientific societies. Since then, he has led departmental studies on experiential learning at N.C. State and institutional studies at Elon University, and helped other institutions to improve experiential practices and create experiential learning requirements. For example, he recently led studies on student outcomes related to the five "Elon Experiences" that led to the doubling of Elon's Experiential Learning Requirement and other curricular changes. His most recent article on experiential learning can be found in the March 2017 issue of the Journal of Experiential Education (40: 5–23).

Rebecca Frost Davis is the director for Instructional and Emerging Technology at St. Edward's University. Focusing on the intersections of digital pedagogy and liberal education, she is co-editor (with Matthew K. Gold, Katherine D. Harris, and Jentery Sayers) of Digital Pedagogy in the Humanities: Concepts, Models, and Experiments (a digital project under contract with MLA and being openly developed online at http://github.com/curateteaching). At the National Institute for Technology in Liberal Education, she led an initiative to develop digital humanities at liberal arts colleges, and co-authored with Bryan Alexander "Should Liberal Arts Campuses Do Digital Humanities?" in Debates in the Digital Humanities (ed. M. Gold, University of Minnesota Press, 2012). Davis served on the digital working group of the AAC&U General Education Maps and Markers project, serves on the faculty of the AAC&U Institute for Integrative Learning and the Departments, and is a frequent speaker on digital pedagogy, liberal education, and intercampus collaboration.

Jeffery Galle is Associate Professor of English and Director of the Center for Academic Excellence at Oxford College of Emory University. He has recently presented and published essays on inquiry-based learning, assessment of learning, and a number of active learning strategies. A forthcoming book co-authored by Galle on High Impact Practices will be published in July 2015 by Rowman and Littlefield. In literary studies he has presented and published on Christopher Marlowe and Mark Twain. Galle has received a number of teaching awards, ranging from the English Department Award for Excellence in Teaching (1994), to Arts and Sciences Professor of the Year (2006), and the Scott Endowed Professor of Teaching Excellence (1996–1999). At Emory, he was selected to serve as a Distinguished Teaching Scholar (2009). As Director of the CAE at Oxford College, he works with faculty in an array of consultations and programs, including the annual Institute for Pedagogy in the Liberal Arts (IPLA).

Phoebe Godfrey is Associate Professor-in-Residence in Sociology at UCONN. She teaches courses titled Climate Change and Society, Sustainable Societies and Sociology of Food. In her publishing, her teaching, her community activism and her life she attempts to put into practice that which she preaches.

Margaret T. McGehee is Associate Professor of English and American Studies at Oxford College of Emory University. Her research and teaching focus on twentieth- and twenty-first-century Southern women writers, the Atlanta imaginary in fiction, and multiethnic U.S. literature, with a focus on immigration experiences. Her work has appeared in Cinema Journal, North Carolina Literary Review, Studies in American Culture, Southern Spaces, and Gale's American Writers series. She received her PhD in American Studies from Emory University and MA in Southern Studies from the University of Mississippi.

Matthew Moyle is Assistant Professor of French at Oxford College of Emory University, where he teaches French language, literature and culture on all levels. His research focuses on the novels and essays of French author Sylvie Germain, and he has also worked on J.-M.G. Le Clézio, Camus, and the Dardenne Brothers. He is the author most recently of "Le mot « Dieu » comme écho du silence" in Les essais de Sylvie Germain: Un espace transgénérique (CRIN 56), "Écrire le lieu qui s'inscrit:

Topographies toponymiques dans La Peste et La Chute" in A Writer's Topography: Space and Place in the Life and Works of Albert Camus, and "Récits cartographes, cartes palimpsestes" in Cartographier les récits (CERAMAC35).

Patricia Owen-Smith is a professor of Psychology and Women's Studies at Oxford College of Emory University where she has taught for the past 29 years. She holds a Ph.D. in Developmental Psychology with a concentration in child and adolescent development. In 2000 she was named a Carnegie Scholar by the Carnegie Academy for the Scholarship of Teaching and Learning, where her research project focused on models of insight development in the classroom. Dr. Owen-Smith founded Oxford College's first service learning program and currently serves as the faculty director of the Theory Practice-Service Learning Program on the Oxford campus. She also directed the Center for Cognitive-Affective Learning, an initiative sponsored by the Carnegie Academy for the Scholarship of Teaching and Learning. Her current research centers on contemplative practices in higher education.

Deric Shannon is a former line cook, cashier, and fast food worker, now an assistant professor of sociology. His work largely focuses on political economy, food, and ecology, though he has also published widely on pedagogy. His peer-reviewed work has appeared in Educational Studies, Qualitative Report, Sexualities, Peace Studies Journal, and Theory in Action. He has edited, co-edited, and co-authored five books and his work has been translated into Spanish, Turkish, and Polish. He is currently working on his first single-authored monograph, Eating: Adventures in the Sociology of Being Human.

Abbey S. Willis is an instructor and Ph.D. candidate in the Sociology Department at the University of Connecticut, where she also teaches Women's, Gender & Sexuality Studies courses. While her current research focuses on non-monogamies, she writes broadly on political economy, the state in its various forms, and the ways that both affect and are affected by sexuality.

Scott Wurdinger is a professor of experiential education and leadership studies at Minnesota State University in Mankato, and currently serves as the coordinator of the Educational Leadership Doctoral Program. His research interests focus on the use of project-based learning in developing life skills such as critical thinking, problem solving, and creativity, and he has been teaching in higher education for the past 24 years. He serves as a cadre expert for Innovative Quality Schools, which is an organization that authorizes charter schools, and has published articles and books on the topic of experiential learning and education reform.

LIST OF FIGURES

CHAPTER 1

Where We Are: Place, Pedagogy, and the Outer Limits

Deric Shannon and Jeffery Galle

Where are we? This seemingly simple question packs quite a lot of context within it if one allows oneself to think deeply and holistically about it. "Where" evokes a spatial identification, perhaps rooted in geographical location. It might also evoke *temporal* identification—that is, where one is now is surely different than that same spot five centuries ago, perhaps even five seconds. The question, "Where are we?" calls attention to *place*, without which we have no reference for situating existence.

To point to the temporal and spatial embeddedness of place is also to suggest that place is bounded. To answer the question, "Where are we?", one's response sets some necessary limits. It is within these limits that place can give us a sense of our surroundings and who we are. As far in the past as "two thousand years ago, Hippocrates" observed "that our well-being is affected by our settings."[1] Gallagher notes how places can heavily influence our thoughts and behaviors.[2] From the amount of sunlight and darkness in a given place; to the weather patterns we experience; to

D. Shannon (✉)
Department of Sociology, Oxford College of Emory University, Oxford, USA

J. Galle
Department of English, Oxford College of Emory University, Oxford, USA

© The Author(s) 2017
D. Shannon, J. Galle (eds.), *Interdisciplinary Approaches to Pedagogy and Place-Based Education*, DOI 10.1007/978-3-319-50621-0_1

1

the settings we can see, hear, taste, touch, and smell; place has been connected with everything from development processes to which social groupings had the capacity for greater resource extraction throughout history.[3]

But this raises some interesting questions about the bounded-ness of place, of its limits, or perhaps of the limits that we impose on notions of place. Low and Lawrence-Zúñiga's collection on anthropological approaches to space and place argue that we might begin with the body and then travel outward as we define place—that is places are *embodied* as they are experienced by persons.[4] Is place, then, bounded by the sensory experience of a body? That would indeed be an extremely limited space for a place to exist, if place ceases at the edges of where we can no longer hear, see, touch, and so on.

It is also possible that the experience of a similar locale can be differentiated based on the cultural *meanings* or symbolic understandings of it as a place. Richardson, for example, notes that the cultural understandings of being-in-the-market and being-in-the-plaza in his ethnographic work in Cartago, Costa Rica, bring about separate considerations of place based on the symbolic meanings of *being* in each setting: "in the market, a factlike world is constructed; in the plaza, a more aesthetic one emerges."[5] If place is, in part, bounded by meaning then that is to say that it is social constructed, culturally negotiated.

We might define place, then, as a socially constructed and negotiated setting bounded by time and space, tied in intimate ways to sensory experience. One of the primary purposes of the volume you are reading right now is to engage with, stretch, and play with that definition (in the context of philosophies of teaching), implanted and engaged in the body of ideas we call "place-based education" (PBE). Here we trace the roots of PBE, note some contemporary tensions in the field, then create some of our own tensions by way of introducing the chapters that follow.

PLACE-BASED EDUCATION

Every people gives, so to speak, new clothing to the surrounding nature. — Élisée Reclus

One might root PBE in early work on childhood education with a particular concern for creating time to get kids out of the classroom and into their communities and natural environments, with an eye toward sustainability education and ecoliteracy. David Sobel observed how place had a central role in identity development for children in his work making maps with them, asking them to note, for example, their favorite places in their neighborhoods.[6] Following this, a number of people began taking note of teachers getting students into their surrounding communities, connecting them to a sense of place.[7]

Out of, and within, this concern for connecting students to their local environments and communities, Sobel defined PBE as follows:

> Place-based education is the process of using the local community and environment as a starting point to teach concepts in language arts, mathematics, social studies, science, and other subjects across the curriculum. Emphasizing hands-on, real-world learning experiences, this approach to education increases academic achievement, helps students develop stronger ties to the community, enhances students' appreciation for the natural world, and creates a heightened commitment to serving as active, contributing citizens. Community vitality and environmental quality are improved through the active engagement of local citizens, community organizations, and environmental resources in the life of the school.[8]

This focus on the surrounding environment and community was seen as a remedy to schooling that centered on abstractions in classrooms, typically to the exclusion of the adjacent environs. Indeed, Smith and Sobel argue that place- and community-based education can serve as a remedy, of sorts:

> to one of the most serious but generally unspoken dilemmas in American education: the alienation of children and youth from the real world right outside their homes and classrooms. What's real for many young people is what happens on their computer monitors, television screens, and MP3 players. Caught in an interior and electronically mediated world, they are losing touch with both the society of flesh-and-blood humans and the natural world that supports our species.[9]

Demarest uses "teacher portraits" to examine and assess place-based curriculum design.[10] She similarly focuses on experiential forms of learning that draw children out of the classrooms and into the communities and social ecologies of which they are a part.

In Grunewald's provocative piece on critical pedagogy and PBE, he argues that the two philosophies of education are mutually supportive and should be synthesized.[11] For scholars of sustainability, the case for doing so seems intuitive. Sustainability, broadly conceived as consisting of environmental, social, and economic pillars, ties environmentalism with issues of equity and participatory social forms. Critical pedagogy, evolving from Marxism and critical theory's concerns with structural inequalities seems a good fit with educational models that stress the need for ecoliteracy and a desire to connect students with efforts to build resilient communities (and Grunewald makes this case quite convincingly).

Grunewald also notes a tension in his synthesis of PBE and critical pedagogy—the tendency for PBE to be associated with the rural and critical pedagogy to be paired with the urban. He argues that "[i]n recent literature educators claiming place as a guiding construct associate a place-based approach with" educational forms largely focused on rurality. He continues, "[o]ne result of these primarily ecological and rural associations has been that place-based education is frequently discussed at a distance from the urban, multicultural arena, territory most often claimed by critical pedagogues. If place-based education emphasizes ecological and rural contexts, critical pedagogy-in a near mirror image-emphasizes social and urban contexts and often neglects the ecological and rural scene entirely."[12] However, this tension is addressed in the array of chapters contributed to Grunewald and Smith's excellent collection on contemporary PBE, being particularly attentive to processes of globalization.[13]

Another tension arising in PBE, particularly on colonized land, is between settler educators and forms of education and the ways they might conflict with indigenous understandings. That is, we might ask questions about who owns a place. How did they come to own it? Perhaps more pointedly, how did we come to believe that places could be "owned" and whose bodies and knowledges have been brutalized in the process, rendered illegible, and/or invisible?

These, and adjacent concerns, are central in McCoy, Tuck, and Mckenzie's collection, asking scholars to consider indigenous, postcolonial, and decolonizing perspectives as they relate to pedagogies of place.[14] They argue that "the ongoing colonization of land and peoples are in fact embedded within educators' and researchers' practices and understandings of (environmental) education around the globe."[15] The pieces in their collection center the fact that place is politicized, often colonized, and that the "neutral" teaching of place so often emphasized by environmental educators erases violent processes both within our histories and present moment(s).

Thus, PBE arose in response to larger concerns about the alienating effects of non-permeable classroom walls that separated students from their communities rather than embedding them within the ecologies where they are located. This form of pedagogy asks teachers to be cognizant of the question we began this discussion with: Where are we? It also invites teachers and students alike to see education as a part of the life of communities and ecosystems and not abstracted from them. But PBE has not been conceptualized without tensions. Its past focus on outdoor education and ecoliteracy can evoke an emphasis on the rural at the expense of the urban. And place-based educators can likewise unintentionally reinscribe patterns of colonialism when they do not maintain a commitment to non-static and non-essentialist indigenous knowledge(s) or when they do not engage in larger process of decolonization.

Here and There

We hope to raise some new tensions in this collection. Over the course of the last two years we have asked scholars to write on concerns traditionally held by place-based educators, but we have also requested that some stretch the concept of place. All of the collected chapters speak to place in the context of *higher education*, perhaps focusing on an arena within PBE that is often underemphasized. Our sections, titled simply "here" and "there," are meant to note that some of the contributions to this collection are easily located within PBE while others take the idea of place and modify or play with it in ways that we find provocative.

We begin with Deric Shannon's reflections on teaching sociology, in part, on a multi-acre organic farm. Shannon argues that the farm provides an important backdrop for conversations about ecology, community, and specific concepts significant in the sociology of food and sustainability. Next, Patricia Owen-Smith argues for *interiority* as place, emphasizing introspection and mindfulness in a practice that begins with the body and the self, an argument gaining traction among environmental and sustainability educators. Scott Wurdinger outlines *how* educators might go about creating their own places into educational projects. Shane Burley invites readers to consider the role of power and place in documentary film education and construction. Jeffrey Scott Coker uses the Elon University Forest as a case study for place-based science education. Finally, Jeffery Galle suggests ways that educators might use their campuses creatively in the context of PBE.

We begin our stretching of place with Matthew Moyle's work on using travel to investigate the places students might read about in literature. William Armaline argues that *inside of the classroom* we might build democratic space for engaging with larger operations of power and environmental destruction located within the geographies and lives of our students. Abbey S Willis maintains that in a globalized age, "place" becomes a flexible concept and one might not need to leave the classroom to investigate the world and its attendant power relations in very material ways. Jill Petersen Adams and Margaret Thomas McGehee explore travel to investigate processes of trauma and peace in search of justice and community. Rebecca Frost Davis investigates the emerging digital ecosystem as a place to learn about local communities and larger processes of globalization. Phoebe Godfrey and Jasmine Brown use student/teacher dialogues to argue for what they call "heartfelt hope" as a place-based pedagogical practice in teaching and learning about climate change.

We understand that the focus on the local, on the outdoors, and on leaving the classroom make some of these contributions idiosyncratic in the context of PBE. Travel courses take students away from the communities in which they live to learn about a different place—or, perhaps to learn *within* a different place. Viewing the internet as a place could, no doubt, emphasize an arena for learning that might seem, at first glance, to mitigate against community engagement or nature education. Similarly, remaining in the classroom as a strategy to investigate the local—or even collapsing the global and local and arguing that there is no coherent separation between the two—could be seen as pushing the notion of *place* into incomprehensibility.

But it is our desire to provoke and to allow some flexibility around the notion of place. First and foremost, this collection focuses on higher education—typically institutions that transient students filter in and out of, while moving on to live out their lives elsewhere. This means that place and locality are already elastic in these institutions, even while the schools themselves are connected intimately with their natural surroundings and communities. Secondly, one might question the limits of the local: Is it defined, for example, in the US by town, city, county? Should it be defined, perhaps, by bioregion or subsections thereof? Without some degree of elasticity to the local, and without its direct engagement and relation to the global, localism can easily turn into a fetishization—and a reactionary one at that. One need only investigate the racist tinges of the recent "Brexit" campaign or Donald Trump's campaigning against "globalism" to see how localism—disconnected from a principled internationalism—can be (mis)used for quite destructive ends.

Nonetheless, we believe that the focus on local processes in PBE is appropriate and, importantly, necessary for resilient and decent communities. Decentralization can increase the capacity for popular participation in community institutions. An emphasis on the local can empower groupings to take responsibility for their surrounding environment and the relations of domination within them. And, as noted by the famed environmentalist Murray Bookchin years ago, our ability to realize an ecological society is intricately connected with our capacity to create just and equitable communities with the capacity for face-to-face interactions.[16] Stretching place, expanding it, and recognizing place *here* and *there* might be a beginning in an internationalist and anti-parochial localism and a pedagogy of place with a capacity for education as part of a longer process of social transformation.

NOTES

1. Gallagher, *The Power of Place*, 12.
2. Ibid.
3. This is especially present in the geographical determinism of Diamond's *Guns, Germs, and Steel*, although he contests the critique.
4. Low and Lawrence-Zúñiga, *The Anthropology of Space and Place*.
5. Richardson, "Being-in-the-Market Versus Being-in-the-Plaza."
6. Sobel, *Children's Special Places*.
7. See, for some examples, Smith, "Rooting Children in Place."; Abbot-Chapman, "Time Out in 'Green Retreats' and Adolescent Wellbeing."; Smith, "Going Local."; Vickers and Matthews "Children and Place."; Wilson, "A Sense of Place."
8. Sobel, *Place-based Education*, 11.
9. Smith and Sobel, *Place- and Community-based Education in Schools*, viii.
10. Demarest, *Place-based Curriculum Design*.
11. Grunewald, "The Best of Both Worlds."
12. Ibid, 3.
13. Grunewald and Smith, *Place-based Education in the Global Age*.
14. McCoy, Tuck, and McKenzie, *Land Education*.
15. Ibid, 1.
16. See especially, Bookchin, *The Ecology of Freedom*.

BIBLIOGRAPHY

Abbot-Chapman, Joan. "Time Out in 'Green Retreats' and Adolescent Wellbeing." *Youth Studies Australia* 25.4 (2006): 9–16.

Bookchin, Murray. *The Ecology of Freedom: The Emergence and Dissolution of Hierarchy.* Palo Alto, CA: Cheshire Books, 1982.

Bookchin, Murray, and Dave Foreman. "Defending the Earth: A Dialogue Between Murray Bookchin and Dave Foreman." *The Anarchist Library* (1991). Accessed October 29, 2016, https://theanarchistlibrary.org/library/murray-bookchin-and-dave-foreman-defending-the-earth-a-debate.

Demarest, Amy B. *Place-based Curriculum Design: Exceeding Standards through Local Investigation.* New York: Routledge, 2015.

Diamond, Jared. *Guns, Germs, and Steel: The Fates of Human Societies.* New York: Norton, 1999.

Gallagher, Winifred. *The Power of Place: How Our Surroundings Shape Our Thoughts, Emotions, and Actions.* New York: Harper Collins, 1993.

Gruenewald, David A. "The Best of Both Worlds: A Critical Pedagogy of Place." *Educational Researcher* 32.4 (2003): 3–12.

Grunewald, D., and Gregory A. Smith (eds.). *Place-Based Education in the Global Age: Local Diversity.* New York: Routledge, 2010.

Low, Setha M. Lawrence-Zúñiga, Denise (eds.). *The Anthropology of Space and Place: Locating Culture.* Malden, MA: Blackwell, 2003.

McCoy, Kate, Eve Tuck, and Marcia McKenzie (eds.). *Land Education: Rethinking Pedagogies of Place from Indigenous, Postcolonial, and Decolonizing Perspectives.* New York: Routledge, 2016.

Richardson, Miles. "Being-in-the-Market Versus Being-in-the-Plaza." In *The Anthropology of Space and Place: Locating Culture.* Setha M. Low and Denise Lawrence-Zúñiga, eds. Malden, MA: Blackwell, 2003.

Smith, Gregory. "Rooting Children in Place." *Encounter* 11.4 (1998): 13–24.

Smith, Gregory. "Going Local." *Educational Leadership* 60.1 (2002): 30–33.

Smith, Gregory, and David Sobel. *Place- and Community-based Education in Schools.* New York: Routledge, 2010.

Sobel, David. *Children's Special Places: Exploring the Role of Forts, Dens, and Bush Houses in Middle Childhood.* St. Paul, MN: Zephyr Press, 1993.

Sobel, David. *Place-based Education: Connecting Classrooms and Communities.* Great Barrington, MA: Orion, 2014 (orig. 2004).

Vickers, V.G., and Catherine Matthews. "Children and Place." *Science Activities* 39 (2002): 16.

Wilson, Ruth. "A Sense of Place." *Early Education Journal* 24.3 (1997): 191–194.

PART I

Here

CHAPTER 2

Teaching on the Farm: Farm as Place in the Sociology of Food and Sustainability

Deric Shannon

Place-based education has deep roots in environmental education and human interaction with (and alteration of) place. As one element of ecoliteracy, pedagogies of place ask us to be aware of where we are, the ecosystem in which we are embedded, the human systems that are a part of that ecosystem, and the webs of connectivity that make up all activity. As opposed to viewing classrooms, or the schools of which they are a part, as place-less appendages, disconnected from the social relationships that give them meaning and possibility, pedagogies of place ask teachers and students alike to be attentive to the communities in which they are rooted.[1]

Many authors in this collection take that notion of place and stretch it, demonstrating the elasticity of place in a globalized world. Indeed, Willis argues that we might use the classroom as a place to recognize the global in the local (and vice versa) and problematize the very notion of a stable place that is not at once everywhere and also particular. Adams and McGehee write about using travel as a way to be introduced to places (and their connected

D. Shannon (✉)
Department of Sociology, Oxford College of Emory University, Oxford, USA

D. Shannon, J. Galle (eds.), *Interdisciplinary Approaches to Pedagogy and Place-Based Education*, DOI 10.1007/978-3-319-50621-0_2

events) that might be unfamiliar to students, an idea that Moyle tackles as well in the context of teaching literature. Owen-Smith invites readers to consider *interiority* as place, a sort of critical engagement with the self.

This chapter, however, is nestled within what might be considered more familiar ground for scholars who use place-based education. Since I am a scholar in the sociology of food and sustainability, questions around community, ecology, and the connections between our forms of life and the places that we inhabit are central to both my scholarly work *and* my teaching. As I've noted elsewhere, notions of justice touch on central concerns within scholarship on food and sustainability.[2] And those concerns cannot be coherently separated from ecoliteracy, human interactions with each other and the non-human world, and place.

For sociologists of food and sustainability, the farm can be an important site for instruction rooted in a connection to place. This reflects a general trend in higher education, as well, as more and more institutions of higher education use farms—and student farms, in particular—as centers for research and teaching.[3] Teaching on the farm and using farm work as a supplement to sociology classes focused on food and sustainability gives students a chance to leave the classroom, interact with each other, put their hands in the soil, and nurture the growth of food and the organisms necessary for its growth. It affords us an opportunity to use place in a way that puts students, teachers, the land bases, and the larger social ecosystem(s) into direct contact.

For this reason, I developed courses on the sociology of food and sustainability that have been taught, in part, on a small organic farm owned and operated by my school. For two years, I have taught classes within the classroom, the barn, and the fields (including farm work as well as tours) to use the farm as a place and, perhaps, to learn alongside the farm with students. In this chapter, I outline four concepts that are centrally important to the sociology of food and sustainability and how I use the farm as a *place* to emphasize them.

LAYING THE FIELD: THE FARM

I work at Emory University's Oxford College, a small two-year residential institution that focuses on undergraduate education and concentrates on the freshman and sophomore year. The farm itself sits a few blocks from the College. It has a rotation of cover crops and vegetables, compost piles, refrigerator systems in the barn on the property, and a small honeybee operation. All of it is overseen by our farmer/educator, Daniel Parson, who has been central to the development of many courses and course-components that integrate the farm into their work on our campus, including my own.

The farm is certified-organic and focused on the sustainable production of foods. This falls in line with the College's commitments to sustainability, aligned with the larger University's sustainability initiatives. The College has described the farm as "a living laboratory for students," which seems to me to be a fair assessment, particularly given my own involvement in its use for teaching.[4] This is important, not only as a descriptor for the farm but also to understand how it serves as a place for learning about food and sustainability.

Perhaps not without irony, the farm sits in the middle of a USDA-defined food desert. It is a part of a larger agricultural-ecological system and contains within it social relationships extending well beyond the farm driveways, fields, and walkways. The farm has a community-supported agriculture (CSA) program, plugging into area social life in production, distribution, and exchange. It produces food for our dining services and for our nearby sister campus in Atlanta, reducing food miles and providing students with local food options. People involved in the operations of the farm, from students to our farmer/educator to professors, have attended meetings with Health Department officials, non-profits, and community groups who are attempting to find creative ways to address the problems that emerge as a result of the local food desert. Collaborators on the farm also deliver fresh vegetables to local food pantries. All of this is to say that the farm has a sociologically interesting and compelling place within the local ecosystem and should serve as a backdrop for the discussion that follows.

MICRO AND MACRO

A central task in sociology is to demonstrate the differences and links between macro- and micro-level thinking. Macro analysis tends to focus on larger, institutional forces, while micro analysis tends to look at the quotidian and how we symbolically create meaning in our lives together. Of course, each way of looking at the world comes with its own set of advantages and drawbacks. *Boundless,* an online collection of educators and subject-matter experts, puts it thusly:

> Micro- and macro-level studies each have their own benefits and drawbacks. Macrosociology allows observation of large-scale patterns and trends, but runs the risk of seeing these trends as abstract entities that exist outside of

the individuals who enact them on the ground. Microsociology allows for this on-the-ground analysis, but can fail to consider the larger forces that influence individual behavior.[5]

C. Wright Mills thought it was important that we connect the micro, lived, daily experiences in our lives to the macro-level institutions and processes that inform much of our daily interactions. That is, his notion of the *sociological imagination* was based on our capacity to understand that the micro and macro are inextricably linked:

> The facts of contemporary history are also facts about the success and the failure of individual men and women. When a society is industrialized, a peasant becomes a worker; a feudal lord is liquidated or becomes a businessman [sic]. When classes rise or fall, a man is employed or unemployed; when the rate of investment goes up or down, a man takes new heart or goes broke. When wars happen, an insurance salesman becomes a rocket launcher; a store clerk, a radar man; a wife lives alone; a child grows up without a father. Neither the life of an individual nor the history of a society can be understood without understanding both.[6]

Similarly, but with a less determinist bent than Mills, Errico Malatesta suggested that the micro and macro link was *reciprocal*, and understanding that nexus was integral to *social change* when he argued that "[b]etween man [sic] and his social environment there is a reciprocal action. Men make society what it is and society makes men what they are, and the result is therefore a kind of vicious circle. To transform society men must be changed, and to transform men, society must be changed."[7]

Students in sociology courses are typically asked to reflect on their own daily lives and the institutional processes that shape them, investigating this micro-macro link. The farm provides a perfect metaphor for this. Especially on organic farms, cover crops are used to enhance soil health and as a form of reducing unwanted weeds or insects. In the early fall, I walk out with my students some distance from a field of cover crops, point to the field, and ask my students what they see. Their replies typically range from things like, "A field of buckwheat," or perhaps, "a field with a cover crop," for those who know what process they are looking at. Next, we walk into the field with the cover crop and we all get down on one knee in the soil and, again, we discuss what we see. The world looks very different from this perspective, as students describe insect activity, pollinators buzzing between flowers, worms and ants traveling on or through the soil, and roots and plant material as connective tissue between the various activities of the rest of the living system surrounding them.

Of course, it is not a perfect metaphor, but it helps students understand both micro and macro approaches to sociology as well as how *place* informs our understanding of the world. Consider, for example, the political economy in which we live. From a macro point of view, we might see the large institutional features of capitalism such as markets, states, wage labor, or private property as large-scale representations of how our society operates. From a distance, that seems to be a pretty accurate portrayal. But in our small-scale, local, and daily lives smaller interactions and institutional operations are at play, as people engage in the activities of work/wage-earning, the command relationships of most workplaces, the reproductive labor in the home that allows for a workforce to continue to exist, and the small day-to-day interactions that make up our larger political economy. Likewise, it can allow us to see that those economic relations are not necessarily totalizing and that we, at times, produce living alternatives to the social relationships that make up capitalism.[8]

Like the insects, soil, and plant material in the close-up view of the cover crop, the farm, and by extension the College and the students, are part of a much larger ecosystem. This exercise highlights not only the farm as a metaphor for micro and macro analyses in sociology but also the crucial dimension of *place* in both the farm and the lives of those present in the class. A cover crop on a farm can serve as a visual metaphor for place, analytical distinctions within sociology, and much more—showing, in part, the strength of the farm as a pedagogical place ripe, as it were, with its own possibilities for learning and instruction.

DIVERSITY

Another such possibility is for discussions of diversity, again using the farm as a metaphor for social life. In sociology, we typically discuss diversity as a trait within every human society with a variety of social impacts. We often point out the benefits of multi-racial and ethnic groups living alongside one another, learning from each other and sharing cultures in a rich tapestry. We teach our students about differences rooted in wide arrays of gender and sexual identities, age groups, ability, and so on and their historical construction(s). And many of us discuss the limits of diversity under institutions that allow some groups to dominate others and, concomitantly, the limits of notions like tolerance or acceptance without being attentive to how power is organized in our social world.

An organic farm out in the country might seem like an odd place for discussions of diversity and/or multiculturalism. In Gruenewald's excellent essay on place-based education and critical pedagogy, he states that "place-based education is frequently discussed at a distance from the urban, multicultural arena, territory most often claimed by critical pedagogues."[9] But this misses the diversity in the *rural*, places that are strikingly multicultural and diverse, though often in ways that are distinct from urban life. And it misses out on key ways that the farm, as a place and particularly where I live in the rural American South, zigzags in and across racial, ethnic, gendered, and religious cultures—particularly where small community farms continue to doggedly persist, despite the agricultural tendency toward industrialization.

It is there, in the small scale, local, organic farm that one can find a powerful metaphor for multiculturalism and diversity. Even the *language* of farming captures this. Referring to industrial monoculture forms of farming, Alkon and Agyeman write:

> Picture a field of corn stretching out into the horizon. Each evenly spaced stalk is genetically identical. Each needs exactly the same amount of water, fertilizer, sunlight, and time as every other. And each is ready for harvest at exactly the same moment. For this reason, the cultivation and collection of this field can be entirely mechanized. Heavy machinery has crossed this field many times, laying seed, applying fertilizer, and eventually gathering many tons of corn. Mechanized production is necessary on a farm of this size, as hand cultivation would be prohibitively expensive. This approach to farming, called a monoculture, ensures that the finished product will always meet the specifications required for processing, which will transform it into everything from animal feed to Coca-Cola.[10]

A small organic farm provides an excellent working alternative to the forms of monoculture described earlier.

Opposed to large-scale, monoculture, capital-intensive forms of farming (that are dominant in the US), putting students on a small, polyculture, labor-intensive farm can buttress positive notions of diversity and strength in difference. The latter forms of farming promote biodiversity, utilizing a wide variety of lifeforms, soil, water, sunlight, and so on in conjunction with each other to produce desired outcomes. By embracing this diversity, students see the farm putting these principles to work. This is easily comparable to social tendencies that more or less embrace difference or that promote their own form of monoculture—whether that hinges on nationalist notions of belonging or the kinds of gray sameness present in many forms of capitalist and consumerist cultural production.

EPISTEMIC DISTANCE

Sociologist of food and agriculture, Michael Carolan, argues that there are epistemic barriers that keep us from recognizing the benefits of the sustainable production of food and the costs of conventional production. We are removed from the processes of production that go into creating the food we consume and the *long-term* benefits of sustainable food production (e.g. soil health, biodiversity, etc.) are *temporally* distant compared to the *immediate* benefits of the conventional production of food (e.g. near-immediate pest removal with chemical pesticides, etc.). This epistemic distance could have "an impact" on "our ethical orientation toward distant phenomena, as it makes it easier for us to act with moral indifference toward those faraway people, places and things that provide us...with what we eat."[11]

The farm, as a place, decreases the epistemic distance between the food my students consume and the production processes that go into creating it—particularly since a portion of our cafeteria meals come directly from the farm and because my students help raise the crops. In this way, the farm becomes not only a place but also a *workplace*. Here might be lessons about epistemic distance as well as workplace dynamics and political economy, ideas that fit quite well together in our globalizing world.

The concept of epistemic distance can be applied well beyond food. While my students do indeed get a lesson in the distance between the production processes that go into creating their food and what they experience at the point of consumption, this lesson invites them to consider all manner of place-based questions. In our contemporary political economy, where neoliberal policies have deregulated industry and the movement of commodities and capital (all the while heavily regulating and restricting the movement of workers), our epistemic distance from all manner of commodities is lengthened. Most students who take the time to look inside of their t-shirts or jeans will find that they were created in so-called "free" trade enclaves in places like Singapore, Indonesia, China, or some other place that has offered tax holidays and super-exploitation to the companies who hire workers in the race-to-the-bottom to maximize profits.[12] The farm as a place invites questions like "Where does my food come from? What went into creating it?" in an immediate sense. But indirectly, students might begin asking questions like "Where do most of my goods come from? Why? What processes went into creating them?" and, crucially, "Are other methods possible?" This allows students to connect the local, everyday places we inhabit with those who do not share our same physical or social locations. Just as food travels from farms (or other workplaces) through complex supply chains, so too do our clothes, electronics, cars, canisters, bins, footballs, toys, and so on. Places, indeed workplaces, allow us insight into entire social ecosystems in which we live.

Structural Inequalities in Food Supply Chains

Using the farm as one link in a web of social relationships that make up the food supply chain invites students to make all sorts of connections. When students consider the farm, like engagement with *any* place-based pedagogy, they have the capacity to consider how it functions in a web of social-ecological relations. Students at Oxford College's farm see the produce they help raise travel to their cafeteria, to our sister campus in Atlanta, to food pantries locally, to farmer's markets down the street, as well as in Atlanta, and so on. These webs of relation also provide an opportunity for students to reflect on the larger food supply chains that make up most of the food that we consume in the US and their impact on various groups, showing structural inequalities at work.

From political economic practices designed to support large corporations at the expense of family farmers, to the imperial project of neoliberalism, to food workers in production, preparation, and service trying to eke out a living on low wages, food—and farm—are never far from issues of economic inequality.[13] And, of course, this is also true of basic questions of access to food, with some scholars critically engaging in such access as an issue of food security[14] or, in the case of some activists and scholars, reframing the issue as one of food sovereignty.[15]

If we use the farm and food supply chains as places to investigate relations of social inequality tied to race, gender, sexuality, age, ability, and other axes of difference, it is likewise easy to locate where we might place that lens all along contemporary food supply chains. The environmental harms of industrial capitalism, generally, and its conventional farming practices, specifically, are not distributed equally and often fall along recognizable patterns of inequality—scholars have coined the term "environmental racism" to highlight this. Similarly, gender norms across societies and norms around sexuality, age, and ability often reflect relations of inequality around food preparation and production (i.e. who is supposed to farm, prepare, and cook food and in what contexts) as well as consumption (i.e. who is worthy of having access and eating and in what contexts).

From Farm to Community

Place-based education has a long history in environmental education, in particular, because of the way that it invites learners to be cognizant of where they are and the ecosystem within which that place is nestled. Agriculture carries with it an important connection to environmental education, in part because contemporary conventional farming methods are implicated in soil degradation, a loss of biodiversity, and even emissions responsible for climate change. Because of food and farming's particular connection to ecology, the farm provides a place that can offer unique insights following in the tradition of place-based education.

Because of this, I developed my sociology of food and sustainability curriculum on a small organic farm connected to my larger workplace. Earlier in this chapter, I outline ways that this farm has served as an important focal point in my own place-based method of instruction. The farm provides metaphors for discussing micro and macro sociology, their connections, and their limits. Issues of diversity and multiculturalism are buttressed by discussions of *biodiversity* and ecological interdependence on the farm. Students are able to decrease the epistemic distance between their consumption of food and its production by working on the farm and are called to connect that distance to other commodities they consume. Finally, farms and the food supply chains of which they are a part provide space for reflection and investigation into larger relations of inequality among humans.

But, I think, the real magic in using the farm as a place for instruction, reflection, and critique is its place within the larger community that it serves. For us, this means serving and learning on a small-scale, local, labor-intensive, organic farm. I think scholars of food can often fetishize the local at the risk of overestimating its importance and losing sight of the global. And localism, as an ideology, leaves much to be desired in terms of political action, particularly if it is treated as some kind of panacea to social ills (i.e. is local exploitation of workers in a market society really the preferable alternative to global exploitation or are there perhaps better ways of looking at social problems?). This problem might also be present in scholarship on place-based education.

Compelling studies, however, have shown that small and local farms *tend toward* better community outcomes than their large, industrial counterparts.[16] The strength of place-based pedagogy, after all, in part resides in its ability to provide a sense of place set within a community. These communities include not only students, professors, workers, children—humans—but also the ecosystems that we inhabit and interact with. Given the challenges facing humanity in terms of ecological degradation and the decline in living systems, we might emphasize this method of instruction that allows us to consider needs from people to mountaintops to mighty redwoods to the tiniest of ladybugs and microscopic organisms—all within a fragile web of interdependence. And the farm is an excellent place to begin.

NOTES

1. See e.g. Sobel, *Place Based Education.*; David Orr, *Ecological literacy*; Smith, "Place-based education"; Theobald, *Teaching the Commons*; Theobald and Curtiss, "Communities as Curricula"; Sarkar and Frazier, "Place Based Investigations and Authentic Inquiry."
2. See Shannon, "Operationalizing Food Justice and Sustainability"; Shannon, "Intersectionality, Ecology, Food: Conflict Theory's Missing Lens"; Shannon, "Ecology, Food, and Holistic Politics."
3. See especially Sayre and Clark, *Fields of Learning.*
4. "Organic Farm Becomes a Reality at Oxford."
5. "Levels of Analysis: Micro and Macro."
6. Mills, *The Sociological Imagination*, 3.
7. Malatesta, *Life and Ideas*, 178.
8. Gibson-Graham, *The End of Capitalism (As We Knew It)*; White and Williams, "Escaping Capitalist Hegemony."
9. Gruenewald, "The Best of Both Worlds," 3.
10. Alkon and Agyeman, *Cultivating Food Justice*, 1.
11. Carolan, *The Sociology of Food and Agriculture*, 140.
12. Davies and Vadlamannati, "A Race to the Bottom in Labour Standards?"
13. Leonard, *The Meat Racket.*; Raj Patel, *Stuffed and Starved*; Shiva, *Stolen Harvest.*
14. See especially Carolan, *Reclaiming Food Security.*

15. See especially the term's use by La Via Campesina at http://viacampesina. org/en/, last accessed July 12, 2016.
16. See Carolan's breakdown of a number of studies in Michael Carolan, *Sociology of Food*, 95–103.

BIBLIOGRAPHY

Alkon, Alison Hope, and Julian Agyeman (eds.). *Cultivating Food Justice: Race, Class, and Sustainability*. Cambridge, MA: The MIT Press, 2011.

Carolan, Michael. *The Sociology of Food and Agriculture*. New York: Routledge, 2012.

Carolan, Michael. *Reclaiming Food Security*. New York: Routledge, 2013.

Davies, Ronald B., and Krishna Chaitanya Vadlamannati. "A Race to the Bottom in Labour Standards? An Empirical Investigation." *IIIS Discussion Paper* No. 385(2011). Accessed July 12, 2016, http://www.tcd.ie/iiis/docu ments/discussion/pdfs/iiisdp385.pdf.

Gibson-Graham, J. K. *The End of Capitalism (As We Knew It): A Feminist Critique of Political Economy*. Minneapolis, MN: University of Minnesota Press, 1996.

Gruenewald, David A. "The Best of Both Worlds: A Critical Pedagogy of Place." *Educational Researcher* 32.4 (2003): 3–12.

Leonard, Christopher. *The Meat Racket: The Secret Takeover of America's Food Business*. New York: Simon and Schuster, 2014.

Boundless. "Levels of Analysis: Micro and Macro," *Boundless*, accessed July 11, 2016, https://www.boundless.com/sociology/textbooks/boundless-sociol ogy-textbook/sociology-1/the-sociologicalapproach-25/levels-of-analysis-micro-and-macro-161-2417/.

Malatesta, Errico. *Life and Ideas: The Anarchist Writings of Errico Malatesta*, ed. and trans., Vernon Richards. Oakland, CA: PM Press, 2015.

Orr, David. *Ecological Literacy*. Albany: State University of New York Press, 1992.

Patel, Raj. *Stuffed and Starved: The Hidden Battle for the World Food System*. Brooklyn: Melville House Publishing, 2007.

Sarkar, Somnar, and Richard Frazier. "Place Based Investigations and Authentic Inquiry." *The Science Teacher* 75.2 (2008): 29–33.

Sayre, Laura, and Sean Clark (eds.). *Fields of Learning: The Student Farm Movement in North America*. Lexington, KY: University Press of Kentucky, 2011.

Shannon, Deric. "Operationalizing Food Justice and Sustainability." *Theory in Action* 7.4 (2014): 1–11.

Shannon, Deric. "Ecology, Food, and Holistic Politics." In *Animals and the Environment: Advocacy, Activism, and the Quest for Common Ground*. Lisa Kemmerer, eds. New York: Routledge, 2015.

Shannon, Deric. "Intersectionality, Ecology, Food: Conflict Theory's Missing Lens." In *Emergent Possibilities for Global Sustainability: Intersections of Race, Class, and Gender*. Phoebe Godfrey and Denise Torres, eds. New York: Routledge, 2016.

Shiva, Vandana. *Stolen Harvest: The Hijacking of the Global Food Supply.* Cambridge, MA: South End Press, 2000.

Smith, Gregory A. "Place-based education: Learning to be where we are." *Phi Delta Kappan* 83 (2002): 584–594.

Sobel, David. *Place Based Education: Connecting Classrooms and Communities.* Great Barrington, MA: The Orion Society, 2005.

Theobald, Paul. *Teaching the Commons: Place, Pride, and the Renewal of Community.* Boulder, CO: Westview Press, 1997.

Theobald, Paul, and Jim Curtiss. "Communities as Curricula." *Forum for Applied Research and Public Policy* 15.1 (2002): 106–111.

White, Richard J., and Colin C. Williams. "Escaping Capitalist Hegemony: Re-reading Western Economies." In *The Accumulation of Freedom: Writings on Anarchist Economics*. Deric Shannon, Anthony J. Nocella, and John Asimakopoulos, eds. Oakland, CA: AK Press, 2012.

Wright, Mills, C. *The Sociological Imagination*, 40th ed. Oxford, UK: Oxford University Press, 2000, orig. 1959.

CHAPTER 3

Reclaiming Interiority as Place and Practice

Patricia Owen-Smith

Pedagogies of place are grounded in the position that *place* is the epicenter of being and of experience. They call forth an understanding of how the world functions and how our lives are part of the spaces we inhabit. Therefore, place is where " . . . our identity and our possibilities are shaped."[1] *Critical* place-based learning models argue specifically that the study of *place* must include student voice and agency in the learning process, engagement with critical questions and dilemmas confronting the self and community, relational trust, student identity and belongingness, safe spaces for discourse and reflection, and an ethical commitment to social justice.[2] More recently, an alternative understanding of place pedagogy emphasizes the *embodiment* of experience in place.[3] From this perspective an inquiry of place becomes "enfleshed" with an embodied understanding. A personal understanding of "the lived terms of inquiry" guides classroom practice.[4]

As most place-based educators note, the ultimate power of place-based education (PBE) as a pedagogical approach rests in the profundity of "sensuous experience, relationship and meaning-making."[5] In the above words of Ortiz, it rests in *being*. Therefore, the nurturing of relational ontologies based on care and emotional experiences are requisites.[6]

P. Owen-Smith (✉)
Psychology and Women's Studies, Oxford College of Emory University, Oxford, USA

© The Author(s) 2017   23
D. Shannon, J. Galle (eds.), *Interdisciplinary Approaches to Pedagogy and Place-Based Education*, DOI 10.1007/978-3-319-50621-0_3

Ironically, actual practices that support these dimensions and return the student to the self and to the place of interior knowing required for place-based pedagogies are often absent in the PBE classroom. Somerville, Power, and de Carteret observe that modern education is one centered on *placelessness* and an "ahistorical and monolithic version of knowledge."[7] Paradoxically, PBE may not be exempt from this notion of placelessness in its methods. Some scholars suggest that the absence of interiority in PBE has done profound harm. As Rushmere maintains, the crisis of ecological domination emerges from the violence of abstraction and removal of relationship promoted by educational institutions and practices:

> Part of the solution is not only thinking through domination per se, but also feeling our way through it in the double sense of working with our senses and emotions. Thus we are not only engaging in a "rethinking of the process and substance of education at all levels," but also a re-feeling of it.[8]

The purpose of this chapter is to (1) discuss the theoretical underpinnings of PBE as firmly grounded in an understanding of the student with *both* an interior and exterior self; (2) consider the idea that many of our current classroom practices, particularly those in PBE courses, fail to acknowledge interiority as fundamental to learning; (3) argue that PBE, in particular, calls for an attention to methods that unambiguously privilege interiority as place; and (4) explore contemplative practices as approaches that might deepen and expand a place-based pedagogy.

Theoretical Approaches to PBE

Conceptualizations of PBE are, more times than not, associated with such pedagogical models as experiential learning, problem-based learning, outdoor education, environmental and ecological education, indigenous education, and democratic education, all of which privilege the connection of place with the self and the other. The notion of place embedded in each of these pedagogical models is the clear conceptualization of the learner as an experiencing, thinking, and feeling human being, one with an exterior *and* interior self. Paulo Freire, one of the most influential educational theorists in the twentieth century and one consistently referenced in the PBE literature, posited a "critical consciousness" and a "decolonization of the mind" as goals for teaching and learning.[9] His phenomenological method is grounded in the idea that access to our interior selves is the requisite for *liberation and the transformation* of the world.

Other educational theorists emerging from the education reform movement in the 1960s echoed Freire's perspective. The constructivist theory of Piaget and Vygotsky, transformative learning theory of Mezirow, feminist theories advanced by Gilligan, as well as Belenky, Clenchy, Goldberger, Tarule, and hooks, experiential or holistic learning theory of Kolb, and developmental theories of Kegan and Perry led to a burgeoning of questions about who students are and how they learn. These questions led to a narrative that emphasized the growth of the whole person. Terms such as *connected knowing, interiority,* and *engagement with the self and others* introduced a new vocabulary in higher education. Each of these individuals conceptualized education as focused on the mind, body, *and* spirit of the student and, like Freire, virtually all of them have contributed to the development of a PBE theoretical model.

PBE's theoretical nod toward transformation, liberation, and contestation is grounded in an acknowledgment of the student's inner life as a critical venue to learning. Incongruously, the actual classroom practice of place-based pedagogies is often inattentive to and dismissive of the interior self as the place where these processes begin. Attention to the wholeness of the body as a classification of thought and analysis continues to be obscured, maintaining what Bush refers to as the continuation of higher education's "dualistic alienation of body from mind, emotion from intellect, humans from nature, and art from science."[10] Specific classroom practices that access interiority remain untapped, and the master systems and narratives that marginalize and dismiss the wisdom, compassion, and self-care critical to PBE and all transformative pedagogies are sustained. As Wakeman argues:

> A critical pedagogy of place provides the framework to discuss and concurrently tease apart the relationships between power, place, education, diversity, biodiversity, and the environment. What remains almost absent in the existing literature, though, is how to practice a critical pedagogy of place beyond using the practices of decolonization and reinhabitation.[11]

A CONTEMPLATIVE RESPONSE

Contemplative educators respond directly to Wakeman's question in positing age-old practices that center on interiority as the critical source and place for personal and intellectual growth. Teacher, poet, and writer

Mary Rose O'Reilley observes that some of our classroom practices "crush the soul" and consistently asks "what spaces [might we] create in the classroom that will allow students freedom to nourish an inner life?"[12] Professor and psychiatrist Robert Coles observes that the fundamental questions asked by each of us are those that reside within our interiority. He sees "overwrought language and overwrought theory" as the place where we lose our humanity and where our sensibilities die"[13] Barbezat and Bush emphasize awareness, attention, and introspection as critical to the student's comprehension of course material and development of self-awareness.[14] Art Zajonc asks if an education of critical reasoning, writing, speaking, and scientific and quantitative analysis is sufficient. He suggests that "the sharpening of our intellects with the systematic cultivation of our hearts [might be] of equal if not greater importance."[15] Tobin Hart advocates for "a new kind of liberal arts... [one] that brings us to the center of our *humanitas*... [and unlocks] virtue, genius, and delight."[16] Gunnlaugson, Sarath, Scott, and Bai advocate for the contemplative dimensions of "presence, discernment, and equanimity" as those that might transform "disengaged forms of academic analysis and disenchanted and instrumental habits of mind and life."[17]

Contemplative educators call for an integral model of knowing that canvasses both interior and exterior epistemologies. They argue that first-person modes are not in conflict with the more traditional, third-person classroom approaches in many of our classrooms, but rather complement, enrich, and expand. They see such practices as silence, reflection, witnessing or beholding, listening, dialog, journaling, and self-inquiry as prototypical and critical to the classroom. All are grounded in introspection, mindfulness, and self-reflection and serve as an important means for accessing the place of interiority. A detailed description of these practices is beyond the scope of this chapter. However, their central core is the disruption of unproductive habits that will, in turn, allow for the development and maturation of awareness and the cultivation of compassion, both of which are central to the integrity of a PBE model. It is important to note that contemplative educators recognize that no one contemplative method fits all students, all teachers, all classes, all disciplines, and all pedagogical goals. Contemplative scholars also remind us that contemplative practices are not intended to take the place of additional types of productive pedagogical methods. However, they do maintain that a content-driven contemplative dimension can be engendered across all disciplines and pedagogical models.

Many contemplative practices might be recognized by PBE teachers under the rubrics of *transformative, critical, experiential,* and *engaged* learning. What, then, specifically shifts and marks such practices as introspective or contemplative and differentiates them from certain other transformative practices? For contemplative educators, attentiveness to that which one is trying to understand is the root of all contemplative practices. Mah y Busch observes that critical pedagogies specifically, as well as many other of the transformative modes, employ word-based, linear dialectics whereas contemplative modes appreciate the dialogical or a "wordless dimension of experience," one that is "...inherently more relational and multidimensional than a dialectic."[18] Drawing from the work of literary theorist M. M. Bakhtin, Mah y Busch discusses dialogism as consisting of numerous subjectivities that coexist; it is not about speech (though conversation can be dialogic). He continues to suggest that while the dialectic is critical to analytical thought and discursive practices in the classroom, its limitation rests in its consistent privileging of words over wordlessness. Hobson and Morrison-Saunders continue the discussion by attending to the ways in which we consider our teaching practices. They hold that "...the conceptions and system of conceptions that we use in teaching and learning change what we observe and notice."[19] They urge us to consider what is left in and what is left out of higher education's conversations about teaching and learning. Such an admonition is particularly compelling in place-based pedagogies given its emphasis on observation and notice.

Zajonc holds that the "cultivation of attention" is central to all learning paradigms and yet, ironically, excluded by conventional pedagogy. This void leaves students without that which leads to creativity, insight, balance, and imagination; therefore, it leaves them without access to the place of their interiority.[20] In speaking of contemplative exercises as a return to the understanding of the student as a whole person, Barbezat and Bush articulate four distinct objectives of contemplative practices: (1) focus and attention building that sustain mental stability; (2) location of the place of self in the content of the course that deepens understanding of the material; (3) compassion and connection to others that lead to the moral and spiritual characteristic of education; and (4) inquiry into the nature of the self and the mind. Therefore, Barbezat and Bush see the contemplative dimension as grounded in a critical first-person inquiry, one that accesses and engages the place of interiority, attends to the production of knowledge in this particular place, and offers a much needed portal for the birth of insight, creativity, and personal resonance in the classroom.[21] If we consider the theory of PBE, each of these objectives is also at the heart of a critical and embodied place-based model.

A CONTEMPLATIVE IMAGINATION OF PLACE

Contemplative scholars cast an understanding of place seldom discussed in the literature outside the contemplative gates. For these educators, space is place. O'Reilley asks how we might make space in our classrooms that will allow students the freedom to nurture an inner life.[22] We have multiple examples for filling spaces and gaps in our classroom, but almost none for their creation. William Powers illuminates this perspective in his use of email as an analogy for the dearth of space in our lives. In both the composition and reading of emails, the central point is "...almost *not* to be thoughtful, not to pause and reflect. To eliminate the gaps."[23] Similarly, developmental theorists in the tradition of Robert Coles insist that the inner lives of students are central to understanding cognitive development.[24] They are quick to ask how we might access these inner lives when our classrooms are filled, overflowing, and often deafening with verbosity.

Silence is the wellspring for and the place from which all contemplative practices emerge. In spite of higher education's reluctance to embrace silence as an important method in teaching and learning, there are those individuals who have espoused its significance outside of contemplative pedagogies. Constructivist theorist Lev Vygotsky might be one of the first of these individuals to speak of silence in learning, suggesting that cognitive maturation moves from external vocalization to internal or "silent," private speech. According to Vygotsky, "...inner speech is for oneself; external speech is for others."[25] In this conceptualization, opportunities for silence create places in the classroom for self-awareness and learning. Likewise, Bruneau put forward the notion of "slow time" or a reflective, inner place that affords the time to think in the classroom.[26] More recently scholars such as Claxton have expanded both Vygotsky's and Bruneau's notions of silence by emphasizing the "knack of delicate inward attention" or focusing, a "thinking at the edge that leads to...the development of a broad epistemic culture" in our classrooms.[27] Kirsch speaks of the use of silence as "...in line with what a number of composition scholars suggest about the power of silence as a rhetorical tool."[28] This "rhetoric of silence" has been popularized by many such teachers including Cheryl

Glenn, who talks of silence as a "rhetorical art...a creative or ethical resource within the college classroom and for college writers."[29] Similarly, Ann French Dalke defines silence as an alternative way of knowing that is the center of the learning process. She states: "...when we do not speak, we may listen, hear, understand, even communicate in other ways. If language distorts, silence may open us to revelation."[30] Kalamaras advances an epistemological model evolving from silence. Silence for Kalamaras is "...a generative condition for discourse theory...[and] for writing theory and practice."[31]

Ollin articulates place in terms of a "silent pedagogy" that centers on the instructor's silence in the classroom, allowing students the possibility of a fresh gaze at an idea or a question.[32] His research highlights teachers' reports of silence. Some teachers recounted that their use of Power Point presentations is centered on images without words explaining that if communication is effective on the slide, "vocalisation was extraneous." Other teachers reported that this approach facilitated students' thinking for themselves as opposed to being told or directed by words.[33] However, Ollin also notes that the use of silence as place can be multimodal and, therefore, not limited to the absence of talk. These included (1) writing in silence as "...the opportunity for more measured thought and a more permanent record of that thinking"; (2) visual silence as "visual images used without vocalization and visual images used without verbalization"; and (3) spatial silence, "...a giving space for students to think or feel, by removing the immediacy of the teacher's presence" and a space to silently "...settle in, for example, to a new situation, a new experience or task..."[34]

Marilyn Nelson echoes this notion of place as embedded in silence by beginning all of her classes at West Point with a five-minute period of silence, what she sees as relevant to teaching poetry as a "slow art." She describes the creation of this constructed place and its relationship to the course: "They turn off the lights, loosen their ties; some of them take off their shoes and sit cross-legged on the floor. I set the timer. We close our eyes; we enter silence."[35] From this place of silence her military cadets begin to write their poetry. In reflecting on this contemplative understanding of place in teaching poetry in a military institution, Nelson describes the experience and place of silence in the classroom: "I hope that by teaching these twenty-eight cadets how to find and hold interior quiet, I am giving them the wherewithal of wise conflict resolution. Perhaps poetry will help them to lead others toward peace."[36]

Silence creates a place from which such contemplative practices as attention, reflection, listening, writing, and reading emerge. When we as a community of learners (both instructors and students) construct space in our classroom hour through moments of silence, we also build an openness that facilitates a deep-learning process. Mah y Busch discusses space in this manner:

> It is a quality. A living quality of experience. Whether we describe political liberation or the moment a student, in sudden realization, gasps "a- ha," what we actually appreciate in each example is the quality of spaciousness that has occurred. It is not the degree of depth or distance. Spaciousness is the quality of having enough room.[37]

Renee Hill sheds an additional understanding of space as a place. Hill turns to the work of Bradford Grant who emphasizes "negative space," which is "the space above, under, between, and around objects, like the three dimensional dough left behind once the gingerbread cookies have been removed. The 'not object' space." Hill expands Grant's conceptualization by suggesting that we squander our negative spaces with our busyness and harried lives and fail to notice the place of space that is present.[38] The classroom structure is no exception. As teachers, we have been acculturated toward filling up the room with activity and our own words. We might ponder the questions: How much space and what type of place may we allow in our classrooms, and where do we hold contemplative dimensions if there is no such space? How do we engage in O'Reilley's notion of "the practice of [classroom] hospitality" if we are not fully present to the spaciousness of the moment, one another, the self?[39] To construct space in our classrooms is not to abandon irresponsibly the work of the classroom nor to marginalize the lecture, discussion groups, learning teams, and all other pedagogical methods that we hold dear in our teaching lives. Rather, it is a pause (perhaps just a moment), a breath, and a deepening of presence that allows contemplative practices, as well as all of our classroom methods, to flourish. Pema Chodron speaks of a pause as a "transformative experience" and one that allows us to connect with a "fundamental spaciousness."[40] For Chodron, it is "the practice of not immediately filling up space just because there's a gap."[41]

Kegan approaches place as a type of "holding environment" or a supportive space, a supportive classroom, where students are nurtured or "held" as they move through developmental changes.[42] Zaretsky describes place as consisting of sustained "pauses" imagining that such pauses might "...bump [his students] into new thoughts not just about history but also their own selves [and] better prepare them to bump into other selves: be they historical actors, fictional characters or our fellow men and women."[43] Similarly, Patterson sees a pause as a place that might facilitate a close observation of what is arising in the self. She observes that "by stretching open the spaces that might prematurely fill with conclusions, contemplative pedagogies [that begin with a pause] make room for discipline based content..."[44] For many teachers, pauses provide an unmonitored place for reflection, creativity, and imagination with no interruption or imposition.

Silence gives birth and maturity to the contemplative practices of mindfulness, attention, reflection, listening, reading, and writing. Each create spaces and places where deep knowing, ethical discernment, and the cultivation of awareness of self and others are possible.

A place-based education calls for a wisdom-based education that instrumentalizes the learning of unselfishness, service, and cooperation. The contemplative practices of concentrated awareness, the extension of this awareness to other beings, and the accompanying sense of connectivity with these beings are gateways to the development of compassion and the moral, ethical imagination. The contemplative classroom, imbued with its emphasis on deep awareness, attention, and appreciation of a shared world, provides a critical context in which students might explore their moral imaginations and ethical dilemmas. It affords a portal for a place-based pedagogy grounded in an ethic of care and compassion. Educational researcher Encarnacion Soriano connects the ethical stance to a reinvention of education in the global world, arguing that one of the major challenges confronting education is the development of student values that will contribute to their citizenship in a democratic world. For Soriano, our students, as participants in and constructors of the twenty-first century, are called upon to coproduce "a universal and transcultural moral," one centered on social justice, human rights, and a resistance to major ethical offenses.[45] Contemplative methods offer a place whereby an ethical consciousness, compassion, and a moral attitude might develop. A contemplative approach to PBE bridges the gap often seen between the theory and practice of place-based pedagogies and offers great promise for a re-envisioned academy of honor, veracity, and relevance for the twenty-first century.

NOTES

1. Gruenewald, "Foundations of Place," 619.
2. McInerney, Smyth, and Down, "'Coming to a place near you?'"
3. Somerville, "A Place Pedagogy," 326.
4. Latta and Buck, "Enfleshing Embodiment," 315.
5. Rushmere, "'Placing' Caring Relationships in Education," 85.
6. Ibid., 81.
7. Somerville, Power, and de Carteret, "Landscapes and Learning," 360.
8. Rushmere, "'Placing' Caring Relationships in Education," 87.
9. Freire, *Pedagogy of the Oppressed*.
10. Bush, "Contemplative Higher Education in Contemporary Life," 223–224.
11. Wakeman, "Power in Place-Based Education."
12. O'Reilley, *Radical Presence*, 2.
13. Swick, "Robert Coles and the Moral Life."
14. Barbezat and Bush, *Contemplative Practices in Higher Education*, 23.
15. Zajonc, "Love and Knowledge," 2.
16. Hart, "The Inner Liberal Arts."
17. Gunnlaugson et al., "An Introduction," 5.
18. Mah y Busch, "A pedagogical heartbeat," 126.
19. Hobson and Morrison-Saunders, "Reframing Teaching Relationships," 774.
20. Zajonc, "Contemplation in Education," 24.
21. Barbezat and Bush, *Contemplative Practices in Higher Education*, 11.
22. O'Reilley, *Radical Presence*, 8.
23. Powers, *Hamlet's Blackberry*, 53.
24. Coles, *The Spiritual Life of Children*.
25. Vygotsky, *Thought and Language*, 225.
26. Bruneau. "Communicative silences."
27. Claxton, "Thinking at the Edge," 360.
28. Kirsch, "Creating Spaces," 8.
29. Glenn, *Unspoken*, xiii.
30. Dalke, *Teaching to Learn/Learning to Teach*, 53.
31. Kalamaras, *Reclaiming the Tacit Dimension*, 60.
32. Ollin, "Silent Pedagogy and Rethinking Classroom Practice, 273.
33. Ibid.
34. Ibid.
35. Nelson, "Aborigine in the Citadel," 548.
36. Ibid., 552.
37. Mah y Busch, "A Pedagogical Heartbeat."
38. Hill, "Honor the Negative Space."
39. O'Reilley, *Radical Presence*, 8.
40. Chodron, *When Things Fall Apart*, 41.

41. Ibid., 43.
42. Kegan, *The Evolving Self.*
43. Zaretsky, "An Appeal for Silence in the Seminar Room."
44. Barbara Patterson, "Sustaining Life," 158.
45. Soriano, *Rethinking Education for a Global, Transcultural World,* 53.

BIBLIOGRAPHY

Barbezat, Daniel, and Mirabai Bush. *Contemplative Practices in Higher Education.* San Francisco, CA: Jossey-Bass, 2014.

Bruneau, Tom J. "Communicative Silences: Forms and Functions." *Journal of Communication* 23.1 (1973), 17–46.

Bush, Mirabai. "Contemplative Higher Education in Contemporary Life." In *Contemplation Nation: How Ancient Practices are Changing the Way We Live,* edited by Mirabai Bush, 221–236. Kalamazoo, MI: Fetzer Institute, 2011.

Claxton, Guy. "Thinking at the Edge: Developing Soft Creativity." *Cambridge Journal of Education* 36.3 (2006), 360.

Coles, Robert. *The Spiritual Life of Children.* Boston, MA: Houghton Mifflin Co, 1990.

Dalke, Ann French. *Teaching to Learn/Learning to Teach: Meditations on the Classroom.* New York: Lang Publishing, 2002.

Freire, Pablo. *Pedagogy of the Oppressed,* 30th ed. New York: Continuum, 2000, orig., 1970.

Glenn, Cheryl. *Unspoken: A Rhetoric of Silence.* Carbondale: Southern Illinois University Press, 2004.

Gruenewald, David A. "Foundations of Place: A Multidisciplinary Framework for Place- Conscious Education." *American Educational Research Journal* 40.3 (2003), 619–654.

Gunnlaugson, Olen, Edward S. Sarath, Charles Scott, and Heesoon Bai. "An Introduction to Contemplative Learning and Inquiry Across Disciplines." In *Contemplative Learning and Inquiry Across Disciplines,* edited by Edward S. Olen Gunnlaugson, Charles Scott Sarath, and Heesoon Bai, 1–11. New York: New York Press, 2014.

Hart, Tobin. "The Inner Liberal Arts." (Presentation to the Leadership Council Meeting), Spring 2011.

Hill, Renee. "Honor the Negative Space." *Journal for Contemplative Inquiry* 1.1 (2014), 135–140.

Hobson, Julia, and Angus Morrison-Saunders. "Reframing Teaching Relationships: From Student-Centered to Subject-Centered." *Teaching in Higher Education* 18 (2013), 773–783.

Johnson, Jay T. "Place-Based Learning and Knowing: Critical Pedagogies Grounded in Indigeneity." *GeoJournal* 77.6 (2010), 829. doi:10.1007/s10708-010-9379-1.

Kalamaras, George. *Reclaiming the Tacit Dimension: Symbolic form in the Rhetoric of Silence.* Albany: State University of New York Press, 1994.

Kirsch, Gesa E. "Creating Spaces for Listening, Learning, and Sustaining the Inner Lives of Students." *The Journal of the Assembly for Expanded Perspectives on Learning* 14 (2009), 56–67.

Latta, Margaret M., and Gayle A. Buck. "Englishing Embodiment: 'Falling into Trust' with the Body's Role in Teaching and Learning." *Educational Philosophy and Theory* 40.2 (2007), 315–329.

Mah Y Busch, Juan D. "A Pedagogical Heartbeat: The Integration of Critical and Contemplative Pedagogies for Transformative Education." *The Journal of Contemplative Inquiry* 1 (2014), 113–134.

Margaret, Somerville, Kerith Power, and de Carteret Phoenix. "Landscapes and Learning" Place Studies for a Global World." *Children, Youth and Environments* 21.1 (2011), 360–362.

McInerney, Peter, John Smyth, and Barry Down. "'Coming to a Place Near you?' The Politics and Possibilities of a Critical Pedagogy of Place-Based Education." *Asia-Pacific Journal of Teacher Education* 39.1 (2011): http://dx.doi.org/10.1080/1359866X.2010.540894.

Nelson, Marilyn. "Aborigine in The Citadel." *The Hudson Review, Inc* 53.4 (2001), 543–553.

O'Reilley, Mary Rose. *Radical Presence.* Portsmouth, NH: Boynton/Cook Publishers, 1998.

Ollin, Ross. "Silent Pedagogy and Rethinking Classroom Practice: Structuring Teaching Through Silence Rather Than Talk." *Cambridge Journal of Education* 38.2 (2008), 265–280.

Ortiz, Simon. "Indigenous Language Consciousness: Being, Place, and Sovereignty." In *Sovereign Bones: New Native American Writing,* edited by E. L. Gansworth, 135–148. New York: Nation Books, 2007.

Patterson, Barbara. "Sustaining Life: Contemplative Pedagogies in a Religion and Ecology Course." In *Meditation and the Classroom,* edited by Judith Simmer-Brown and Fran Grace, 155–161. Albany, NY: State University of New York Press, 2011.

Rushmere, Andrew. "'Placing' Caring Relationships in Education: Addressing Abstraction and Domination." *Paideusis* 16.2 (2007), 81–88.

Schultz, Katherine. *Rethinking Classroom Participation: Listening to Silent Voices.* New York: Teachers College Press, 2009.

Somerville, Margaret J. "A Place Pedagogy for 'Global Contemporaneity'." *Educational Philosophy and Theory* 42.3 (2010), 326–344.

Soriano, Encarnacion. *Rethinking Education for a Global, Transcultural World.* Charlotte, NC: Information Age Publishing, 2015.

Swick, David. "Robert Coles and the Moral Life." *Mindful.* August 24, (2010): np.

Wakeman, Heather. "Power in Place-Based Education: Why a Critical Pedagogy of Place Needs to be Revived and How Narratives or Collective Biographies Support Its Practice." Doctoral Projects, Masters Plan B, and Related Works, University of Wyoming, 2015.

Zajonc, Arthur. "Love and Knowledge: Recovering the Heart of Learning Through Contemplation." *Teachers College Record* 108.9 (2006), 1741–1759.

Zajonc, Arthur. "Contemplation in Education." In *Handbook of Mindfulness in Education*, edited by K. A. Schonert-Reichl and R. W. Roeser, 17–27. New York: Springer-Verlag, 2016.

CHAPTER 4

Turning Your Place into Projects

Scott D. Wurdinger

Place-based learning has evolved over the years with roots stemming from environmental education and occurred within urban, suburban, and rural contexts.[1] Its primary focus was to use environmental education as a way to improve the place or community in which one lived. Certain scholars have defined it as performing a service to the community, which in turn helps students learn about the history, values, and decisions that helped that particular community.[2]

More recently, community has become as significant as environmental education in helping define place-based learning. According to the Place-Based Education Evaluation Collaborative (PEEC), place-based learning "focuses on using the local community as an integrating context for learning at all levels."[3] Wurdinger suggests that it includes the incorporation of a local community's history, culture, and people, and in order for students to learn about these things they must leave the classroom and engage in direct experience with places like schools, organizations, businesses, and natural surroundings in their community.[4]

S.D. Wurdinger (✉)
Experiential Education and Leadership Studies, Minnesota State University, Mankato, USA

© The Author(s) 2017
D. Shannon, J. Galle (eds.), *Interdisciplinary Approaches to Pedagogy and Place-Based Education*, DOI 10.1007/978-3-319-50621-0_4

EXPERIENTIAL LEARNING AND PLACE-BASED LEARNING

Place-based learning is one of several experiential approaches to learning that is guided by certain principles including: "promoting hands-on learning, using a problem-solving process, addressing real world problems, encouraging student interaction with each other and the content, engaging in direct experiences, and using multiple subjects to enhance interdisciplinary learning."[5] With this process students are actively pursuing their learning, are provided freedom to explore and discover knowledge, and may collaborate with peers in seeking answers to problems. One of the primary underlying themes behind this teaching approach is encouraging students to take control of their own learning by becoming actively engaged participants.

Figure 4.1 depicts five common experiential approaches to learning that show how one approach incorporates the one before it when moving from the inside to the outside rings. For example, a place-based learning activity like creating a community park would include providing a service to the community, solving multiple problems as the park is being built, and collaborating with others to complete the project.

Project-based learning, depicted in the triangle, shows that it is possible to incorporate this approach into all of the other approaches to varying degrees. Project-based learning is often at the center of place-based

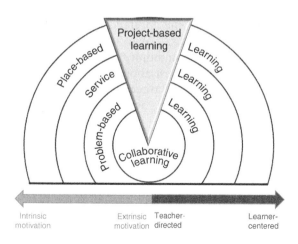

Fig. 4.1 Project-based learning infused

learning because most place-based learning activities are actually projects. The approaches in the outer rings tend to be more student centered because they require students to leave the classroom and interact with community members, and therefore are often more intrinsically motivating. Collaborative and problem-based learning tend to be more teacher directed occurring in classroom settings and are more extrinsically motivating.

By using a little creativity, educators can create place-based projects that students can begin to develop in classroom settings, and then venture out into the community to complete them. There are multiple potential projects that students can work on in college classrooms, and with all the technology available today, they can reach out to community organizations and complete much of the planning phase right in the classroom. Projects can be small, requiring one class session to complete, or they can be big, requiring the entire semester to complete.

Projects are at the heart of place-based learning: "Place based educators want to advocate for an integrated curriculum that emphasizes project based learning, teacher collaboration, and extensive use of community resources and volunteers."[6] A project often denotes a product that is created having useful application, and the learning process that occurs when developing and completing projects requires students to solve multiple problems along the way to completion.

For example, conducting restoration for a local hiking trail entails creating a plan to determine what parts of the trail need to be restored, where the trail might be eroding, what type of material will be needed to restore the trail, how to transport the material to the trail locations, tools that will be needed to transport and move materials, and the number of people that will be needed to do the work. Questions and problems will crop up during the process of completing the project, which might require several trial and error attempts during each phase of the process before the project is completed.

The learning theory that occurs with place-based learning stems from John Dewey's "pattern of inquiry."[7] Dewey's pattern of inquiry consists of six steps. His explanation of this theory, however, is similar to the scientific method, which suggests that a relevant problem causes perplexity and a desire to find an answer (step one), followed by the creation of a plan (step two), testing the plan against reality (step three), and reflecting on its worth (step four). The testing phase of this learning theory is what makes the learning experiential because students must execute their plan to determine if it works. Responding to instructor questions and reciting back information in traditional classroom settings allows students to talk, but learning becomes experiential when they create plans to solve problems and test them in real-world scenarios. For example, creating a piece of artwork or building a model off a blueprint requires students to develop plans and test them to determine their worth.

When students are in the process of completing a place-based project, they go through the process of identifying problems, developing plans, testing them against reality, and reflecting on them. This process challenges students cognitively as they attempt to construct the project and, in many cases, solve multiple problems they encounter during the process.

Place-based projects can be complex, which may entail going through multiple trial and error attempts before the project is completed. Each time students go through this cycle (problem, plan, test, reflect), the process requires them to solve problems and learn from their mistakes. Figure 4.2 shows how the place-based learning process begins in the present and leads students out into the future as they undergo multiple problem-solving episodes. They become discoverers of knowledge, and each cycle requires them to practice and learn skills such as problem solving, creativity, time management, responsibility, work ethic, and self-direction. The skills they learn from going through this process are important life skills they can use the rest of their lives.

Collateral Learning

In 1938 John Dewey wrote an influential book titled *Experience and Education* in which he discusses the importance of collateral learning:

> Collateral learning in the way of formation of enduring attitudes, of likes and dislikes, may be and often is much more important than the spelling lesson or lesson in geography or history that is learned. For these attitudes are fundamentally what count in the future. The most important attitude that can be formed is that of desire to go on learning.[8]

This is what happens with place-based learning. In learning environments where students are given freedom to determine their own place-based projects from their own interests, as well as freedom to work on projects at their own pace, they begin to learn how to learn and learn how to

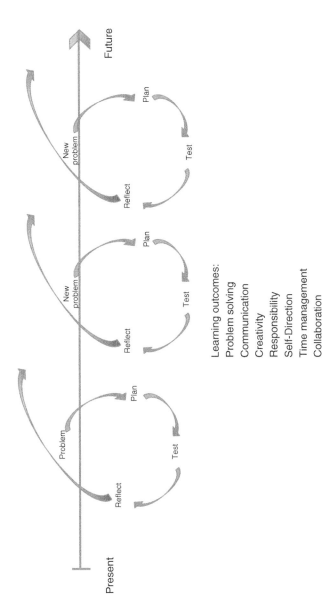

Fig. 4.2 Place-based learning process

become self-directed learners. They are working on completing a project, but as a result they learn other skills as by-products of the process.

Problem solving and critical thinking, for example, tend to be fundamental skills that students use and learn during this process.

STUDENT PROJECTS

Turning the place where you live into projects is not difficult. Communities are filled with needs, stories, and events that can easily be turned into projects. During a conversation with the late Sigurd Olson, who lived in Ely, Minnesota, and was a well-known Minnesota nature writer, we discussed the history of Pine Island, which is a tiny island located on Burntside Lake near his cabin. He told me that the island was never logged because it was hidden in the middle of numerous other islands on the lake. White pines, highly coveted trees for their wood, were gigantic in size on this island and were estimated to be between 150 and 300 years old with a two- to three-foot diameter at the base.[9] These trees were extremely valuable in the late 1800s when logging was at its peak, but luckily they were not discovered until after the logging era ended, allowing future generations to enjoy their beauty.

Olson's story could easily be turned into a project for students. For instance, college students in a biology or history course could count the number of trees on the island, take their girth measurements to estimate their age, photograph them, create a presentation on the importance of preserving these trees, and present it at a local town-hall meeting. This project would allow them to learn how to conduct research on the history of this island and the logging era, learn how to age a tree, practice photography skills, learn to collaborate with peers and take responsibility for completing their project tasks, and practice their communication skills during their presentations.

Reaching out to individuals who live and work in a community and asking them questions about the history and current needs of their organizations and businesses provides opportunities to create meaningful projects for students. Communities are filled with projects that not only can help educate students, but can also fulfill a need, as well as educate others who live in the community.

What follows consists of examples of projects that students completed in college courses. These projects can be easily adapted for your own classrooms. The course topics focused on experiential learning and leadership and were taught at a university in South Central Minnesota. These students were encouraged to think about projects that could improve their own educational environments where many of them worked. Community organizations are always in need of improvements and are rich with the potential for creating a variety of projects.

Several students who reached out to local community members created wonderful projects that benefited not only the organizations but also numerous individuals associated with these organizations. The first four projects described below were created to enhance the learning of the students at local schools or universities. The second four projects were community projects. With these projects students reached out to community members working in different organizations and identified a need, which their projects fulfilled.

Healthy Snack Shop

Students in my classes have completed a number of place-based projects that evolved out of their own school environments. One teacher, for example, decided to create a contest for her students to determine what they believed was a relevant problem that needed to be fixed at their school. The students brainstormed a list of problems, and through a process of elimination they decided that the school needed more options for healthy snacks. They voted to create a healthy-snack shop because they wanted alternatives to what was currently being offered to them at their school. Her class decided that they would create and run the shop.

This place-based project created a number of challenges and problems, which students had to overcome as they worked toward the creation of this shop, which required a fair amount of problem solving and collaboration. Students had to find out what kinds of foods were healthy and appealing to the student body, how much they should charge for these foods, where they would purchase the food they would sell, how to create a schedule for working the snack shop, and what they would do with the proceeds. They had to test out their ideas when they began selling food to see how to run the shop and adjust their ideas as they proceeded. This project allowed students to learn skills like problem solving, organization, and communication.

It also allowed them to learn how to run a small business and how to take on responsibilities for doing tasks and completing them. This type of learning is more rigorous and meaningful because it has a direct impact on their lives. Students tend to take ownership of their learning when they identify and create the project.

This project probably impacted their lives in other ways as well. For instance, they may have learned more about health and nutrition and changed their eating behaviors, or learned more about the importance of effective communication when running a small business. Skills like communication and collaboration are critical in order to survive in today's world.

The process of completing this particular project required students to consider multiple topics. Students learned about nutrition, marketing, economics, communication, and business practices, which is an interdisciplinary approach to learning. In traditional classes educators often compartmentalize subject matter and tend to break down content into small bits and pieces in order to provide students with just the necessary information they need for tests. When students take on the challenge of creating a complex project, they need to take a broader perspective and consider a wide range of topics. Each topic creates its own set of problems to solve, and solving these problems creates a rigorous learning environment for students.

Kilowatt Hour Cost Saving

Another college student decided to create a project based on electricity being used at the university. Specifically, he decided to determine the approximate cost of electricity per day in Armstrong Hall, the building where I teach my courses, and determine ways for the university to cut down on electrical costs. This was a difficult time-consuming process that was not completely accurate. But it at least gave the facilities director an approximation on how to cut back on costs. His project was based on the electricity being used by the lights only in the classrooms. He did not include the use of technological appliances such as computers and classroom projectors.

I am neither an electricity nor math expert, but he was and truly enjoyed working on his project. He used the following formula to determine the approximate cost of electricity when classrooms were not in use:

wattage × hours used ÷ 1000 × price per kWh = cost of electricity

In order to determine the amount of electricity being wasted, he first decided to walk through all three floors of the building several times each day for a month and record the number of rooms with lights on that were not in use. He was able to receive a copy of the building's schedule to determine when each room was in session with classes. When he found a room that was not in use with the lights on, he assumed the lights would be on until the next class session. This is where it was a little inaccurate because someone could walk past the room and shut off the lights. Each time he walked through the halls of the building, he would multiply the wattage of each fluorescent tube by the number of minutes or hours used when the room was empty. He then divided this number by 1000 and multiplied it by the cost of electricity.

He did this for one month and averaged the total cost for one month by nine months during which time the fall and spring semester classes were in session. He then set up a meeting with the Vice President of Facilities Management and discussed his findings with him. To my knowledge this meeting resulted in one significant change. Although the vice president of facilities left the university not long after his meeting with this student, I did notice motion-sensor lights in most of the classrooms the following fall semester. This one change may have cut down the costs significantly.

This project took place right in the building where this student was taking his classes. He took his immediate place and turned it into an in-depth project. What did he learn from this project? When he first started the project, he thought it would be fun to use his interests in math and science to calculate energy waste in the building. But once he started the project, he realized there could be very practical applications for the university. He not only learned how to conduct some research but he also learned how to organize his thoughts into a presentation. He was able to practice research skills, organizational skills, and communication skills. Knowing the personality of this student, the most challenging piece of his project was probably the presentation he gave to the vice president.

Historical Crayon Rubbings

One of my students was a history buff and created a project based on the history of the university. He spent most of his time in the library-archives section reading information about the university and writing down major events that occurred since the inception of the university. As a way to document the history for his classroom presentation, he decided to walk around the university and use crayon rubbings of monuments, cornerstones, building names, and other important historical events. Crayon rubbings is a simple but effective process when bringing living history into the classroom. He took waxed butcher paper and placed the wax side down on things like a cornerstone date of a building, and then took a crayon the long way and rubbed it over the year, creating a rubbing of the date.

Back in the late 1960s and early 1970s my university had a lab school that was highly innovative. As part of this student's project, he asked if the students in the class could walk over to the old lab-school site, which has since been transformed into a daycare center, and do some crayon rubbings. He wanted students to see the community garden (definitely ahead of its time) that was located in the center of the lab school and do their own rubbings of various artifacts located in this garden. After doing their rubbings, the students were asked to share their rubbings with the rest of the class. As students shared their rubbings, this student explained the history behind each artifact. This was a unique experience for all the students and made an impression on them regarding the history of the university they were attending.

At the end of this course students presented their projects to the class in order to practice their public speaking and communication skills. His presentation consisted of showing a variety of rubbings from all over campus and an explanation of each rub. He walked the rest of the class through a chronological timeline of all of the major events that occurred on this campus through his rubbings. He had rubbings of building cornerstones, monuments, such as that for the Vietnam War, and the names of students who had tragically died in accidents. His presentation was informative and emotional. Everyone in the class, and I include myself, learned a great deal about our university.

The students in our program come from all across the country, but this student was fairly local from a town 30 miles away, so he may have been more interested in the university's history than others in the class. However, by the end of his presentation, everyone was interested in the history. His presentation was highly creative and well conceived. This student enhanced his creative thinking skills as well as his organization and communication skills. History often gets a bad rap and is accused of being boring, but this student brought the people and places on this campus alive and captured everyone's attention in the class.

Mini Ecosystem

One of my students created a guidebook that identified all the vegetation for a small piece of property that was on the edge of the university boundary. The property was approximately 75 feet by 75 feet in size, so it was fairly small. He surveyed all the plants, bushes, and trees and created a map and a key that identified all the vegetation. The beginning pages of the guidebook consisted of a step-by-step process that allowed individuals to identify plants, bushes, and trees on their own. The guidebook was simple to use and consisted of a process of elimination. So if a tree did not have certain characteristics associated with its leaves or bark, then the guide would direct you to another page.

The guidebook also included a key to identify animal tracks. During the time he spent on this property, he discovered that mice, squirrels, wild turkeys, and whitetail deer frequently walked through this area. This student was an excellent artist. So he drew pictures of these animals with their associated track prints next to them in the book.

The guidebook also included a section that explained the history and evolution of plant growth in immature and mature forests. Interestingly, this piece of property was a fairly mature forest because it consisted of older trees with large canopies that shaded the understory, therefore not allowing smaller plant growth to occur. He also explained the importance of maintaining a healthy ecosystem and how interconnected and important plant and animal species are to one another.

He piloted the guidebook during his class presentation by placing each student next to a plant, bush, or tree and asked everyone to go through the process of identifying his or her vegetation using the guidebook. He asked his peers to use the guidebook with a critical eye by writing down suggestions on how to make the book easier to use. He was pleasantly surprised to learn that his guide was fairly easy to use and most of the students were able to identify their vegetation. The primary purpose behind his project was to teach people about the interconnectedness of the ecosystem and to engage students in discussions about how ecosystems are being threatened today by human progress.

Since this student was not from Minnesota, he learned about the local vegetation and wildlife. He also learned how to write a guidebook that was user-friendly for students. He practiced and honed his writing and communication skills and contacted publishers to learn the process on how to publish his book.

Dakota Uprising

For the most part, the small city I live in has a wonderful history, except for one horrific event. Mankato, Minnesota was the site of the largest mass hanging of Native Americans in the United States, which occurred in December of 1862 when 38 men were hung simultaneously.[10] There was a large Native American population in this area in the 1800s, whom the federal and state governments slowly cheated out of their land. Treaties were signed but not honored and money was promised but never paid.

By the mid-1850s the Native Americans could no longer maintain their way of life because they were forced onto smaller pieces of ground with limited wildlife to hunt and were not given the money they were promised in order to feed their families. The multiple years of false promises reached a boiling point in 1862 when four Native Americans shot and killed five settlers. This episode was the beginning of a series of killings and battles in the Minnesota River Valley, where many Native Americans and White settlers lost their lives.

There have been several faculty members at my university who wrote books on this event, so one of my students read all the books, talked to one of the authors, and decided to create an interactive children's book for upper-elementary students. She detailed some of the major events that happened during the Dakota uprising in her book in order to give students an understanding of some of the history that occurred in their own city.

My student was an exceptional artist and drew pictures of some of the key people, including Little Crow, the chief that attempted to prevent the uprising, Henry Sibley, who was the governor of the state at the time, and several others. She also drew pictures of buffalo and other wildlife to show students the connection between animals and spirituality for Native Americans, as well as what they hunted to provide food for their tribes. She left open spaces in her book for students to draw their own pictures of settlers, Native Americans, and wildlife.

She showed her book to several local elementary school teachers, who asked her if she could photocopy her book so that they could use it in their classrooms. I asked her how her meetings went with the school teachers and she informed me that she felt as if their knowledge deepened after her meetings with them.

Food Bank Awareness

One student who was volunteering at a local food bank wanted to conduct a public awareness campaign for her project. So she spoke to the director of this organization and asked if this would be beneficial for the organization. Since the food bank was not well known in the community, they decided that the campaign was a great idea and would potentially increase the amount of food donated to the organization.

She created a brochure that explained the mission of the organization, as well as the specific rules that are enforced when giving away food to individuals in need. The brochure also explained how much food they give away each year, as well as future goals for donations.

When the brochure was finished, she did a media blitz to get the word out to community organizations. She started with businesses that she thought might want to donate food, such as grocery stores, large restaurants, and bakeries. She also publicized the food bank on the local TV station and asked that businesses consider giving people discounts if they brought in a certain number of nonperishable items.

Her project was a huge success! The donations poured into the food bank. There were multiple businesses that gave discounts to those who brought in food items. To this day, there are still many businesses that on certain days or special events offer discounts if you bring food in. For example, every winter the downhill-skill area identifies at least one night during the winter when individuals receive a lift ticket discount if they bring in a certain numbers of food items. Since conducting that campaign, the food shelf has outgrown its building and is now located in a much larger facility.

This student learned that a small brochure, along with a tremendous amount of leg work, could have an enormous impact on her community, and that a significant impact could occur over a relatively short period of time. She was in our program for three years and became a familiar face in the community due to meeting numerous business owners and appearing on the local TV station several times while promoting the food bank.

Nature Center Curriculum

One of my graduate students identified a need in the community, which focused on renovating and creating new curriculum stations at a local nature center. He contacted the director and set up a meeting at the center. The center had been in disrepair for a few years after the local school district decided to discontinue its funding for educational programming.

He visited the nature center, had conversations with the director, and identified a series of ideas that could result in new learning stations at the center. This student was an artist, so he painted beautiful wall murals with plant- and animal-identification activities. His enthusiasm caught on in my class and soon he had several other students helping him with this project. During one class session, students broke into small groups and began brainstorming ideas and creating plans for different stations, identifying specific tasks that each group could work on before the next class. The result of this brainstorming session was to create a squirrel obstacle course and video and audio activities about birds and insects.

During the rest of the semester, they worked on these projects and slowly completed them. Through the process they learned better communication skills, how to work in teams, how to be responsible for doing their individual tasks, and how to manage their time to complete the tasks. The project was such a success that some students continued to work for the nature center after the semester course had ended.

Science Museum

My city has a children's science museum, which continues to expand and grow in popularity. The museum was moved into a bigger building and staff were looking for more curriculum ideas, so one of my students met with the director and asked if she was interested in having him create three indoor agricultural systems: an aquaponics system, a vermicomposting system, and a grow-shelves system. She agreed and he was off and running. He was tasked with building these systems within a given space in the museum with a somewhat limited budget for the materials.

The aquaponics system was built with a large aquarium and grow shelves. The system works as follows: the fish produce waste, which the worms and microbes turn into fertilizer. The fertilizer is then used to grow plants that are directly above the aquarium in growing shelves. The plants are typically leafy vegetables like lettuce and kale. The plants then filter the water, which returns to the aquarium.

He built the vermicomposting system out of wood and screen material. The container has wooden slats separated by space so that air can flow into the compost material to help break down food waste. The container is filled with composting dirt, fungi, and worms. Food waste from vegetables and fruits is placed in the container and the worms, bacteria, and fungi break down the food waste into composting dirt. The dirt is then used in the grow shelves to grow more vegetables and fruits. The grow shelves for the vegetables and fruits are located in a different part of the museum, where they are exposed to a lighting system.

After he finished constructing the three agricultural systems, he created four lesson plans to go with them. His lessons were all hands on and included seed identification, planting seeds in small containers, worm composting with the use of magnifying glasses to view the decomposing process, examination of the differences between traditional and aquaponic growing systems, and aquaponics water testing. His lesson plans were formatted using the following headings:

     I. Leading Question
    II. Subject Area/General Topic
   III. Grade Level
   IV. Learning Objective
    V. Engage
   VI. Explore
  VII. Explain
VIII. Elaborate
   IX. Evaluate
    X. Evoke Emotion
   XI. Materials Needed
  XII. Background Information

Most of the lesson-plan headings are self-explanatory, but this student wanted to make this a hands-on lesson, so he engaged people by having them plant seeds in their own cups. In small groups they explore their own questions and explain how they believe seeds grow. They evaluate their questions and ideas, and emotion is evoked by having them discuss questions about people that don't have enough food to eat.

I remember asking him in an email message what he believed were the most important lessons learned from his experience working with the children's museum. Here is his response:

> I honed my communication skills, communicating on a very regular basis by email, phone and in person with a program team that wanted and needed immediate response to make decision. I learned to manage my time effectively to be available when needed for logistical support and troubleshooting. Further, I learned to create program budgets and to manage funds appropriately to maximize effectiveness of limited funds.

I also gained a great deal of knowledge on aquaponics, meeting with local experts and researching 100s of aquaponics designs. I learned to consider not only the most efficient aquaponics designs but what design would work best in a museum setting.

I also worked on my problem solving skills, trying to develop a physical space and programming with limited funding and a constantly changing vision of the AgLab site by the leadership team.

I developed a great deal of life skills through the implementation of this project as well as experience creating programing and specifics skills on aquaponics systems. This is just a short list of what I learned.

Summary

Place-based projects that are of interest to students have the potential to transform their lives and lead to other learning experiences. Experiences like these can change lives when they stretch out into the future and inspire students to learn and discover new knowledge. Rigor requires that students do something with information. They need to apply it by demonstrating what they know or telling others what they know. Rigor requires students to show or tell others what they know and explain details of the project.

Rigor should result in invigoration where students are excited about learning and are motivated to do work on their own. They will be more excited about finding answers and solutions to problems when the learning has direct relevancy to their lives.

Place-based learning is more challenging to implement than other approaches because it requires spending some time away from the college classroom. However, much of the work can be completed in classrooms. But implementing the project will require students to be at the place where the project will occur. It also requires some upfront time on the instructor's part. In many cases instructors will need to contact community organizations and make arrangements for the project to occur.

This approach has tremendous potential for students to learn life skills. Doing place-based projects allows students to collaborate with peers, take responsibility, communicate with peers and community members, solve problems, and ultimately learn how to learn. If instructors want students to learn important skills that they can carry with them after they graduate, then they must tap into students' interests and allow them the freedom to pursue projects that are relevant and meaningful to them.

Notes

1. Sarkar and Frazier, "Place Based Investigations and Authentic Inquiry."
2. Henthorn, "Experiencing the City."
3. "PEEC—The Placed Based Education Evaluation Collaborative."
4. Scott Wurdinger, *The Power of Project Based Learning.*
5. Wurdinger and Carlson, *Teaching for Experiential Learning,* 8.
6. Sobel, *Place Based Education,* 19.
7. Dewey, *Logic,* 101–119.
8. Dewey, *Experience and Education,* 48.
9. Tefft, "Transformed by Burntside Islands SNA."
10. Lawrence, *The Peace Seekers.*

Bibliography

Dewey, John. *Experience and Education.* New York, NY: Free Press, 1938a.

Dewey, John. *Logic: The Theory of Inquiry.* New York, NY: Holt, Rinehart, and Winston, 1938b.

Henthorn, Thomas. "Experiencing the City: Experiential Learning in Urban Environments." *Journal of Urban History* 40, no. 3 (2014): 450–461.

Lawrence, Elden. *The Peace Seekers: Indian Christians and the Dakota Conflict.* Sioux Falls, SD: Pine Hill Press, 2005.

"PEEC—The Placed Based Education Evaluation Collaborative." *Place-Based Education Evaluation Collaborative.* December 12, 2003. http://www.peec works.org/PEEC/PEEC_Concept_Full_12-11-03.pdf

Sarkar, Somnar, and Richard. Frazier. "Place Based Investigations and Authentic Inquiry." *The Science Teacher* 75, no. 2 (2008): 29–33.

Sobel, David. *Place Based Education: Connecting Classrooms and Communities.* Great Barrington, MA: The Orion Society, 2005.

Tefft, Bill. "Transformed by Burntside Islands SNA." *The Ely Echo.* March 3, 2012. http://www.elyecho.com/articles/2012/03/03/transformed-burnt side-islands-sna

Wurdinger, Scott. *The Power of Project Based Learning: Helping Students Develop Important Life Skills.* Lanham, MD: Rowman and Littlefield, 2016.

Wurdinger, Scott, and Julie. Carlson *Teaching for Experiential Learning: Five Approaches that Work.* Lanham, MD: Rowman and Littlefield, 2010.

CHAPTER 5

The Story of Here: Documentary Film Education, Teaching Narratives, and Drawing from the Critical Perspective of Place

Shane Burley

As the 2008 financial crisis began rumbling through the lives of millennial undergraduates, it seemed like the era of arts education as a component of the university experience might be receiving its fatal blow. The predicament of contemporary higher education has affected most academic fields, yet there has been a certain unmitigated assault on the arts since the contemporary American job market is not as welcoming to candidates from non-STEM fields. For those in arts education, the new turn is toward embedding educational programs with practical skills that can lead directly to long-term career potential. This has always been the pedagogical praxis inside of many film education departments, where fine arts programs are often composed of a series of practical industry "trade" tracks like video editing, lighting and cinematography, sound design, and animation.

For film students, the ability to develop a "video narrative" is one of the most central practical industry skills they can learn. While the narrative

S. Burley (✉)
Independent Scholar, New York, USA

© The Author(s) 2017
D. Shannon, J. Galle (eds.), *Interdisciplinary Approaches to Pedagogy and Place-Based Education*, DOI 10.1007/978-3-319-50621-0_5

visual storytelling of traditional filmmaking attracts numerous students to the field, this is not reflected in the current state of commercial video production. Instead, nonfiction film and video dominates through broadcast news, reality television, broad documentary content, educational videos, and a huge range of industrial and commercial enterprises. While all of these projects stray from the conceptual auteur theory driving much of the "film school culture" that ties directly to the film festival circuit, these projects are pieced together with much the same narrative structure as anything in "black box" theaters. To maintain a student's professional trajectory, there must be an attempt to drive home the basics of narrative structure and the ways that it can apply to nonfiction production where there is no script dictating what happens in front of the lens.

For students learning narrative structure for video presentation, screenwriting materials often stress a particular film language that the audience has a specific relationship to. For nonfiction production, narratives must include the ability to develop a critical perspective on the events they portray so as to create something that is both unique and challenging. Nonfiction production has, at its heart, subjectivity to it through the choices of its artists. This is not tangential to the narrative structure of nonfiction projects, but it is *fundamental* to it. The challenge to educators is to then create a perspective in student filmmakers whereby they can analyze a real-world story, create a critical perspective that fleshes out their own values and social theory, and then pieces those elements together into a package that can be understood and experienced by a diverse audience.

When attempting to develop a critical pedagogical approach to students who are looking to develop a unique skillset, it is useful to use existing approaches in critical inquiry as a gateway to understanding key concepts. Moving into the use of *places* themselves can offer a scaled-down model for how to tell nonfiction stories that highlight social struggles. Broad histories of places themselves are subject to constant revision as social values develop in response to cultural movements and offer their own narratives that remain vibrant and relevant to the experiences of those living there. An application of a critical pedagogy of place(s) offers film educators particularly, and those in arts education broadly, a model from which to work with when developing the ability to take real-world events and reshape them in a critical narrative context.

To look at the use of critical place-based education in teaching narrative structure to nonfiction film students, I will first outline what this narrative structure is that students must adopt. This rests documentary film directly into the critical analysis of form used to discuss narrative film, where elements of story structure have to be imposed so the audience can understand and interpret the events in the film. This notion of story structure is applied to real-world events in documentary, which is at odds with much of the popular conception of documentary film as an "unbiased observer." It is from this position that the histories of places can provide a model for how to create narrative arcs out of lived experiences and to develop a socially critical eye in how those stories are told.

NARRATING FILM STUDIES

The influence of Marshal McLuhan on Film Studies, as in all branches of Media Studies, cannot be overstated, especially when considering the function of nonfiction media. All technology is viewed as a natural extension of the body and its essential functions. And all media, from language to smart phones, are considered technology, in his vernacular.[1] Media are a natural extension of what the body needs; with journalism and nonfiction media being the extension of the internal drive to observe, categorize, and report, furthering the body's access to key necessities. Moreover, the "real world," as it is experienced through the senses, is transposed to a narrative form so as to be understood. While avoiding the issue of biological necessity and narrative form, humans generally observe and report events in a narrative structure. When a consistent narrative structure is lacking in the transmission of information, they generally apply a narrative structure internally.

In a certain sense, documentary film aims to inhabit the "invisible editing" popularized in Classic Hollywood cinema, whereby the narrative of chronological events is delivered to the audience. Likewise, as David Bordwell has noted, the fabula (chronological sequencing) is part of what the viewer constructs during their interpretation. Classical narrative structure uses the film primarily for the transmission of story arc, the encouragement of the audience to interpret the images as a coherent story, and to use the appropriate and minimal number of filmic techniques necessary for the story's transmission. What is important is how the audience can participate with this process by interpreting a number of techniques of film language that they have become comfortable with through a lifetime of interacting with popular media.[2] Though documentary and narrative film may have dramatically different production processes, their exhibition is remarkably similar, which has a direct influence on their audience's collective consciousness. Audience members often expect, even unconsciously, an experience that will draw on the same semiotic patterns within the two film types. Documentary has then been pulled along with the expectations of Classic Hollywood, as has most production forms. While the narratives that audiences understand may evolve and change during moments of avant-garde rupture in the production norm, the general pattern for narrative is as baked into the audience as it is in the production methods that are industry standards.

Narrative structure has been critical to the "dramatic arts," especially where sequential storytelling is the central tenant. Film scholar Howard Suber notes the narrative drive is about applying logic and certain "cause and effect" to incidents of life that we may assume to lack these characteristics.

> In dramatic structure, everything is regarded as meaningful and everything is intentional, because dramatic structure operates like Newtonian physics— everything has a cause, and for every cause there is an effect. Accidents and coincidences occur all the time in real life, and the history of individuals and entire societies often turns on them. But dramatic structure is based on the fundamental assumption that what individuals do *determines* what happens— not fate, God, history, accidents, or coincidences. The logic of life, as we all learn through experience, is that all too often there *isn't* any logic. Ironically, a drama that tries to simulate this lack of logic stands a good chance of being called unrealistic. What audiences seek in drama is a structure they seldom find in real life.[3]

Documentary and nonfiction films are more dramas than they are records, with the editing and pre-production processes often likened to that of screenwriting. We must assume *causality* to the events and characters in our stories, and apply a narrative structure to them that we see akin to narrative films. In nonfiction film we do this by ascribing certain values, making choices about what is important, and deciding what events preceded others in a way to suggest that causality. This is not to impose causality where there is none, but to understand that certain sequencing suggests that correlation, and to represent events in ways that we think are both honest and in line with the filmmaker's perspective. In essence we have to attach the human experience of understanding through narrative to the real world, even if it is a uniquely human concept of sharing and interpretation.

What this does is then challenge the role of the documentarian as the observer, a notion that is largely a falsehood developed rhetorically during the early development of mobile 16-mm film cameras. During the 1960s–1970s, it became more practical to shoot in real-world situations with minimal artificial light and for long periods. The notion proposed by people like Frederick Wiseman was that the filmmaker would observe, documenting their observations, and a narrative or set of ideas would develop naturally out of that. Instead, many today would say that even this period of observation during Cinema Verite was about the imposition of narrative on the subject by the filmmaker, even if the filmmaker strove toward objectivity and fairness. One lesson we can take out of this is that the narratives that are applied to real-world subjects have to be done so with a certain reverence for the facts and an honest attempt to portray things as they are even if the application of filmic conventions do not allow for a pure "observe" ideal.[4]

Nonfiction production finds itself almost wholly built around theoretical interpretations of the theatrical documentary, meaning the documentary with the same artistic intentions as narrative films. Documentary Studies, as an interdisciplinary approach to Film Studies that draws on fields like journalism and visual anthropology, is not conceived of so narrowly. Nonfiction film has always had a shifting social role, from having a "reporting" function to one of ethnographic documentation to one of topical education and training.

When considering documentary and nonfiction film production from a theoretical standpoint, it intersects with narrative film theory through its relationship both to formalist and neo-realist approaches. While traditional formalism stresses the visibility of the tools of film language, from lighting to editing decisions, the documentary film draws attention to form only in its attempts to use aesthetics to draw out deeper themes of the material.[5] The realist alternative was intended not to overtake the formalist approach, but to create a counter-filmic culture where the "real world" in its approach and consequences was to be highlighted. As Siegfried Kracauser's work outlines, this is the triumph of "content" as the correct driving factor of "material aesthetic," an approach that put it at odds with the largely formalist community of theoretical film writing.

The medium of film, in Kracauser's theory, is a mélange of subject matter and subject treatment, of cinematic raw material and cinematic technique. This mélange is unique in the aesthetic universe because instead of creating a new "world of art" the medium tends to turn back to its material. Instead of projecting an abstract or imaginative world it descends to the material world. The traditional arts exist to transform life with their special means, but cinema exists most profoundly and most essentially when it presents life as it is. The other arts *exhaust* their subject matter in the creative process; cinema tends on the contrary to *expose* its matter.[6]

Film has the ability to accurately represent reality as well as to transform it, and the best approach to film was one that stripped itself of excessive stylistic flairs in favor of clear representation. The realists would then focus on content above form, just as documentarians are expected to do. This does not mean that form is not apparent to the audience, as is obvious with the filmic techniques that documentaries use to express things like statistics or to make long exposition more dynamic. Instead, that form is slavish to content. Realist narrative cinema may even attempt to crossover into documentary, or mimic its conventions.

To a degree, this realism represents the general *aspirations* of contemporary nonfiction production while formalism represents the actual production itself. Content is the driving factor in all but the most abstract documentary films, yet it is generally understood that film does not necessarily portray "the real" objectively by virtue of the medium's technology. Instead, perspective is critical since the "story" of the film is not necessarily present just in the real world events; it has to be crafted in the construction of the final film product. This puts the messaging itself above "the real" in front of the camera, which is the case even in the most "hands off" Cinema-Verite approaches to production. The filmmaker has to make choices about what is important and package it into an arc that the audience is able to understand and experience. These choices are form, even if they do not use complex filmic devices.

Nonfiction film adapts more to the purpose rather than a particular theoretical approach, even if those film theories do drive preferences in production styles. The position of realism in the public discourse around documentary has led to a common understanding of nonfiction film purely as uncritical documentation, a notion that is ahistorical. The documentary's purpose is instead in the mechanisms driving its production. That purpose could include things like the financial backing, the institutions invested in its production, and the artistic perspective of the filmmaker. The perspective itself could be labeled as propaganda or critical engagement depending on the degree to which editorialism drives artistic decisions and in what direction that perspective takes. The narrative itself is always a matter of perspective, and one that needs to be cultivated consciously so as to have the film reflect thoughtful decisions about its intent.

PLACING THE NARRATIVE

In the development of a narrative perspective, looking at places themselves can help to create a particular narrative structure. As the history of *towns* and *regions* becomes a more common way to look at contemporary historical issues, and the acknowledgement that dominant narratives often leave behind minority stories and the experiences of traditionally marginalized peoples, there has been a prevalence of "narratives" used to tell the stories of particular places. Towns, especially ones smaller than culturally influential cities, have collective narratives applied to them to create an understanding of what the place is and why it has been significant.

In the same way that a town or place may apply a narrative to itself, students learning filmic structure in documentary are attempting to apply a narrative to real-world events. Learning from the narratives of place is a somewhat arbitrary choice, but it scales down the world of complex, interweaving narratives so as to look at something more manageable to understand how that narrative was produced. It allows students to see how a critical story arc can be applied to historical events, both recent and distant, just as they are attempting to do with their own subject matter. This is to say that they bring intention and perspective into a topic and are finding ways of scaling it down and transferring it into a "story" format so that it can be understood by viewers, just as the histories of places are.

There are a number of ways that these regional histories can be brought into the classroom for practical instruction. As students begin to adapt to an understanding of formal narrative structure, bringing in historical events using places as key characters allows for this transfer of life experiences to narratives. The use of historical documentary in the classroom, that is documentaries made up primarily of archival material and oral histories, again allows students to imprint the narratives that exist in an understood history of a place to the filmic structure. Here students look first at how a place has changed, using a key component of that as the critical point of catalyzing action. Then they can develop a traditional three-act structure (or an alternative narrative structure) looking at where the place was before, during, and after the primary event. This relation is already present when the historical analysis of a place already acknowledges that a few key historical events were the heartbeat that defined what that place was and is.

Deindustrialization, prominent social movements, or the assassination of a political figure can all be these central moments for a city, and hence for the narrative implicit to the place. Whether students then develop projects that center on the narrative of a town or a person or broad concept, the principles remain the same.

When developing narrative structures out of places themselves, the critical pedagogical framework already exists where a critical space can form around the interpretation of events. Narrative itself is an inherently critical space since the choices of what to include and where a "story" is carves out a unique perspective, one that puts the events and existing narratives up to scrutiny. Just as a place-based critical pedagogy is used to develop a broad critical approach to social systems, problems, and solutions, the use of this approach in the teaching of narrative can create a narrative space that is equally critical.

Stan Denski puts the debate inside of media education as one of the *reproduction* versus the *production* of knowledge. On the one side, the reproduction of knowledge is necessary for giving the students practical skills, such as the ability to put video content into a narrative structure that audiences can understand. This reproduction of skills reflects all of the dominant narratives, structures of power, and social systems that have helped to create that media praxis, and therefore takes part in the reproduction of those systems.

The production of knowledge, as the alternative, is the direct challenge to all of the social signifiers that are implicit to the knowledge that is being reproduced. The production of knowledge would be a critical space where new perspectives and ideas, which could challenge the fundamental basis of the previous understanding, can be developed in the student.[7]

> As a media teacher, I had encountered a moment of crisis in the transmission/reproduction of a variety of video production "facts." In response, I changed roles, in effect, from one of *teacher* concerned with the *reproduction* of production "knowledge" to one of the (media) *theorist* now concerned with the *production* of theory capable of addressing this crisis.[8]

To combine these two roles, one of the *reproducer* and one of the *producers*, Denski says his role has become "schizophrenic." Teachers are often put into a struggle between the necessity of imparting practical skills and the need to challenge the institutions those skills seek to serve. If narratives must be applied to real-world situations, then critical narratives drawn from histories may provide an option for attempting both pedagogical tracts.

Histories of places are ever-changing based on increasing evidence and found records as well as the changing narratives that shift the interpretation of the events. If we want students to use their approach to film and narrative as one that can live up to the greatest aspirations of art as a form of challenge, then they will need to adopt those lessons of critical inquiry.

This can mean adopting ideas like intersectionality where a given narrative chooses to highlight the way that experiences of oppression intersect with each other, where both the dominant narrative and a single-minority narrative could not be sufficiently critical. Instead, the narrative could reflect the diverse ways that the social systems portrayed in a story affect the subjective experiences of those affected. As many histories, even of resistance and social progress, often erased the experiences of queer and gender nonconforming people, these are now being put back into the critical histories of places as the narratives that excluded them are now seen as obviously deficient. In the same way, critical approaches to the narrative about real events provide students with tools to critically challenge the ways they are portraying events and characters. This keeps students in line with much of the greatest ideals of the observer, where their critical engagement can allow them to better represent fairness and accuracy (though never pure objectivity).

Developing collective consciousness shifts the approach to narrative even further as new concepts require a complete historical audit of our understandings of particular places. Environmental destruction and the impending threats of climate change have shifted a backward narrative about American industrialism and economic growth, one that has been optimistic, even on the radical left, for most of the twentieth century, must now be tempered, at the least, with criticism if not outright pessimism. Today, the histories of many large economic centers are now seen within the criticism of extractive industries. Likewise, the story of economic development in the US is hampered by deindustrialization, the decay of the Rust Belt, and the destruction of many manufacturing unions. Now the stories of places like Detroit are not ones purely of American ingenuity and entrepreneurship, but a story of the declining working class, the long-term environmental risk of manufacturing, and the ongoing racial divide that failed to live up to the promises of the civil rights movement. Those stories have changed dramatically over time as their conditions changed, and this fact provides a key example for students about how lasting narratives require inquiry, deconstruction, and reasonable speculation about the future.

The role of film in challenging the world and the role of the filmmaker in making choices about that challenge is critical when developing student artists that intend to take on this professional and social role. As John W. Higgins opens with in his paper, "Video Pedagogy as Political Activity," critical pedagogy is closely aligned with the teaching of video production in that a certain critical discernment has to be built into the filmmaker in their sense of narrative structure if we are to truly live up to the nature of the medium.

> The education of students in the techniques of video and audio production is essentially a political act. It involves a manner of structuring reality as defined culturally; this arranging, if unquestioned, normally follows a mode of "seeing" reality as presented by Western commercial broadcast television. To actively work in opposition to this method of structure is to declare oneself politically as against the mainstream. To uncritically follow and imitate the dominant mode of production is similarly to make a political statement: to perpetuate the status quo of visual representation.[9]

Higgins goes on to warn educators about the alignment between form and content and how cultural perspectives and values are represented in production choices. Teaching a hegemonic study of film form, from production methods to narrative structure is a form of cultural hegemony, one that perpetuates contemporary systems of power. For teachers looking to build a sense of narrative in students, turning toward the critical pedagogy of place presents a position to challenge dominant perspectives, whether racial or national or otherwise, in the film production form that has dominated the industrial sphere. Higgins looks to Paulo Friere for solutions to this problem, attempting to apply a dialectical teaching method where "problems" in teaching material are generated from the students and the lines are blurred between "student" and "teacher."[10] This can be a difficult proposition when imposing difficult praxis, such as the application of narrative structure to real-world events, but it also presents opportunity to expand the scope of what regional narratives are possible for teaching students. Higgins references the differences in film narratives by Native

Americans specifically, who in early film production reflect an alternative narrative sensibility to the conventionally Euro-centric film world. This serves the purpose to still build a narrative sense in the students, one that is then imposed on real-world subjects, but it helps to expand our notions of what a narrative can be. Place-based critical pedagogy lends to the deco-lonization inherent in critical pedagogy as a philosophy of teaching, where students are forced out of the classroom and into the community for "reinhabitation." The reclaiming of the commons, the re-establishment of schools into their communities, and often the reclaiming of identity for traditionally marginalized peoples, are all presented options through place-based education, and ones that can be tapped into when using place-narratives as models for filmic ones.[11]

This educational praxis continues to challenge the homogenizing force of the classroom, and how that limits the work students do to productions that reinforce dominant institutions.[12] The lived counter-colonial forces themselves, such as indigenous communities rediscovering roots or collective houses experimenting with new home lives, have developed narratives of struggle and resistance both implicitly and explicitly. To draw from those places, those spaces of creation, is to draw on a narrative that is inherently critical, and when used as a model in educa-tion outlines where critique and social challenge is built into the search for the story.

For the critical pedagogy of place, the narrative itself is already of prime importance. The inclusion of multiple voices adds to the critical context in which the dominant institutions are viewed in, which brings it back to personal experience rather than the impersonal record of monolithic institutions.

> When teachers allow a space for multiple voices to be heard and encourage diverse voices in place-based education, then students come to understand who they are in the context of where they are ... This is important, because when students confront local social and environmental issues through direct experience, then these issues gain personal meaning, and conse-quently, students become more committed to social and ecological changes in their local places ... As a result, engaging with personal stories in place has the potential to increase the number of diverse stakeholders and activists in social and ecological problem solving. Stories reveal how power influences identity and ways of life in places, and they also provide an opportunity for students to be empowered to develop solutions to such issues.[13]

The place-based pedagogical method that the above quote suggests is to create a critical context for a variety of disciplines, but it also shares the root of the narrative purpose in the film studies context. While the stories are teased out as a way of creating a critical stance, they are still brought out as clear narratives. This again lends to a dual purpose: of teaching students how to find a narrative arc in factual events *and* how to build a critical eye key for making that narrative arc unique, powerful, and useful.

New Intersections

As educators try to mix interdisciplinary approaches into the arts, specifically film education, options increase for employing critical place-based pedagogy in the teaching of film narrative techniques. Much of the difficulty inside of arts education in the current market is that departments are pressed to reflect the needs of a changing workforce. Rather than setting the expectations for what is important in higher education, industry has a reflexive relationship where the skills required in the job market dominate what students will need to make their degrees valuable. Inside of film departments this means practical lighting skills, cinematographic techniques, understanding increasingly complex post-production software, and how to work with exponentially intensifying photographic equipment. Plainly put, departments need to focus on getting students unique tools for entry-level positions in the film industry rather than giving them the skills necessary for being critical artists. This is a part of the ongoing struggle over the role of the academy in society, and how responsive education should be to standards set by industry. A great deal has been written about the attacks on the arts as a non/para-commercial institution in civil society, yet this is still a reality for many who are looking to create art on the disappearing public grants from arts organizations.

While creating practical skills training is crucial for making film education an area of study that can lead into sustainable careers, the foundation of Film Studies as a discipline is in the art form's ability to be transformative, expressive, and impactful on society. Without this, the trades that compose its practical production form are robbed of the essence that has made the "magic of the movies" that has driven the industry and the young artists enrolling in these increasingly popular academic programs.

This requires a broader, more encompassing project that recenters the arts as a driving factor behind moral, philosophical, and political discourses. The film, as a more commercial branch of the arts, is presented with an even more unique task of continuing to exhibit itself as a medium that can challenge dominant structures of power rather than just reinforcing them by replicating the existing modes of commercial entertainment. This project "begins at home," so to speak, in that the role of the arts as a form of critical inquiry has to remain central to pedagogy in film departments if it is ever to exist in the broader society.

Part of this interdisciplinary approach to the arts, and to film studies, would be to put the filmmaking process at the service of other disciplines. From ecological education to tools in community health and labor organizing, the filmmaking process can apply narratives that are already built in service to larger social goals. Place-based pedagogy can then draw these elements together, uniting the development of community narratives for the filmmaking in the same way that those community narratives inform social service decisions. Part of reframing the discipline to be inclusive to critical pedagogy broadly will be the reinforcement of the art as a tool with multiple approaches, some of them already built on the critical pedagogical tradition.[14]

Critical inquiry can then be further adapted into film education by using interdisciplinary approaches to form and content, where the lessons of allied disciplines like visual anthropology, journalism, critical history, comparative literature, and critical theory can all lend to a multidimensional view of nonfiction/documentary film as a medium. If film education can borrow from the critical perspectives of other disciplines it can help to make the adaptation of narrative one that is simultaneously looking toward evolving the film form and letting students succeed in a commercially competitive market.

Through looking at Documentary Studies, I have discussed how place-based education can have an additional application in developing a critical narrative sense in students. By looking at how narrative is structured, what purpose it serves, and how it uses the tools of film language, documentary lives in much of the same world as the rest of narrative filmmaking. Students must develop the ability to apply a narrative structure to a world where neat narratives are not necessarily built in, and this subjectivity requires a critical sense of the world that can sequence stories. The histories of places, the way that they tell stories of resistance and failure, can be an element in this, and can provide an example for how to apply a broad range of narrative forms to the real world in ways that can be as challenging as the film form allows.

NOTES

1. McLuhan, *Understanding Media*, 103.
2. Bordwell, "Classical Hollywood Cinema," 25–30.
3. Suber, *The Power of Film*, 354. Italics in original.
4. Barnouw, *Documentary*, 231–252.
5. Andrew, *The Major Film Theories*, 78.
6. Ibid., 108.
7. Denski, "Critical Pedagogy and Media Production," 3–7.
8. Ibid.
9. Higgins, "Video Pedagogy as Political Activity," 1.
10. Ibid., 1–10.
11. McInerney, Smyth, and Down, "Coming to a Place Near You?," 4–6.
12. Gruenewald, "The Best of Both Worlds," 8–10.
13. Wakeman, "Power in Place-Based Education," 26.
14. Graham, "Art, Ecology and Art Education," 375–387.

BIBLIOGRAPHY

Barnouw, Erik. *Documentary: A History of the Non-Fiction Film*. New York and Oxford: Oxford University Press, 1993.

Bordwell, David. "Classical Hollywood Cinema: Narrational Principles and Procedures." In *Narrative, Apparatus, Ideology*, edited by Philip Rosen. New York: Columbia University Press, Vol. 1986: 17–34.

Denski, Stan W. "Critical Pedagogy and Media Production: The Theory and Practice of the Video Documentary." *Journal of Film and Video* 43, no. 3, Pedagogies of Production (Fall 1991): 3–17.

Dudley, Andrew, J. *The Major Film Theories*. London: Oxford University Press, 1976.

Graham, Mark A. "Art, Ecology and Art Education: Locating Art Education in a Critical Place-Based Pedagogy." *Studies in Art Education* 48, no. 4 (2007): 375–391.

Gruenewald, David A. "The Best of Both Worlds: A Critical Pedagogy of Place." *Educational Researcher* 32, no. 4 (May, 2003): 3–12.

Higgins, John W. "Video Pedagogy as Political Activity." *Journal of Film and Video* 43, no. 3, Pedagogies of Production (Fall 1991): 18–29.

McInerney, Peter, John Smyth, and Barry Down. "'Coming to a Place Near You?' The Politics and Possibilities of a Critical-pedagogy of Place-based Education." *Asia-Pacific Journal of Teacher Education* (January 15, 2011): 3–16.

McLuhan, Marshall. *Understanding Media: The Extensions of Man*. London and New York: The MIT Press; Reprint edition, 1994.

Suber, Howard. *The Power of Film*. Studio City: Michael Wiese Productions, 2006.

Wakeman, Heather. "Power in Place-Based Education: Why a Critical Pedagogy of Place Needs to be Revived and how Narratives or Collective Biographies Support This Practice" (master's thesis, University of Wyoming, 2015).

CHAPTER 6

Pedagogy and Place in Science Education

Jeffrey Scott Coker

The Role of "Place" in Science

The natural sciences seek to understand nature through rational and evidence-based processes. Since nature is essentially place moving through time, the sciences are grounded by a sense of place in the most literal sense.

On one hand, it seems somewhat obvious that natural science should be grounded by place. A chemist studies molecules that exist in a place; a biologist studies organisms and ecosystems that evolved in a place over millions of years; even astronomers operate in their place among the stars.

On the other hand, even while grounded by place, modern science drifts quickly toward abstraction. In the examples above, molecules cannot be seen by the naked eye, one cannot directly observe organisms as they evolve over millions of years, and other stars are light-years away. There is often a gap between the objects of scientific study and our lived experience that must be bridged using technology, theoretical models, and imagination. As a result, scientists must be able to mentally frameshift between the concrete and the abstract, between things that can be directly experienced in a place and things that cannot. Every place-based discovery such as evolutionary process in the Galapagos Islands[1] or effects of climate change

J.S. Coker (✉)
Elon Core Curriculum, Elon University, Elon, USA

© The Author(s) 2017
D. Shannon, J. Galle (eds.), *Interdisciplinary Approaches to Pedagogy and Place-Based Education*, DOI 10.1007/978-3-319-50621-0_6

on Greenland glaciers[2] is matched by a non-place-based discovery such as the structure of DNA[3] or creation of an invisibility cloak.[4]

There is another reason why scientists must balance place-based and non-place-based ways of thinking: to see both the proverbial forest and the trees. Place-based investigations are necessary to see how systems operate as a whole. Such studies tend to be contextualized, messy, multivariate endeavors with a more practical purpose. By contrast, non-place-based investigations in science often abandon place with a calculated purpose— the isolation of one experimental variable from another in order to tease apart cause-and-effect relationships. Such studies often occur in laboratories or other carefully controlled environments. As Claude Bernard noted in his classic book that launched experimental medicine, a scientific investigator may be an observer "who applies methods of investigation, whether simple or complex, to the study of phenomena which he does not vary and which he therefore gathers as nature offers them,"[5] or s/he may be an experimenter "who applies methods of investigation, whether simple or complex, so as to make natural phenomena vary ... to make them present themselves in circumstances or conditions in which nature does not show them."[6]

Overall, it follows that the practice of science includes a productive tension between place-based and non-place-based investigation. Both are important. The former offers immediate relevance to the real world and a holistic view, while the latter provides the power to discern causality and discover the inner workings of nature piece by piece. One is severely handicapped without the other. It is their integration—abstract joined with concrete, theory joined with practice, basic research joined with applied research—that usually leads to the greatest understanding and progress. That is when the computers of Silicon Valley erupt from the theoretical learning machines of Alan Turing and others.[7]

Given the actual practice of science, it seems logical that science education would include place-based (in addition to non-place-based) investigations and help students to navigate back and forth between place-based and non-placed-based approaches.

Place-based Science Education

In their influential book *Scientific Teaching*, Handelsman, Miller, and Pfund summarize the state of college-science teaching by saying, "The national reports recommend that college courses retool their goals to highlight conceptual understanding, interdisciplinary context, authentic scientific experience, and interpersonal skills."[8] Place-based pedagogies are well suited to address these goals, particularly at the introductory level.

Place-based education involves learning through authentic interactions within a local community or natural environment. Sobel further described place-based education as "emphasizing hands-on, real-world learning experiences"[9] that ultimately create "a heightened commitment to serving as active, contributing citizens."[10] Smith suggests that place-based education involves common elements including attention to local phenomena, students acting as creators of knowledge, student agency related to what is studied, and instructors acting as guides and co-learners.[11]

A place-based approach contrasts with pedagogies that are applied in an "isolated, disconnected, imaginary, and abstract fashion,"[12] which describes a large percentage of college-science courses. The "lecture-lab" model remains the most common pedagogy for teaching introductory college science. Lecture often seeks to deliver factual information in a perfected form, which seems noble on the surface, but turns out to be relatively ineffective as a pedagogy and leads to low retention of information.[13] As Dewey summarized the organized presentation of facts, "The necessary consequence is an isolation of science from significant experience."[14] Isolated laboratory exercises can seem equally abstract because students often have no experience with or connection to the objects of study. While abstractions do play a role in science for the reasons stated earlier, a curriculum based on abstraction is likely to come across as irrelevant to students, especially at the introductory level. Without the meaning-making that happens through student agency in an authentic place, students may remain unable to solve a scientific problem even when they have experience with the "scientific method."[15]

At the other extreme, it would be a disservice to students (and to science) to romanticize that science education should always be embedded in an authentic natural or community setting. For example, one does not build the best bridge only through the study of bridge-building. More reductionist laboratory studies of material strength, compression, tension, and so forth are also needed. Likewise, one cannot discover a treatment for disease without careful laboratory studies that remove the scientist from the authentic disease environment for at least some period of time. A call for an entirely place-based approach to science education would not mirror professional practice in most instances.

Just as balance between place-based and non-place-based study typifies actual scientific process, so should it typify science education. A student accustomed to investigating authentic problems in a place and then following those investigations back into a laboratory would be well prepared for the practice of modern science.

Place-based pedagogy is applicable across scientific disciplines. For example, Haywood highlighted its importance in pedagogies that employ public participation in scientific research.[16] Sarkar and Frazier offer examples related to meteorology (effects of local ground cover on weather conditions), civil engineering (effects of temperature on sidewalk cracks and joints), and biology (grasshopper behavior in a school yard).[17] Food science,[18,19] geography,[20] mobile computing,[21] earth science,[22] local impacts of climate change,[23] and others have also been subjects of place-based pedagogies. Many of these examples illustrate that place-based education tends to lead to an interdisciplinary or multidisciplinary approach. An authentic problem quickly transcends disciplinary boundaries, requiring a broader set of information sources and ways of thinking.

AUTHENTIC INQUIRY IN NATURAL ECOSYSTEMS

In a century of climate change, growing population, and expanding human control of the environment, environmental and nature-based education is more important than ever. Place-based education is uniquely suited for learning about nature, embodying the mantra, "Think globally, act locally."

Unfortunately, a decline of fieldwork in nature has been observed in many regions.[24,25] Authentic fieldwork has been replaced by paper-based and computer-based simulations for three reasons. First, as universities and their surrounding communities grow, development engulfs universities until natural areas are subdivided further and further. Eventually the nature experiences on or near campus become nearly pointless, aside from the memory of natural areas destroyed. Second, as Smith pointed out, textbooks and other pedagogical materials are written for a national market and so they are often unhelpful for interpreting nature locally.[26] Third, the proportion of life scientists who are highly trained in fieldwork has steadily dropped over the last century as genetics and molecular biology have become more prominent.

Despite the obstacles, the educational benefits of study in authentic local ecosystems warrant special attention. Previous studies have shown that study in natural settings builds ecological knowledge, hands-on experience, a sense of place, and inquiry skills.[27,28,29,30] Most importantly for science education, nature is an excellent setting for doing authentic scientific process—real investigations that develop and pursue questions, experimental designs, and analysis that are designed by students. As numerous national scientific organizations have pointed out over the last 20 years, "inquiry into authentic questions generated from student experience" should be the central strategy for teaching science,[31] and not the acquisition of content.

Authentic scientific inquiry in nature also tends to connect with the larger world in a way that lectures and laboratory studies (by design) do not. In a beautiful essay, David Orr likened place-based environmental education to Thoreau's transformative time at Walden Pond: "Walden is a model of the possible unity between personhood, pedagogy, and place."[32] Orr pointed out that a place cannot be understood without interdisciplinary thinking and making connections across a "complex mosaic of phenomena and problems."[33] "Places are laboratories of diversity and complexity, mixing social functions and natural processes. A place has a human history and a geologic past: it is a part of an ecosystem with a variety of microsystems, it is a social, economic, and political order: they import or export energy, materials, water, and wastes, they are linked by innumerable bonds to other places."[34]

Examples of place-based science education in the literature often involve learning within natural settings, whether through a focus on a natural environment itself or instead on the interplay between humans and (the rest of) the environment. Previous studies have utilized a wide variety of ecosystems such as wetlands,[35,36] bayous,[37] revegetation projects[38] deserts,[39] and oceans,[40] as well as more human-controlled environments such as nature centers, backyards, and parks.[41] Natural ecosystems tend to be utilized that are close to campus and easily accessible for students.

Forests, in particular, are very important ecosystems on local and global levels, and they typically have rich environmental and cultural histories. Thus, they are excellent sites for place-based pedagogies.

CASE STUDY: ELON UNIVERSITY FOREST

By the early 2000s, Elon University was well on its way to becoming one of the many universities without easy access to a functioning natural ecosystem. Only one intact forest remained within walking distance of campus.

Luckily, the last site was substantial (58-acres) and had significant ecological value. Much of the area was old growth hardwood forest exceeding 120 years of age—older than the university itself—with some patches exceeding 200 years and constituting a "forest of continuity" (an area that has likely never been cut). There were also open fields, rocky outcrops, hills, and seasonal bogs, and a creek. An interesting history of land use was also apparent, as partly shown in Fig. 6.1. Some of the land had been farmland that was abandoned in the early 1960s and grew into a mid-successional pine forest. The forest was also penetrated by utility easements for sewer and power lines, which themselves harbor unique ecosystems because of differing management practices. Overall, the diversity of ecosystems and an interesting cultural and land-use history provided substantial educational opportunities.

Faculty approached the administration with a proposal to set aside "Elon Forest" as a permanent site for experiential, place-based learning—an opportunity within walking distance for students to experience nature firsthand during classwork, research, service, and reflection. The forest would also create a valuable psychological and aesthetic resource for the university and surrounding community. The spirit of the idea spoke to the highest values of the university, including community, stewardship, and global awareness. On October 22, 2010, the Trustees formally voted to preserve Elon Forest, enacting the proposal's vision.

Elon Forest was conceived through a broad lens, which anticipated a wide array of pedagogies that could be employed and disciplines that could be engaged across the arts and sciences. A forest is many things at once. It is a home for animals big and small, worthy of study by wildlife biologists, entomologists, and so on. It is a refuge for a wide diversity of trees and herbaceous plants, worthy of study by botanists. It has an interesting land-use history dating back to indigenous peoples, worthy of study by historians. It is a collector of garbage and pollution from surrounding areas, worthy of study by sociologists and environmental scientists. It has substantial economic value as a piece of real estate, worthy of study by economists. Math is everywhere. Artistic inspiration is everywhere. Spirituality whistles through the trees.

One example of pedagogy in Elon Forest occurs in Reinventing Life, an introductory biology course for the general student population that explores the impacts of humans on the natural world. Students in Reinventing Life are oriented to the forest through a walking tour that outlines the natural history, successional stages, energy and nutrient

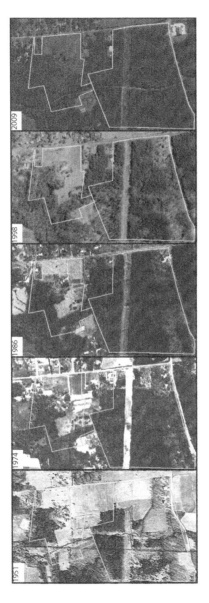

Fig. 6.1   Aerial photography of land use in Elon University Forest from 1951 to 2009 illustrates how the interplay of ecological, cultural, and historical factors are needed to understand the current forest

Composition by Dr. Ryan Kirk

cycling, and basic biology of the forest. Examples of the five major ways that humans are destroying biodiversity globally are all observed firsthand: habitat destruction, habitat fragmentation, invasive species, pollution, and overharvesting. Finally, the impacts of climate change are readily observable in the forest as shown by changing species densities and other changes.

After this orientation, student teams are provided with a set of ecological tools (measuring tapes, scales, soil-sampling equipment, water-testing strips, and so forth) and asked to design their own experiments in Elon Forest. Student teams spend a day of class coming up with an answerable question, designing an experiment to address the question, and then seeking the approval of the instructor to move forward with it. After approval, students spend the next week carrying out the experiment and collecting data. Another week is spent analyzing data and figuring out how to present it in a professional manner using basic statistics, tables, and graphs. Finally, teams present their findings in a series of class presentations, followed by students asking questions of one another focused around how to design and analyze experiments of one's own design.

As an example, one ambitious student group of communications majors decided to compare microbial diversity between various surfaces in the forest and others in human-built places (an experiment they affectionately named "Project Ewww"). After acquiring petri dishes and learning some basic techniques, they designed a simple experiment with a control and several replicates for each surface. They had a fantastic time, putting in far more time than the class called for simply because they had become enamored with the project itself. Some of the results changed how they thought about places around them—who knew that the invisible diversity in a forest was so great, or that toilet seats are often cleaner than food trays! Affected by the experience, one of those students went on to win a journalism award several years later for a story on a related public health topic.

Elon Forest allows Reinventing Life students to integrate learning in several different ways. First, it provides tangible, local examples of global phenomena such as biodiversity loss, climate change, and nutrient and water cycling. Second, students are able to complete their own authentic experiments in a natural setting from beginning to end, from asking a question to presenting results. Third, student investigations often cross disciplinary boundaries as they explore how and why humans have impacts on natural ecosystems. All of these modes of integration are empowered by the place-based pedagogy.

Many students have reported that this is their first experience doing an authentic scientific investigation. In addition, many students (probably about half) bridge the place-based versus laboratory-based divide of authentic science through their own experimental designs. For example, groups may elect to collect soil, water, or larval samples in Elon Forest and then analyze them using basic equipment in the lab. The contextualization of the forest brings the laboratory alive in ways that students have never experienced before. All of a sudden, it all connects—the field and the lab, science and society, the questioning and the process for finding things out, and the excitement of authentic discovery.

Elon Forest has also been the site for numerous investigations in science courses for majors: organism surveys to measure abundance and diversity, studies of water and soil quality, using geographic information systems to designate property boundaries and areas within the forest, landscape history studies, and student-designed projects of all sorts. The possibilities are endless.

A wealth of research opportunities are also available for students (and faculty). Research in the forest was greatly empowered by the granting of permanent natural status in 2011. Prior to that, faculty would not create permanent research plots or put forward substantial time/resources out of fear that the forest would be cut down and the research destroyed. Since 2011, however, an explosion of longer term research has taken place related to virtually every category of living or nonliving elements of the forest.

Learning in the forest has also extended into the arts and humanities. For example, philosophy classes have used it as a place for (and a subject for) reflective thought. Art and communications students have used it for inspiration and as the subject of paintings and videography, while physical education classes have used it to talk about the relative benefits of naturally maintained spaces versus actively managed outdoor spaces. Teacher education students have studied reptiles and amphibians to practice inquiry-based teaching methods.

Finally, the management and maintenance of campus ecosystems can also be a fertile area of learning.[42] Students are involved in decision-making processes for Elon Forest, including membership on the committee that manages it. Service-learning experiences are also available in the form of kudzu removal, trash pick-up, and so on. Each service experience doubles as a research opportunity related to the best methods for maintaining a forest and/or the human impacts on natural systems.

All of this activity occurring in one place (instead of many) further magnifies the integrative learning and educational impact. Students and faculty are able to make connections across investigations and disciplines that might not be possible otherwise. The fragmentation of knowledge that can occur through highly focused studies is overcome (or at least reduced) by a collaborative pedagogy of place.

CONCLUSION

Pedagogies of place are especially valuable for science education because they contextualize and integrate learning that would otherwise be abstract and fragmented. They provide local examples of global (or universal) phenomena, allow students to complete their own experiments from beginning to end, and cross disciplinary boundaries. The mental framework that develops around a place is complex and interdisciplinary, serving as an excellent platform for learning that prepares students for effective citizenship and professional success.

As one might learn from Henry David Thoreau's Walden, Michael Faraday's candle, or William Blake's grain of sand, one place can be a window on the universe. A single place such as Elon Forest can serve as a starting point to learn about practically anything.

NOTES

1. Darwin, *The Origin of Species.*
2. Mouginot et al., "Fast Retreat of Zachariæ Isstrøm."
3. Watson, *The Double Helix.*
4. Ni, "An Ultrathin Invisibility Skin Cloak for Visible Light."
5. Bernard, *An Introduction to the Study of Experimental Medicine*, 15.
6. Ibid., 15.
7. Turing, "Computing Machinery and Intelligence."
8. Handelsman, Miller, and Pfund, *Scientific Teaching*, 2.
9. Sobel, *Place-Based Education*, 7.
10. Ibid.
11. Smith, "Place-Based Education," 593.
12. Sarkar and Frazier, "Place-Based Investigations and Authentic Inquiry," 30.
13. Handelsman, Miller, and Pfund, *Scientific Teaching*, 13.
14. Dewey, *Democracy and Education*, 220.
15. Sarkar and Frazier, "Place-Based Investigations and Authentic Inquiry," 29.
16. Haywood, "A 'Sense of Place' in Public Participation in Scientific Research."
17. Sarkar and Frazier, "Place-Based Investigations and Authentic Inquiry," 29–33.

18. Membiela, DePalma, and Suarez Pazos, "A Sense of Place in the Science Classroom."
19. Sperling and Bencze, "Reimagining Non-Formal Science Education."
20. Oyana et al., "Nurturing Diversity in STEM Fields Through Geography."
21. Zimmerman and Land, "Facilitating Place-Based Learning in Outdoor Informal Environments with Mobile Computers."
22. Miele and Powell, "Science and the City."
23. Gold et al., "Lens on Climate Change."
24. Barker, Slingsby, and Tilling, *Teaching Biology Outside the Classroom.*
25. Smith. "Issues and Trends in Higher Education Biology Fieldwork."
26. Smith, "Place-Based Education," 588.
27. Glasson et al., "Understanding the Earth Systems of Malawi."
28. Orr, "Place and Pedagogy."
29. Semken and Freeman, "Sense of Place in the Practice and Assessment of Place-Based Science Teaching."
30. Sukhontapatipak and Srikosamatara, "The Role of Field Exercises in Ecological Learning and Values Education."
31. National Research Council (NRC), *National Science Education Standards,* 31.
32. Orr, "Place and Pedagogy," 183.
33. Ibid., 186.
34. Ibid.
35. Sukhontapatipak and Srikosamatara, "The Role of Field Exercises in Ecological Learning and Values Education."
36. Wilson and Stemp, "Science Education in a 'Classroom without Walls.'
37. Gautreau and Binns, "Investigating Student Attitudes and Achievements in an Environmental Place-Based Inquiry in Secondary Classrooms."
38. Borgelt et al., "Using Digital Narratives to Communicate about Place-Based Experiences in Science."
39. Semken and Freeman, "Sense of Place in the Practice and Assessment of Place-Based Science Teaching."
40. Borgelt et al., "Using Digital Narratives to Communicate about Place-Based Experiences in Science."
41. Zimmerman and Land, "Facilitating Place-Based Learning in Outdoor Informal Environments with Mobile Computers."
42. Way et al., "Greening the American Campus."

BIBLIOGRAPHY

Barker, Susan, David Slingsby, and Stephen Tilling. *Teaching Biology Outside the Classroom, Is it Heading for Extinction?* Shrewsbury, UK: Field Studies Council/British Ecological Society, 2002.

Bernard, Claude. *An Introduction to the Study of Experimental Medicine.* New York: Dover, 1865/1957.

Borgelt, Kym Brooks, Jane Innes, Amy Seelander, and Kathryn Paige. "Using Digital Narratives to Communicate about Place-Based Experiences in Science." *Teaching Science*, 55, no. 1 (2009): 41–45.

Darwin, Charles. *The Origin of Species.* New York: Barnes and Noble Classics, 1859/2004.

Dewey, John. *Democracy and Education.* New York: Free Press, 1916/1997.

Gautreau, Brian T., and Ian C. Binns. "Investigating Student Attitudes and Achievements in an Environmental Place-Based Inquiry in Secondary Classrooms." *International Journal of Environmental & Science Education*, 7, no. 2 (2012): 167–195.

Glasson, George E., Jeffrey A. Frykholm, Ndalapa A. Mhango, and Absalom D. Phiri. "Understanding the Earth Systems of Malawi: Ecological Sustainability, Culture, and Place-Based Education." *Culture and Comparative Studies*, 2006. doi: 10.1002/sce.20148.

Gold, Anne U., David J. Oonk, Lesley Smith, Maxwell T. Boykoff, Beth Osnes, and Susan B. Sullivan. "Lens on Climate Change: Making Climate Meaningful Through Student-Produced Videos." *Journal of Geography*, 114, no. 6 (2015): 235–246. doi: 10.1080/00221341.2015.1013974.

Handelsman, Joe, Sarah Miller, and Christine Pfund. *Scientific Teaching.* New York: W.H. Freeman, 2007.

Haywood, Benjamin K. "A 'Sense of Place' in Public Participation in Scientific Research." *Science Education*, 98, no. 1 (2013): 64–83. doi: 10.1002/sce.21087.

Membiela, Pedro, Renee DePalma, and Mercedes Suarez Pazos. "A Sense of Place in the Science Classroom." *Education Studies*, 37, no. 3 (2011): 361–364. doi: 10.1080/03055698.2010.506340.

Miele, Eleanor A., and Wayne G. Powell. "Science and the City: Community Cultural and Natural Resources at the Core of a Place-Based, Science Teacher Preparation Program." *Journal of College Science Teaching*, 40, no. 2 (2010): 40–44.

Mouginot, Jeremie, Eric Rignot, Bernd Scheuchl, Ian Fenty, Ala Khazendar, Mathieu Morlighem, A. Buzzi, and John Paden (2015). "Fast Retreat of Zachariæ Isstrøm, Northeast Greenland." *Science*, 350, no. 6266 (2015): 1357–1361. doi: 10.1126/science.aac7111.

National Research Council (NRC). *National Science Education Standards.* Washington, DC: National Academy Press, 1996.

Ni, Xingjie, Zi Jing Wong, Michael Mrejen, Yuan Wang, and Xiang Zhang. "An Ultrathin Invisibility Skin Cloak for Visible Light." *Science*, 349, no. 6254 (2015): 1310–1314. doi: 10.1126/science.aac9411.

Orr, David. "Place and Pedagogy." *The NAMTA Journal*, 38, no. 1 (2013): 183–188.

Oyana, Tonny J., Sonia J. Garcia, Jennifer A. Haegele, Timothy L. Hawthorne, Joe Morgan, and Nekya Jenise Young. "Nurturing Diversity in STEM Fields through Geography: The Past, the Present, and the Future." *Journal of STEM Education*, 16, no. 2 (2015): 20–29.

Sarkar, Somnath, and Richard Frazier. "Place-Based Investigations and Authentic Inquiry." *Science Teacher*, 75, no. 2 (2008): 29–33.

Semken, Steven, and Carol Butler Freeman. "Sense of Place in the Practice and Assessment of Place-Based Science Teaching." *Science Education*, (2008): 1042–1057. doi: 10.1002/sce.20279.

Smith, Debbie. "Issues and Trends in Higher Education Biology Fieldwork." *Journal of Biological Education*, 39, no. 1 (2004): 6–10.

Smith, Gregory A. "Place-based Education: Learning to be Where We Are." *Phi Delta Kappan*, 83 (2002): 584–594.

Sobel, David. *Place-Based Education: Connecting Classrooms & Communities*. Great Barrington: The Orion Society, 1994.

Sperling, Erin, and J. Lawrence Bencze. "Reimagining Non-Formal Science Education: A Case of Ecojustice-Oriented Citizenship Education." *Canadian Journal of Science, Mathematics and Technology Education*, 15, no. 3 (2015): 261–275. doi: 10.1080/14926156.2015.1062937.

Sukhontapatipak, Chutamas, and Sompoad Srikosamatara. "The Role of Field Exercises in Ecological Learning and Values Education: Action Research on the Use of Campus Wetlands." *Journal of Biological Education*, 46, no. 1 (2012): 36–44. doi: 10.1080/00219266.2011.554574.

Turing, Alan M. "Computing Machinery and Intelligence." *Mind*, 59 (1950): 433–460.

Watson, James D. *The Double Helix: A Personal Account of the Discovery of the Structure of DNA*. New York: W. W. Norton & Company, 1968/1980.

Way, Thaisa, Chris Matthews, Nancy Rottle, and Timothy R. Toland. "Greening the American Campus: Lessons from Campus Projects." *Planning for Higher Education*, 40, (2012): 25–47.

Wilson, Kimberley, and Kellie Stemp. "Science Education in a "Classroom without Walls": Connecting Young People via Place." *Teaching Science*, 56, no. 1 (2010): 6–10.

Zimmerman, Heather Toomey, and Susan M. Land. "Facilitating Place-Based Learning in Outdoor Informal Environments with Mobile Computers." *TechTrends*, 58, no. 1 (2014): 77–83.

CHAPTER 7

The Potential for Place-Based Learning Experiences on the College Campus

Jeffery Galle

In the intersection of place and belonging lies a significant opportunity for all institutions and particularly residential colleges of modest scale and a long history. Fritz Steele links place and people in a very clear way when he defines the sense of place as "the pattern of reactions that a setting stimulates for a person."[1] The word *pattern* reveals something of Dr. Steele's awareness of the richness of association that a particular place can hold. Indeed, this is one of the fundamental ideas of this chapter: the college is a place of immense importance to the members of the community that inhabit it and as a place the college carries meanings that range across a broad spectrum from the personal, the cultural or group, to the fully public. With its architecture, a substantial history, mature flora upon a unique landscape, a population of interesting, colorful, intelligent people, and the intellectual resources to stimulate deep learning experiences, the residential liberal arts college invites students to develop the richest patterns of personal association.

In *How College Works*, Daniel Chambliss and Christopher Takacs depict the undergraduate experience as a set of successive challenges that each student faces and addresses. Students that develop the sense of belonging,

J. Galle (✉)
Department of English, Oxford College of Emory University, Oxford, USA

© The Author(s) 2017
D. Shannon, J. Galle (eds.), *Interdisciplinary Approaches to Pedagogy and Place-Based Education*, DOI 10.1007/978-3-319-50621-0_7

one of the early challenges, will be more likely to persist, to learn, and to flourish.[2] Students are contextually and also developmentally more than ready to join a new place that embodies their plans and hopes for success at the next stage in life. We may assume that coming to belong happens in a particular way; rather, as Chambliss and Takacs point out, the sense of belonging develops in numerous, often interrelated, ways (common pathways, a favorite professor, a club office, success in a sport, a prestigious program or transformative curriculum, as well as other pathways, or what has been described by Collins as "ritual chains"[3]). Given the resources of the residential liberal arts college and the developmental and contextual realities facing undergraduate students, this essay then urges that we connect the college to the students' need to belong through more intentional (and broader) use of the representations of place that college possesses. Student life and academic affairs can collaborate as Cook and Lewis[4] describe, and they can act independently but along parallel lines of creative effort to establish multiple points of connection to the campus as place for undergraduate students, thereby deepening their sense of belonging while they are learning.

This assertion may appear self-evident at the treetop level, something that colleges already do. Colleges make some use of history and cultural practices, celebrate some aspects of their physical spaces, and certainly everyone enjoys the beauty of the campus. So this is what I am asking: is there a better means to enhance the sense of belonging for students through the intentional development of learning experiences that are curricular, co-curricular, or both? This essay uses the organizing framework of place-based education (PBE) as the means to emphatically address the question in the affirmative.

As students acclimate themselves to all that their arrival entails, the college also presents to them its faces—the scale of the campus and each of its physical spaces, its permanent members[5] (faculty and staff), the culture and traditions of the institution, its academic program, its values, and its sense of community. If we are being thoughtful about this inevitable engagement of student and campus, then we must recognize there is an implicit invitation to educators to imagine and reimagine campus venues for learning and teaching using disciplinary content and place as the guiding organizational principles. To connect the developmental stage and contextual needs of incoming undergraduate students to the richly complex materials of history, physical spaces, and culture within those spaces involves applying the principles and methodologies of place-based education to materials that only rarely (or by happenstance) become instrumental to the learning of students in the community.[6]

The origins of PBE in the 1990s grew from concerns for the environment.[7] Professors took students on site to observe nature and to gather data of the impacts of human practices upon the environment. Such courses enabled students to study these impacts in the way that an expert in the field would. One result is students experienced learning in a much deeper way. Service learning, a second tradition within PBE, also involves taking students out of the classroom, in this case to the "places" of institutional partners where students engage experientially with people in a "live" setting, perform valuable service, and apply the disciplinary content with time given to reflection on their experiences on site. Students report really "getting it" after they serve and then reflect on the ways that course content, disciplinary concepts, informed what happened at the site. Service learning developed from a similar awareness of the benefits that accrue (learning and service) from connections to places external to the college. Community engagement and environmental education are then two of the most useful and good forms of PBE, yet place figures very prominently in other courses as well.

Combining some aspects of these forms of PBE, Jeffrey Coker's essay in this collection focuses on courses and learning experiences developed from Elon Forest. The essay shows how a particular place provides the locus for disciplined study of a complex natural environment and for service. Here, again, is an off-campus site, in this case one that is near the university. Coker explains that the forest has provided the material resources for a number of place-based course designs in the sciences, social sciences, and humanities, indeed learning experiences across the liberal arts. Growing from different historical roots, the development of travel courses within the theme of global learning offers another PBE context. Travel courses that develop deep learning have a similar focus on place, on data gathering, on experiencing learning, and on reflection. What has been common to these varieties and applications of PBE has been a central methodology, a focus on individual places within which physical realities and disciplinary content (from language, to cultural practices, to scientific realities of the natural setting) play an instrumental role in the learning of students.

As Coker and other authors in this collection explain, educators are now enlisting new contexts, venues, and applications of PBE, and the primary reason for this growth is that place itself invites study that often results in deep learning when the experience includes disciplinary content and time for reflection. This essay pushes at the far boundary of PBE by extending the template to the college campus itself, its spaces, culture, and community. Similar to an exploratory trip to the geographical site of a potential PBE course, a potential learning unit developed as part of this course must include the necessary inventory of available materials. In the categories of physical spaces, culture, community, and values, appropriate available resources must be identified and examined for their usefulness in the student learning experience. Following the exploratory process, the actual course unit(s) can be designed.

The rationale for such a unit or course may not be clear at first to faculty accustomed to developing environmental studies courses, the traditional field units of science courses, service-learning, and traditional travel courses. Why add institutions to the list? The underlying purpose is this: applying a PBE analysis to an institution of higher education—its physical campus, its values, culture, and community—will enable explorations for students that make more articulate and conscious their own holistic development as they move forward in independent inquiry into the ways knowledge is constructed through place-based experience and in that vital connection to others and their second home. With a more complete knowledge of available (and untapped) resources, academics and student-life professionals may imagine learning experiences for their undergraduate students. The materials are at hand.

Students leave a very familiar place to enter a new, unfamiliar one, and we know from developmental psychology that they are at a stage where attachment to place is a good possibility.[8] Providing that students connect with significant others along common pathways and enjoy common rituals, then the elements of attachment and belonging will be sufficiently present such that they will become a cohort and emotionally bound to each other within this special place, their second home.[9] That the development of the sense of belonging may involve aspects of place like scale, size, number, and historical significances (all data findings from the book by Rogers and Galle) suggests further exploration is warranted.

A number of compelling factors come into play when students successfully undergo the process of leaving one place, arriving at another, and coming to belong in a meaningful, individual way to this new place. Every space of the residential liberal arts college can become a learning space or a space where this sense of belonging grows. So we can inquire how our programs, courses, and experiences are learning experiences that enhance this connection to place and to the development of belonging. Classroom experiences, the design of common pathways, dining and residence halls, sports events, and facilities—all of these and more invite an integration and coordination that is very seldom undertaken. The college's culture, the way that decisions are made, the common experience of place, and the very *ethos* of the place—all represent the aspects of belonging or disconnect students experience.

To make the idea of this essay more concrete, I will contemplate developing course materials using my own residential liberal arts college as a single case study.

A Sample Case: Oxford College of Emory University and PBE Process

For eight years now I have worked in the community of students, faculty, and staff at Oxford College of Emory University. On the day of my campus interview, I drank in each aspect of the physical place—the physical scale of the campus with its central commons called the Quad, the historic campus that is the original site of Emory College (1836), and the physical beauty of the campus. During ensuing days, weeks, and now years, my original perceptions became textured and the fabric of the campus overlapped with complex, living strands of community and relationships with students, faculty, and staff members. My sense of the place merged with my associations of home and belonging. As a professor and as faculty developer, I have read a great deal about the ways that students learn and the developmental needs of the young people who make up each cohort of students. I have presented work on innovative teaching, and proposed a successful panel on redesign of space for learning, and I have often wanted to make better use of the physical campus and its many dimensions and resources to support student learning.[10]

The backstory of this essay traces to a study of high-impact practices and programs (HIPs) at Oxford College of Emory University.[11] We were tasked by the college dean to update a white paper he had written that included key facts about our graduates—high percentages of students that entered graduate school, assumed positions of leadership in the university, and reported high levels of satisfaction with their Oxford College experience. Conducting extensive interviews with faculty, staff, current students, and graduates led to a larger project than updating the white paper. Soon, we saw that only a book project would capture the patterns that we discerned during the analysis of these interviews. Each chapter of the book described a particular condition or practice across the campus that contributed to the success of the students—high expectations, support through interaction, innovative teaching strategies, undergraduate research experiences, collaborative learning opportunities, leadership development, and others that will be mentioned later in this essay. During the writing of the book, we discussed data findings that our writing neglected, realities that did not seem to fit the focus on high impact practices. Interview comments about other influences upon student experience and learning—the scale of the campus, its size, the numbers of students, the relationships that developed across campus, the connections between the college and the surrounding community, as well as other factors called attention to work that remained to be done. Conversations with other faculty like Deric Shannon about place, pedagogy, and their interrelationships led to further reading in PBE and ultimately to this essay.

Indeed, at this college, the sense of place is very strong, and as director of the teaching center, my work has included many intersecting aspects of place, people, and the culture of learning.[12] In early years here, the question frequently arose of the connections between place in the fullest senses of the word to learning and belonging. From these conversations with my students, or listening to senior faculty talk about experiences years before of their meaning-making moments in the community of Oxford College, or listening to student leaders in freshman seminar talk about their sense of belonging to the college community, or in faculty retreats, even curricular discussions—from all of these and more arose the idea of systematically analyzing these influences and connections.

An exploration of the physical plant reveals a great deal about place, history, and even values. A first look discerns the most prominent sights—a central quad dotted with impressive mature trees interspersed with young saplings, a wide bricked walking path around the quad signaling a common pathway to each of the historical buildings around the quad, nineteenth-century speech-society buildings facing each other across the quad, a single dining hall just off the central green, and Seney Hall, the red brick iconic building that is both classroom and administration building. This architectural configuration suggests a moderate physical scale where the tallest building is the four-story Seney and a respect for disciplinary distinctions with the original signage still visible on low bronze signs—Language Hall, Science Building (which is now Humanities Hall). The provenance of nineteenth-century historical structures is also clearly evident—the bell tower of Seney Hall, beaded woodwork in Candler Hall next to Language Hall (the location of Emory's original library), and signage in front of other historic buildings surrounding the quad reveal the original purpose of each: a small red-brick building with windows near the top of pitched roof is now Admissions, but one learns it served as the natatorium for the college in the nineteenth century. Williams Hall is the gymnasium and one learns it possesses the oldest suspended wooden track in the nation. Near the center of the quad an obelisk statue rises; the name Ignatius Few is etched in the stone. In the exploratory walkabout, one sees not all of the buildings are of nineteenth-century vintage. Some are very new but were built in the style of the primary buildings on the campus. The new library and the science building have been built since 2010 but nestle in among the older buildings perfectly, suggesting that time, attention, and detailed planning were invested in retaining the look of the original campus. The eye records all of these details, and one makes mental notes of them without attaching a great deal of significance to them until the inventory is complete.

TAKING THE INVENTORY

Following the physical walkabout, one might next identify possible materials that could play a part in course or unit development. All materials of significance become part of the inventory. Historical documents and background readings, books about the college, documents vital to the identity of the college, and all materials that embody the culture, traditions, and values of the college can be sought.

Near the beginning of the list specific background readings, resources of historical value could be placed. Two recent books on the college discuss different ways place, continuity, culture, and belonging must be included. Erik Oliver, at the request of the dean of the college, Stephen Bowen, wrote *Cornerstone and Grove*, whose subtitle reveals its focus on place: *A Portrait in Architecture and Landscape of Emory's Birthplace in Oxford, Georgia*. Oliver combines in one narrative three types of histories: the conventional history of the college in terms of great actions of key figures, the memoirs of alumni and emeriti, and finally accounts of the institution's relationship with the surrounding town. Early on, he identifies six elements that form the "continuity" of the college: "(1) small scale, (2) historic buildings, (3) an orchestrated landscape, and (4) rooted people with (5) historical awareness and (6) relationships born of familiarity and longevity."[13] The list of elements that form the continuity of the college also reveals an intertwining of features of place and the people who have inhabited it.

A great portion of Oliver's account of the college focuses on the interrelationships of elements integral to the story—relationships of people (the collegiality of faculty and the bonds between faculty and their students), love of the college and loyalty to its education mission, a continual focus on academic excellence, the valuing of the history and the origins of the college, and an indelible association of architecture with the values of rigor, excellence, collegiality, and loyalty.

Joseph C. Moon, Dean of Student Life, in 2003 published *A Unique Place: Oxford College of Emory University, 1914–2000*. Preceding Oliver's work by a few years, this book provides an abundance of historical information about the origins of the college as the birthplace of Emory College in 1836 and its evolving identity through successive organizational experiments after Emory College moved to the Atlanta campus in 1918. Dr. Moon's book recounts the efforts of key leaders of Emory at Oxford to define the college's identity within the university that grew dramatically after the move to Atlanta. Over succeeding decades, the college at Oxford tried out different academic structures, each with a central focus on academic excellence. Both the Oliver and Moon books also emphasize the advantages created by the college's small size and focus on the first two years and the connection to Emory's research resources and prestige. The current model is clear: a small residential liberal-arts college that focuses on the first two years of the Emory baccalaureate and offers students the advantages of individualized learning on a small residential campus with the resources of a major research university.

As a single item in the inventory, the Moon book offers a great deal in terms of the historical development of the college, the essential decisions that protected it and ensured a brighter future, and the key values that pass to each generation of faculty, staff, and each cohort of students. Moon explains, for example, that the decision not to develop a college football program, for example, is one that Emory (like such institutions as the University of Chicago) intentionally made to underscore its focus on academic excellence. Both of these accounts are on the inventory, and they invite further reflection and analysis. Yet there are many more items to consider.

Other written materials not necessarily of a historical nature may be valuable in an inventory. A number of documents reveal fundamental aspects of the thinking of college leaders. The Ways of Inquiry initial curriculum proposal and the documents associated with the evolution of that curricular innovation represent a topic that is rich with data and invites further analysis. The Liberal Arts Intensive values and outcomes document is another that students may enjoy and benefit from in analysis. For the sake of space, this area "Historical documents" can remain a line item on the inventory signifying much more work can be done.[14]

College traditions play a significant role in forging identity and inviting a sense of belonging.[15] Convocation, baccalaureate, and commencement are ceremonies that can become subjects of study, comparison, and analysis. Similarly, such traditions as Emory's Dooley, student pranks such as positing animals in Seney Hall, and the midnight breakfast where students are served by faculty and staff also invite exploration through their connection to place, identity, and culture. Planned events like fall college retreat and Global Connections, sponsored by the Chaplain's Office, also reflect culture and values.[16] Alternative spring break also expresses the values of the college, as students travel to engage in service work rather than the typical vacation experience. These few examples, and there are many others, are meant to serve as an invitation to think about these college traditions in disciplinary ways. How they might enter the academic or student-life contexts will vary according to the discipline, the program, and the logistics of each.

What do students report about the learning experiences at the college? During the High Impact Practices project,[17] seven key educational practices were identified through extensive interviews with Oxford College juniors and seniors on the Atlanta campus, students who had graduated from the two-year program of the college and had new experiences at Emory to use as the basis for comparison. Faculty, staff, and students were interviewed, focus groups were held, and the seven practices emerged. The expressions of core identity by Moon and Oliver coincided with the majority of discoveries made by six months of interviews and focus groups—intimacy of the campus within which an energy based on high expectations and relationships that students, faculty, and staff share emerges in nearly every conversation. Others are of interest as well—service learning, undergraduate research, student leadership programs, and so on—define the college's integration of curricular and co-curricular experiences. The spaces of the college also emerged in that study as did Steele's sense of place, the spirit of the place, its living history, and relationships. Students characterized the physical dimensions and historical qualities of the college as being "home," "intimate," and "convenient." These comments relate to the beauty of the environment and also to factors of scale and personal safety. Students about to graduate from Emory were two years removed from their Oxford College experience and when many of them said that they remain closer to their Oxford College friends than anyone they had met on the very prestigious, high-energy Atlanta campus, this calls for further exploration and analysis.

These few materials are meant to be considered representative, not comprehensive. Were a faculty or a staff member with teaching responsibilities to undertake a PBE exploratory and inventory, many other materials could be sought, identified, and considered.

From Exploratory and Inventory to Course Development

An exciting discovery for me has been that some existing courses already possess connections to place. Without expressly stating these courses have resulted from a study of the pedagogy of PBE, faculty have creatively connected course content to some aspect of place to address a particular pedagogical need. In leadership development and in campus curricular issues, courses in psychology and mathematics have joined course content and the resources of the college campus to form a learning experience.

Statistics. A math course in statistics undertakes a college project whereby the students focus on a specific local topic of great interest to the college community. Students lead data gathering, analysis, and presentation of results to the college faculty and staff. In recent years, the curricular requirement of the Inquiry courses has become the subject of this college-wide project. This mathematics course has also received the designation as an inquiry course, and I would add that PBE at its best is at work here as well.

Psychology and Leadership Development. A psychology course on the nature and psychology of leadership possesses a unit whereby students identify a problem on campus where leadership could help address it. Students themselves act as change agents by identifying the problem, analyzing it, and creating the means to address it. Students develop leadership skills not only in studying leadership but in demonstrating the problem-solving skills that leadership depends upon.

English and writing. An English course (actually several courses by different professors) have drawn upon the Emory archives in Woodruff Library to enable students to read, analyze, and interpret the recorded journals of previous generations of Emory College students, particularly those from the late nineteenth century.

Freshman Seminar. A student co-facilitated freshman seminar course contains a number of campus materials for students to explore and thereby orient themselves to the college ethos.

Not all of the PBE learning experiences reside in courses offered for credit. In fact, many of the student-life activities and programs focus on key values of leadership and service, values important to the ethos of the college. These programs, like Leadership Oxford, have PBE at their core.

The usefulness and popularity of these successful and much-acclaimed courses clearly illustrate that course assignments, activities, and research projects that rise out of a campus need, a college value, connect students both to learning and to the sense of belonging that I have described all along. Two things should be apparent: the sense of belonging may develop from multiple causes but the one that seems to stand out most prominently is aligning one's work with the college's own recognized needs and values. Chambliss and Takacs describe this as central to the development of the sense of belonging. One could wonder then, why there are not scores of such course elements and units. Indeed, the present successes invite further exploration of alignments of learning, disciplinary content, and the resources of the college itself.

The imagination and creativity of faculty and teaching staff will provide the intellectual energy for future PBE learning experiences. Here I can only suggest the outlines of a few possibilities of them. As an English faculty member at the college I teach a writing course using the memoir as the organizing principle. These exploratory materials and the inventory encourage a course based either wholly or in part on the theme "Oxford College students lives, then and now." My writing students can employ the archival records in Woodruff Library and the books by Moon and Oliver for portraits of students in previous decades and conduct interviews with current students. The insights and comparisons set out in the requisite research paper could provide further connections to the college and could deepen their sense of belonging.

Describing this project on evening walks with my spouse, an administrator at another area college but whose academic background is as a southern literature specialist with a focus on women writers, I asked what elements of the inventory and exploratory interested her. She almost immediately began to describe connections between the nineteenth-century architecture, representations of place, home, and the intersections of public and private in residential colleges of the nineteenth century. I asked her why so much effort was expended on retaining the architectural style: she said that question is a topic worthy of student research projects.

For fear of being too presumptuous of what my colleagues in other disciplines might find interesting or provocative about the college as place, I hesitate imagining what they may see in these (and other) materials of this college for units in new and existing courses. Simply for the sake of practicality, some ideas come to mind quickly: a psychology unit/course involving the sense of belonging as it works in such a residential college compared to a large urban college that Atlanta has in ready supply; a mathematics course focusing on dimensions of scale insofar as scale relates to convenience, safety, scheduling; and ultimately to enhancing the sense of belonging; a history of education course on the development of curriculum within Oxford College over its 175-year history; a sociology course exploring the treatment of equity and justice in different generations of Oxford College students. The creativity of faculty, teaching staff, and students as resources is indefatigable at the college. What course themes can be generated, and what course ideas developed? Some possibilities suggest themselves even in this very cursory look at the inventory: leadership across the generations, social clubs then and now, to mention just two possibilities.

If what Steele argues is true, then one's sense of place includes the fibrous network of individual perceptions that go toward defining that place in the mind and memory of each member of the community—scale (how many minutes it takes to travel from residence hall to classrooms, to the dining hall), aesthetics (what specifically calls for attention and recognition that defines the campus itself), history (the living impact of people who reside in the present in some ways), culture (the customs, events, celebrations, programs that are on the calendar each month, semester, year, and the way that decisions are made, votes taken, curricula and courses and classes experienced), and the community (the successive cohorts of students that arrive, form a unique but common identity, and give way to the next and the next, guided by faculty and staff that remain relatively consistent).

The development of significant units within existing courses or new courses in such a way provides a number of potential benefits. First, exploring the campus in this way develops the sense of belonging in students and other members of the college community as well. A second resulting benefit is many of the learning projects and activities are co-curricular in such a way that academic life and student life collaborate to provide that seamless experience so deeply and enthusiastically endorsed by Cook and Lewis in *The Divine Comity*. Third, students will use an academic lens to explore materials relating to their campus and institution. That means they can experience their own campus through the methods afforded by PBE and learn about their new home more deeply.

A number of recent books descry various aspects of the status quo in higher education. Perhaps the most prominent has been *Our Underachieving Colleges* by the former president of Harvard, Derek Bok. After analyzing a number of factors contributing to the lack of good results—unclear purposes of undergraduate education, faculty attitudes and priorities, and financial incentives for other priorities, to mention a few—Bok in the afterword to the 2008 paperback edition goes on to say, "I remain resolutely optimistic about the prospects at Harvard and else-where for substantial reform in teaching and learning."[18] He anticipates various pressures from accrediting agencies and the presence of enterpris-ing deans and department chairs can result in a truly "creative response" to the current situation. If this occurs, he concludes, "the next 25 years could turn out to be among the most creative and most productive periods in the long history of higher education."[19] A scant two years or so after the publication of this afterword, Bok offered a conference keynote address at Oxford College of Emory University, which was hosting a Ford Foundation supported gathering entitled "Transformative Models in Higher Education."[20] At the conclusion of the seminar, after hearing a detailed presentation of the teaching and learning focus at Oxford College, he characterized the evolution of Oxford through various itera-tions to its current mission as a liberal arts intensive college as a "fortunate historical accident." Perhaps the wry-humored Bok can look forward to the next 25 years at Oxford College when creativity and innovation are fueled by intention and not merely the result of accident and good fortune.

In the past, PBE has taken students to institutions and other sites where they apply the ideas of the experts and in so doing develop their own problem-solving abilities. By extending PBE to the colleges as sites, we can foster a number of outcomes. In these learning experiences within the college campus and culture, students simultaneously enhance their problem-solving abilities, increase their disciplinary knowledge, and further their sense of belonging. In those programs and activities that span academics and student life, the college will also further the ideal of the seamless experience of college life. A third outcome could be that such learning experiences address the fundamental question of the value of a liberal arts education that is so often raised and answered variously by such writers as Andrew Delbanco and Fareed Zakaria.[21]

Sometimes, the most valuable learning does not occur because we take the context for granted. I love the story David Foster Wallace tells during his Kenyon commencement address (2005) of the two young fish who set out for a swim one morning after breakfast and come upon a mature fish who asks them, "How's the water?" The two young fish politely nod in deference to the older fish and swim off to enjoy the rest of their morning. As the two swim away, one turns to the other and asks, "What the hell is *water?*" The very place to which we belong and where our lives take shape is precisely the place we do not acknowledge or even discern. Applying the precepts of PBE to the intricacies and realities of the college itself enables students to name the place and provides deep learning experiences and a sense of belonging.

NOTES

1. Fritz's Steele's *The Sense of Place* is an anchoring text that describes the ways that individual perceptions represent one's relationship to place. A foundational text published before place-based education (PBE) really began, it is often cited in essays, studies, and bibliographies involving PBE. Steele delves into the relationship between individuals and place, including such immeasurable qualities as essence and spirit of a place. Notwithstanding these emphases, Steele's argument focuses on the individual's perceptions that represent one's relationship to a place. See also Wilson, "A Sense of Place."
2. See Chapter 5, Chambliss and Takacs, *How College Works*. The authors argue that students who develop this sense of belonging will persist, even flourish, and learn more deeply. For other attachment to place essays, see Sobel, *Children's Special Places*.
3. See Collins, *Interaction Ritual Chains*.
4. See Cook and Lewis, *The Divine Comity Collaboration*. This seminal book calls for collaborations between student life and academic affairs. Students experience college life as various manifestations of a single thing. We as various kinds of professionals analyze and compartmentalize the campus when it would be "divine" to creatively collaborate to provide seamless

experiences that achieve the learning outcomes the institution seeks. Student life, the academic divisions and departments, the library, and all other units on campus can work together to achieve greater learning experiences for students.

5. On this point of "permanence," I am convinced after nearly three decades of teaching that students associate professors, staff, and the physical campus in a very clear way. We may make many distinctions (about tenure track, adjunct lecturers, or interim and acting positions, for examples) but for students the people who populate their days and years on the campus form the college experience and determine the degree of their belonging.

6. The idea that places foster learning is hardly new; for the privileged few, taking the Grand Tour in past centuries was founded on the idea of learning from places, meeting the people of importance who resided there, perhaps immersing oneself in the language, and experiencing the culture that instructed young nobility to be informed citizens, leaders, or princes.

7. See, for example, Worster, "Sense of Place among New England Commercial Fisherman and Organic Farmers."

8. The literature on place attachment in children and adolescents is fairly abundant. Theories of attachment are offered by Bowlby in *Attachment*, and by Sobel's *Children's Special Places* and *Beyond Ecophobia*.

9. See Chambliss and Takacs, *How College Works* and particularly the section in Chapter 5 on Randall Collins' revision of Emile Durkheim's process of belonging in a religious community.

10. I've presented papers on inquiry-guided learning at Association of General and Liberal Studies (AGLS) and the Association of Core Texts (ACTC), and the Association of American Colleges and Universities (AAC&U). The redesign panel occurred at the AAC&U Annual Conference in 2014.

11. See Rogers and Galle, *How to Be a 'HIP' College Campus.*

12. This idea of a culture devoted to learning is in part attributable to John Tagg's *The Learning Paradigm College* (Bolton, MA: Anker Publishing, 2003. Tagg's important book describes institutions that place learning before all things that institutions can value. His idea that such institutions vary in size, history, setting, and student composition but are similar in the way they arrange activities around the central and unique mission of learning within the college.

13. Oliver, *Cornerstone and Grove*, 12. Through these elements, which are consistent and continual facets of the college as place across more than 175 years of its history, Oliver conveys a sense of its core identity.

14. These materials possess an individual history and meaning for members of the college community. I do not detail those meanings here, for the reason

that readers should see the documents as types for similar kinds of efforts in their own institutions.

15. See Chambliss, *How College* Works, Chapter 5, 79–83, for a discussion of Randall Collins' recapitulation of Emile Durkheim's notion of how emotional solidarity is formed. For a more complete analysis of the role of ritualized activities, see Collins' *Interaction Ritual Chains.*

16. A strong chaplain's office at the college connects to the specific history of Emory College as a Methodist institution and also to the evolution of the office of the Chaplain.

17. See *How to be a 'HIP' College Campus.* The focus of the Moon book on relationships and the six recurring factors of Oliver also emerge in the interviews undertaken during the research for this recent book. The consistency of values across time, at least for those whose stories become part of the histories and indeed the folklore of the college underscore the persistence of institutional identity and place over time.

18. Derek Bok, *Our Underachieving Colleges,* 358.

19. Ibid., 360.

20. This seminar, hosted by Oxford College, attended by Emory administration including President Jim Wagner and Provost Earl Lewis, featured a number of presentations of transformative models in higher education. According to Emory Strategic Plans webpage, participants in the seminar included "representatives of the Gates, Lumina, and Jack Kent Cook foundations, and the Posse Program, MDRC, the National Survey of Student Engagement, the Educational Testing Service, and principals from leading higher education research institutes[, who] left thinking about how others could apply or adapt 'The Oxford Model.'"

21. See Andrew Delbanco, *What College Was, Is, and Should Be* (Princeton, NJ: Princeton UP, 2012) and Fareed Zakaria, *In Defense of a Liberal Education* (Harvard: Harvard University Press, 2015).

BIBLIOGRAPHY

Abbott-Chapman, J. "Time Out in 'Green Retreats' and Adolescent Wellbeing." *Youth Studies Australia* 25.4 (2006): 9–16.

Blaich, Charles, and Kathy Wise. Wabash National Study, 2006–2012, 2013. Accessed, August 30, 2016, http://www.liberalarts.wabash.edu/study-overview/.

Bok, Derek. *Our Underachieving Colleges.* Princeton: Princeton University Press, 2006.

Chambliss, Daniel F. and Christopher G. Takacs. *How College Works.* Cambridge, MA: Harvard University Press, 2014.

Collins, Randal. *Interaction Ritual Chains.* Princeton: Princeton University Press, 2005.

Cook, James H., and Christopher A. Lewis. *The Divine Comity: Student and Academic Affairs* Collaboration. Washington, DC: National Association of Student Personnel Administrators (NASPA), 2007.

Durkheim, Emile. *The Elementary Forms of Religious Life.* Trans. Joseph Ward Swain. London: G. Allen & Unwin, 1915.

Goffman, Erving. *The Presentation of Self in Everyday Life.* New York: Anchor Books, 1959.

Goffman, Erving. *Asylums: Essays on the Social Situation of Mental Patients and Other Inmates.* New York: Anchor Books, 1961.

Grunewald, David A. "The Best of Both Worlds: A Critical Pedagogy of Place." *Educational Researcher* 32.4 (2003): 3–12.

Liu, Eric, and Nick Hanauer. *The Gardens of Democracy: A New American Story of Citizenship, the Economy, and the Role of Government.* Seattle: Sasquatch Books, 2011.

Moon, Joseph C. *An Uncommon Place: Oxford College of Emory University, 1914–2000.* Atlanta: Bookhouse Group, 2003.

Oliver, Erik. *Cornerstone and Grove.* Atlanta: Bookhouse Group, 2009.

Perez, David M. Callejo, Stephen M. Fain, and Judith J. Slater, eds. *Pedagogy of Place: Seeing Space as Cultural Education.* New York: Peter Lang, 2004.

Rogers, Satu, and Jeffery Galle. *How to Be a 'HIP' College Campus: Maximizing Learning in Undergraduate Education.* Lanham, MD: Rowman and Littlefield, 2015.

Smith, Gregory A. "Place-Based Education: Learning to Be Where We Are." *Phi Delta Kappan* 83 (2002): 584–594.

Sobel, David. *Children's Special Places: Exploring the Role of Forts, Dens, and Bush Houses in Middle Childhood.* PLACE: Zephyr Press, 1993.

Sobel, David. *Beyond Ecophobia: Reclaiming the Heart in Nature Education.* Great Barrington: Orion Society, 1996.

Sobel, David. *Place Based Education: Connecting Classrooms and Communities.* Great Barrington, MA: The Orion Society, 2005.

Steele, F. *The Sense of Place.* Boston: CBI Publishing Company, 1981.

Tagg, John. *The Learning Paradigm College.* Boston: Anker Publishing, 2003.

Theobald, Paul. *Teaching the Commons: Place, Pride, and the Renewal of Community.* Boulder: Westview Press, 1997.

Vickers, Valerie G, and Catherine E. Matthews. "Children and Place: A Natural Connection." *Science Activities* 39.1 (2002): 16–24.

Wilson, R. "A Sense of Place." *Early Childhood Education Journal* 24.3 (1997): 191–194.

PART II

There

CHAPTER 8

Stepping off the Page: Teaching Literature with a Pedagogy of Place

Matthew Moyle

Wishing to offer upper-level students in French an opportunity for experiential learning, I considered a short-term travel course a natural choice. I was then faced with the challenge of creating a program that would support the goals of what was primarily a literature course. In a typical advanced-level course, students and I work through literary texts with the goal of introducing them to the French and francophone literary tradition and, just as importantly, of increasing their reading fluency and their capacity to hold nuanced discussions in French. My idea, then, was to design a syllabus with texts in which a sense of place was particularly important and develop a travel itinerary that led us to those places. In this essay, I will first discuss some of the possible pitfalls of pairing travel and literature study; then I will explain how I tried to choose texts and places that would obviate those risks; and finally I will make some comments on the results.

The places that form the setting of literary works—fiction especially, but also autobiography and essay—can never bear more than a resemblance to real ones. The novelist's world may share recognizable features with the world that we know, and the nonfictional text may claim to

M. Moyle (✉)
Humanities Division, Oxford College of Emory University, Oxford, Georgia, USA

© The Author(s) 2017
D. Shannon, J. Galle (eds.), *Interdisciplinary Approaches to Pedagogy and Place-Based Education*, DOI 10.1007/978-3-319-50621-0_8

represent it with more or less precision, but our understanding of textual places is always filtered through the way an author describes it. When we visit the place and remove the filter, we may believe we are gaining a fuller understanding of the place, but we have in fact experienced a different place.

Whenever a kind of literary tourism is practiced, there is a risk, then, of substituting this different place for the one on the page, and of obscuring the literary narrative with the travel experience. This is a particularly salient problem when literature becomes part of the tourism industry. The Mississippi of William Faulkner, such as one can visit it today, is a constructed, commodified version of the author's vision.[1] The tourism industry attempts to create an appearance of authentic life such as readers understand it from Faulkner, instead of confronting visitors with the dissonances between Faulkner's imagination and the true Mississippi then and now. The lines between inspiration and reality can become blurred—the courthouse in Monroeville, Alabama, where Harper Lee set the trial scenes in *To Kill a Mockingbird*, for example, was renovated and redesigned to resemble the Hollywood set of the film adaptation.[2]

Liedeke Plate suggests that the walking tour can be a more authentic practice because it is embodied and experiential: "writers are remembered by tracing their (or their characters') steps through the places described in their books."[3] For example, a course on Jane Austen's London novels allowed students to understand the spatial distance between different neighborhoods where characters lived, offering a more real sense of the London that Austen knew than what they would have seen in films.[4] On the other hand, the walks mapped out by the instructors avoided those parts of Austen's London where the nineteenth century was no longer recognizable: "Portman Square, largely rebuilt with flats and offices, does not resonate with the values and codes of Jane Austen's London."[5] What had been a lower-class neighborhood now has little physical or visual connection with Austen's places.[6] So, when Kaplan states that walking London with Austen's novels in hand allows "Austen's close observations of London life [to be] reflected back to us,"[7] the reflection is in fact a refraction, the insights filtered through the changes urban development has brought.

Kaplan and Plate's studies point to a broader challenge when teaching literature with a pedagogy of place: many of the places we might like to teach are simply not there. In the case of Austen and Woolf in London, urban development has obscured at least part of the reality of certain neighborhoods—we can no longer see what the author saw; certain neighborhoods now signify different things because different kinds of people live there. With respect to my own goals, though, trying to find only places that evoked the time period of my texts to the exclusion of places that had evolved would have risked reducing the text to a historical artifact, silencing some of the multiple narratives present in the texts and places.

Many sites of literary tourism create a second, simplified, narrative that is superimposed upon the original text.[8] Reich and Russell offer two examples: a selective reading, such as the version of *Midnight in the Garden of Good and Evil* proposed at the Mercer Williams House,[9] and the euphemistic references to slavery at the plantation where Kate Chopin lived and wrote.[10] Alternately, the Great Expectations boat ride, a one-time attraction at the Dickens World amusement park, presented disparate elements that vaguely evoked the world of the novel but that were incoherent without piped-in descriptions.[11]

Faced with these numerous examples of the dangers of stepping off the page and into the real world, instructors are challenged to develop a model that allows "being there" to enrich, rather than disrupt, students' understanding of a literary text. One strategy is to frame the course as a "field study" as did Reich and Russell, and to consciously set the narratives of literary tourism against the narratives of the text.[12] Another is to seek out places where the tourist industry is less developed—Flannery O'Connor's Andalusia, for example, where "the void of the physical site is filled by her writing."[13]

My own goals were closest to those of Reich and Russell—I wished to use places to enhance students' understanding of literary text rather than impose new narratives on top of their reading. I insisted that the places we would study contained multiple narratives, and used this quote from Patrick Modiano's Nobel Lecture as a sort of epigraph to our work together:

> With the passing of the years, each neighbourhood, each street in a city evokes a memory, a meeting, a regret, a moment of happiness for those who were born there and have lived there. Often the same street is tied up with successive memories, to the extent that the topography of a city becomes your whole life, called to mind in successive layers as if you could decipher the writings superimposed on a palimpsest. And also the lives of the thousands upon thousands of other, unknown, people passing by on the street or in the Métro passageways at rush hour.[14]

Modiano's words assert the importance of a city's topography, which requires an embodied experience like a stroll to fully appreciate. However, where a programmed walking tour might follow a single, specific narrative of the past, I was struck by the way in which Modiano instead refers to multiple pasts understood as multiple texts each showing the traces of the ones before. Furthermore, the texts in question are linked to lives, not of a single author or character, but rather to the "thousands of unknown passersby." Our overall goal in the course was thus to see how literary texts described places in such a way as to unveil this palimpsest and then to examine how being in the place itself could enhance our understanding of each text—broadly and with respect to the question of the multiple aspects of topography that it brought to mind.

We began the semester with some short texts intending to provide an initial idea of the writing of place in our corpus, including Modiano's Nobel lecture cited above. We then turned to two surrealist texts; first, excerpts from André Breton's *Nadja*, including parts of the essay portion where he describes how out-of-place places, such as the "extremely handsome and extremely useless Porte Saint-Denis"[15] often provoke the surfacing of subconscious thoughts; as well as the beginning of the narrative when the author/narrator's relationship with Nadja is recounted, inscribed in streets, squares and cafés. Next, we turned to Aragon's *Le paysan de Paris*, and specifically his minute description of the passage de l'Opéra, a pedestrian covered gallery on the verge of demolition as part of the last wave of "Hausmannization." Finally, we returned to Patrick Modiano. His *Dora Bruder*, like much of his other work, is set in a Paris that has largely disappeared, to the point that his work has sometimes been characterized as nostalgic[16]; yet the nature of this text insists on the intertwining of past in (or within) present.[17]

Patrick Modiano is an author in search of the past, particularly the Paris of the Nazi occupation. One day, he came across an announcement of a runaway teenaged girl, placed by her father in the *Paris-soir* newspaper in 1942, and was captivated, all the more since the address listed was in a boulevard he used to frequent in his youth. *Dora Bruder*, published in 1997, was the result.[18] It weaves three narrative strands: as much of Dora Bruder's story as Modiano can discover, the story of his investigation, and the story of Modiano's own life. *Dora Bruder* is, thus, not a novel: in fact, Modiano steadfastly refused to make a fiction out of Dora Bruder's life.[19] Yet it nonetheless closely resembles Modiano's other works. His novels typically concern the search for some kind of lost figure—fictional in other cases, real in this one.[20] Modiano is a "seeker of auras," as Kawakami puts it, attentive to the traces of the past, invisible as often as not, in the present-day city.[21] The Paris of his novels is that of Modiano's personal geography.[22] *Dora Bruder* too revolves around Modiano's places, to the point where Annelies Nordholt calls the book a sort of "portrait of the artist as Dora Bruder."[23] Despite having done some detective work of his own and relying on historian Serge Klarsfeld for numerous other details, Modiano writes *Dora Bruder* like a novel.[24] The author fills in gaps in the documentation with his own imagination of what *might have* happened: hypotheses based on the evidence, parallels with his own or his father's life, and his intuitions. These last are often closely linked with places Modiano visits in order to follow in Dora's footsteps.[25]

Many of these places have changed, some have disappeared, and some were so generic, essentially, as to be entirely unremarkable then or now. So, is there pedagogical value in following Modiano while he follows Dora Bruder from place to place?

When Modiano visits sites from Dora's life, "he finds little trace of their presence, except for his own sense of their absence."[26] The hotel where Dora's parents lived, at 41, boulevard Ornano, is anonymous: "A five-story building, late nineteenth century."[27] The café that once occupied the lower floor is gone. Rusting shutters cover some of the windows.[28] For the contemporary visitor, the five-story nineteenth-century buildings could line any number of Parisian boulevards. It attracts Modiano because of associations with his own past: he walked down it with his mother on the way to the Saint-Ouen flea markets a short distance away; he remembered riot police prepared for protests in 1958; he later had a girlfriend in the neighborhood.[29] Thus, it seemed risky to visit the boulevard Ornano with students. Our only association with the street was the newspaper ad Modiano reproduced; we did not have any of the emotional connections Modiano had. Would we grasp the importance of the place for Modiano or how it contributed to the importance of place in the work as a whole? Would they be able to sense the layered writings of a palimpsest[30] that Modiano describes or at least understand why Modiano senses them?

The students did, I think, though not necessarily for the reasons I had imagined. As Green has also pointed out, the boulevard Ornano is today filled with shops representative of immigrant communities,[31] which suggests a loose parallel between Dora Bruder's parents, who immigrated from Austria, and contemporary immigrants. It was this that particularly impressed my students, and which brought the boulevard Ornano out of anonymity. Even though there remains no visual trace of the subject of Modiano's novel, there are nonetheless layers of a palimpsest visible: the stories of the marginalized, written and rewritten across generations.

In November 2014, the mayor of Paris proposed naming a space in the city after Dora Bruder.[32] As such, the green space between two one-way streets, the rue Leibnitz and the rue Belliard, has been baptized "promenade Dora-Bruder." The space chosen is in the same neighborhood, though not particularly close to the boulevard Ornano or to any places Modiano thinks might have been important to Dora. Furthermore, there is a certain slippage between the commemorating of Dora Bruder, as a representative of the "countless victims of Nazi barbarity,"[33] and honoring the literary œuvre of the Nobel laureate. The Council resolution reads " . . . to pay homage to Dora Bruder, and by the same act to Patrick Modiano, by giving the name of Dora Bruder to a place in the Capital . . . ."[34]

Paris street signs almost always include a line or two of text explaining the importance of the namesake. Here, the text of the advertisement from *Paris-soir* that opens Modiano's book is given followed by a reference to the newspaper and then, in parentheses: "in Dora Bruder—Patrick Modiano (1997)." So, while the sign does not exactly give Modiano's text, it again refers to *Dora Bruder* the book as much as it does to Dora Bruder herself. And the notion that the space is named as part of a larger movement to commemorate French victims of the Shoah is entirely absent. Walking the *promenade Dora Bruder* is not following in Modiano's footsteps, but visiting it exposed the book's dual narrative—Dora's life and Modiano's reconstruction of it—and opened a way to discuss the mechanisms of commemoration much more tangibly than if we were in the classroom.

Modiano discovers that Dora Bruder was attending the Saint-Cœur-de-Marie convent school when she ran away. This school no longer exists. What would students take away from a visit to this non-place? In part, they were again able to feel the juxtaposition between Paris past and present—the rue de Picpus where it was located is a mixture of contemporary and older buildings. The Hôpital Rothschild, where Dora was born, is across the street and it too is something of an architectural hodgepodge, new additions and renovations standing next to older parts of the campus. The palimpsest, in short, was represented by the built environment. In addition, there is a public school just up the street, not mentioned by Modiano, which did exist in the 1940s. My students were struck by this building—it seemed older and in somewhat poorer condition than others in the area, and the French flag that flew above its entrance seemed tattered. Also, this school bears a plaque bearing witness to the children deported during the Second World War. This building told the story of Dora Bruder's peers and symbolized the dark days of the Occupation. Taken with the absence of Dora Bruder's site, our visit succeeded in unveiling layers of history written in that street.

Aragon's "Le passage de l'Opéra"[35] also concerns itself with the presence of the past, specifically with a covered shopping arcade on the verge of being demolished in favor of the last of the *grands boulevards* to be completed. Like *Dora Bruder*, it straddles genres—neither novel nor prose poem nor philosophical treatise, it instead performs a "minute cultural geography" of the arcade.[36] Within this, however, there are "a great many little novels barely sketched out," as Anne Roche puts it.[37] Thus, we have the narration of a real entity mixed with the story of the narrator and his thoughts about it, all inspired by the place. But one of the chief impulsions of Aragon's text is the impending destruction of the *passage*. How could we visit a place that wasn't there?

While the Passage de l'Opéra is indeed gone, there remain a few similar *passages* in Paris, which, while smaller than Aragon's subject, have a similar architectural form. Often running between two streets, they feature iron and glass roofs that give them the feel of an aquarium.[38] One such place is the Passage Brady, which links the boulevard Saint-Denis and the boulevard de Strasbourg, not far from the Gare de l'Est in north central Paris. When we were there, students felt that they had left Paris, because the arcade is isolated from the noise of the streets and maintains the curious quality of light that Aragon mentions. It felt like an anomaly, a piece of nineteenth-century space in the middle of twenty-first-century Paris. The incongruities between the moribund and the modern fed surrealist mythology in Aragon's work[39]; in the twenty-first century, the passage Brady is hardly moribund, but it nonetheless stands in stark contrast to the city around it, and we were able to seize on this surprising juxtaposition.

André Breton's *Nadja* is another curious mix of essay and narrative set in the streets of Paris. The narrative portion recounts Breton's relationship with Nadja, an enigmatic woman he meets while walking on the rue La Fayette. For Ishikawa, Nadja points to the mysteries of Paris that already fascinate Breton; such that *Nadja* is as much about Paris as it is about Nadja.[40] Breton has always been interested in the vestiges of a disappeared Paris—for example, he centers his Paris on the medieval Tour Saint-Jacques rather than on the more traditional Notre-Dame.[41] Likewise, Breton often returns to the Porte Saint-Denis for its incongruous presence within the modern city. The gate is a triumphal arch built on the orders of

Louis XIV at the site of one of the gates in the late-medieval city walls. Wide boulevards now line the route of that wall, and as the picture included in *Nadja* shows, the gate sits in the middle of a busy intersection, surrounded by what we think of as typical Parisian buildings. It doesn't fit, and this anachronistic structure jars the senses. For Breton, this kind of dissonance evokes surrealist reflection, and to experience it today, when the anachronism may be even stronger with the increase of automotive traffic, provides students with insights as to what fascinated the surrealists.

Later in the book, Breton recounts his first meeting with Nadja, on the rue La Fayette: "I had just crossed this intersection whose name I forget or never knew, right there, in front of a church."[42] Breton's nonchalant description of the street matched our first impressions. When we came up out of the métro at Gare du Nord and began to walk down the rue La Fayette, it was hard to feel a strong connection with Breton's text—the street feels much like any other. However, the church that Breton evokes looms much larger in person than it does in the text. It breaks the monotony of the streetscape—that nameless spot has a much different feel than the spots around it. My students felt a dissonance between ancient and modern, between secular and spiritual, similar to the Porte Saint-Denis. In other words, seeing the church on this street contextualized the mysterious ambiance of Breton's encounter with Nadja better than Breton did himself. With this understanding of the place, students understood how Breton's fascination with Nadja was consistent with how particular places defined his personal mythology.

My students and I set out with the goal of enhancing our understanding of literary texts by visiting some of their important settings. While we risked anchoring imaginative works too strongly within the real, we were, I think, able to come to a sense of how contemporary Paris reflects the preoccupations of the writers we studied. By visiting places from *Dora Bruder*, we were able to appreciate the lives that Modiano senses, while at the same time facing some of the contradictions of its peculiar genre. Visiting the passage Brady and the Porte Saint-Denis let us appreciate the curious heterogeneity of Paris that inspired the surrealists. While walking the rue Lafayette led us to add a layer of description to Breton's narrative, this enhanced, rather than obscured, our understanding of the text. By stepping off of the page and out of the classroom, we were able to allow the multiple narratives of place to highlight Modiano's multivocal text and the surprises of surrealist mythology. Carefully done, a travel component of a literature course can immeasurably add to students' overall learning experience.

NOTES

1. Watson, "Tourist Trap," 145.
2. Ibid., 147.
3. Plate, "Walking in Virginia Woolf's Footsteps," 102.
4. Kaplan, "London as Text."
5. Ibid.
6. Ibid.
7. Ibid.
8. Reich and Russell, "Taking the Text on a Road Trip," 420.
9. Ibid.
10. Ibid., 422.
11. Marty and Mitchell, "Understanding the Literary Theme Park," 159.
12. Reich and Russell, 418.
13. Ibid., 417.
14. Modiano, Nobel Lecture, 17.
15. Breton, *Nadja*, trans. Richard Howard, 32.
16. Robin, *Le mal de Paris*, 76.
17. We also studied part of a novel by Le Clézio, *Étoile errante*, and three of his short stories ("Mondo," "Lullaby," and "Celui qui n'avait jamais vu la mer"), all set in or around Nice. For space considerations I have chosen to only treat the Paris texts here.
18. Modiano, *Dora Bruder*.
19. Jurt, "La mémoire de la Shoah," 96.
20. Ibid., 94.
21. Kawakami, "Flowers of Evil, Flowers of Ruin," 259.
22. Ibid., 260. See also Robin, 76.
23. Nordholt, "*Dora Bruder*," 79.
24. Morris, "'Avec Klarsfeld, contre l'oubli'," 276, 279ss. See also Nordholt, 78.
25. Nordholt, 85.
26. Green, "People Who Leave No Trace," 444.
27. Modiano, *Dora Bruder*, 7. Quotations from *Dora Bruder* are from Joanna Kilmartin's translation.
28. Modiano, 9.
29. Modiano, 3–4.
30. Modiano, Nobel Lecture, 17.
31. Green, 434.
32. See Cosnard, "En hommage à Modiano, bientôt une promenade Dora-Bruder à Paris." I am grateful to Priscilla Charrat for pointing me to this article.

33. Conseil de Paris,"Extrait du registre," document 2014 V 298. My translation.
34. Ibid. My translation. The discussion in the Council meetings shows a similar tension between honoring Dora Bruder and honoring the novelist. See Conseil de Paris, "Bulletin municipal et départemental," pp. 264–266 and Conseil du XVIIe Arondissement, "Compte-rendu," pp. 14–15.
35. In *Le paysan de Paris*, translated as *Nightwalker* by Frederick Brown.
36. Paris, "Uncreative Influence," 22.
37. Roche, "Le paysan de Berlin," 182. My translation.
38. See Aragon, *Le paysan de Paris*, 9.
39. Smith, "The Arcade as Haunt and Habitat," 18.
40. Ishikawa, *Paris dans quatre textes narratifs du surréalisme*, 80.
41. Ibid., 82.
42. Breton, *Nadja*, 64. Translation modified.

Bibliography

Aragon. *Le paysan de Paris*. Paris: Gallimard, 1926.
Aragon. *Nightwalker*. Translated by Frederick Brown. Englewood Cliffs, N.J.: Prentice-Hall, 1970.
Breton, André. *Nadja*. Translated by Richard Howard. New York: Grove Press, 1960.
Breton, André. *Nadja*. 1928/1962. Paris: Gallimard (Folio), 1977.
Conseil de Paris [Paris Municipal Council]. "Extrait du registre des délibérations, séances des 17, 18, et 19 novembre 2014" (document 2014 V 298). http://www.paris.fr/municipalité/le-conseil-de-paris/.
Conseil de Paris [Paris Municipal Council]. "Bulletin municipal et départemental officiel des débats, séance des 17, 18, et 19 novembre 2014." http://www.paris.fr/municipalité/le-conseil-de-paris/.
Conseil du XVIIe arrondissement [18th District Council]. "Compte-rendu de la séance du lundi 30 mars 2015." http://www.mairie18.paris.fr/.
Cosnard, Denis. "En hommage à Modiano, bientôt une promenade Dora-Bruder à Paris."*Le Monde*, January 20, 2015.
Gould, Marty, and Rebecca N. Mitchell. "Understanding the Literary Theme Park: Dickens World as Adaptation." *Neo-Victorian Studies* 3, no. 2 (2010): 145–171.
Green, Mary Jane. "People Who Leave No Trace: Dora Bruder and the French Immigrant Community." *Studies in 20th and 21st Century Literature* 31 (summer 2007): 434–449.
Jurt, Joseph. "La mémoire de la Shoah: *Dora Bruder*." In *Patrick Modiano*, edited by John E. Flower, 89–108. Amsterdam: Rodopi, 2007.

Kaplan, Laurie. "London as Text: Teaching Jane Austen's 'London' Novels *in situ.*" *Persuasions Online* 32, no. 1 (2011). http://www.jasna.org/persua sions/on-line/vol32no1/kaplan.html

Kawakami, Akane. 2007. "Flowers of Evil, Flowers of Ruin: Walking in Paris with Baudelaire and Modiano." In *Patrick Modiano,* edited by John E. Flower, 257–269. Amsterdam: Rodopi, 2007.

Le Clézio, J.-M.G. *Mondo et autres histoires.* Paris: Gallimard, 1978.

Le Clézio, J.-M.G. *Étoile errante.* Paris: Gallimard, 1992.

Modiano, Patrick. *Dora Bruder.* Paris: Gallimard, 1997.

Modiano, Patrick. *Dora Bruder.* Translated by Joanna Kilmartin. Berkeley and Los Angeles: University of California Press, 1999.

Modiano, Patrick. Nobel Lecture. Translated by James Hardiker. Stockholm: Swedish Academy, 2014. http://www.nobelprize.org/nobel_prizes/litera ture/laureates/2014/modiano-lecture_en.pdf. Original French text at http://www.nobelprize.org/nobel_prizes/literature/laureates/2014/mod iano-lecture_fr.pdf.

Morris, Alan. "'Avec Klarsfeld, contre l'oubli': Patrick Modiano's *Dora Bruder.*" *Journal of European Studies* 36, no. 3 (2006): 269–293.

Paris, Vaclav. "Uncreative Influence: Louis Aragon's *Paysan de Paris* and Walter Benjamin's *Passagen-Werk.*" *Journal of Modern Literature* 37 (Fall 2013): 21–39.

Plate, Liedeke. "Walking in Virginia Woolf's Footsteps: Performing Cultural Memory." *European Journal of Cultural Studies* 9, no. 1 (2006): 101–120.

Reich, Paul D., and Emily Russell. "Taking the Text on a Road Trip: Conducting a Literary Field Study." *Pedagogy* 14 (Fall 2014): 417–433.

Roche, Anne. "Le paysan de Berlin: *Le paysan de Paris* lu par Walter Benjamin." *Recherches croisées Aragon / Elsa Triolet* 8 (2002): 177–186.

Schulte Nordholt, Annelies. "*Dora Bruder*: le témoignage par le biais de la fiction." In *Patrick Modiano,* edited by John E. Flower, 75–87. Amsterdam: Rodopi, 2007.

Smith, Douglas. "The Arcade as Haunt and Habitat: Aragon, Benjamin, Céline." *Romance Studies* 22 (March 2004): 17–26.

Watson, Courtney. "Tourist Trap: Re-branding History and the Commodification of the South in Literary Tourism in Mississippi." *Studies in Popular Culture* 36 (Fall 2013): 145–161.

CHAPTER 9

Public Education Against Neoliberal Capitalism: Illustrations and Opportunities

William Armaline

The following should be understood as an argument for prioritizing public education as a critical terrain of political struggle in the face of neoliberal capitalism and its disastrous effects. This chapter is not unique in suggesting that "critical pedagogy"—an educational approach in fundamental opposition to capitalism and other exploitive social systems—can provide powerful responses to macro social problems, including but not limited to structured inequalities and climate change.[1] Rather than develop the already well-established body of theoretical work on critical pedagogies, the purpose here is to further a *strategic* conversation, asking how the classroom as a political place and critical pedagogy as a model for knowledge and community creation currently play out in illustrative contemporary struggles for social justice and sustainable social systems. Like other chapters in this volume, the goal here is to compliment and illustrate existing conceptual work on "critical pedagogies of place," meant to "explicitly examine the place-specific nexus" of political economy, culture, education, and natural ecosystems.[2]

The urgency of counter-hegemonic, critical resistance to capitalism on all available fronts (including the terrain of public education) is perhaps

W. Armaline (✉)
Department of Sociology and Interdisciplinary Social Sciences, San Jose State University, San Jose, USA

© The Author(s) 2017
D. Shannon, J. Galle (eds.), *Interdisciplinary Approaches to Pedagogy and Place-Based Education*, DOI 10.1007/978-3-319-50621-0_9

demonstrated by our increasing awareness of neoliberal capitalism's social and ecological impacts. Considerable scholarship suggests that capitalism—the dominant global mode of production that continues to prove incompatible with a planet of finite resources—is a central driver of ecological disaster, and that a sustainable future for the human (and many other) species will require systemic alternatives of some sort.[3] In addition, the most recent (fifth) summary report (2015) of the International Panel on Climate Change [IPCC] differs from previous reports in that it insists (1) climate change is *nearly certainly caused by human activity* that produced a drastic increase of greenhouse gases and various other destabilizing pollutants since the dawn of industrial capitalism, (2) solutions to climate change *are as much political as they are scientific*, since avoiding catastrophic (2°C or more) warming involves rethinking the way we produce, consume, and relate to one another and our natural world, and (3) given current international targets (keeping to 1.5°C warming or less), *climate change will present significant challenges to modern human civilization, that will also most certainly exacerbate existing inequalities* (IPCC 2015). The complexity of challenges presented by climate change, both social and ecological, is also made clear in the report, as in relevant scholarship:

> Climate change will amplify existing risks and create new risks for natural and human systems. Risks are unevenly distributed and are generally greater for disadvantaged people and communities in countries at all levels of development. Increasing magnitudes of warming increase the likelihood of severe, pervasive, and irreversible impacts for people, species and ecosystems. Continued high emissions would lead to mostly negative impacts for biodiversity, ecosystem services and economic development and amplify risks for livelihoods and for food and human security.[4]

In other words, climate change presents both direct and indirect threats to our irreplaceable ecosystems and to human civilization as we know it. Scholarship suggests that neoliberal capitalism and its effects on the climate will mutually exacerbate global conflict, primarily over resource and human migration (refugee crises), and global inequality—already measured at staggering levels, thanks to the dominance of neoliberal economic logic and its few, extraordinarily powerful beneficiaries.[5]

At present, only 62 individuals control as much wealth as over half of the global population (3.6 billion). The wealth of this miniscule owning class rose by 45% since 2010, while the bottom 50% of the global population watched their share of wealth fall by 38%.[6] Though "free market" politicians and think tanks commonly counter anti-capitalist critics by pointing to the drop in "extreme poverty" around the world in recent decades,[7] data clearly demonstrate that the global poor are completely excluded from the economic benefits of neoliberal development models and measured "economic growth." As Oxfam reports, "since the turn of the century, the poorest half of the world's population has received just 1% of the total increase in global wealth, while half of that increase has gone to the top 1%."[8] In sum, climate change and extreme wealth inequality present overlapping threats to human civilization that are fundamentally tied to the neoliberal logic of contemporary global capitalism. For those engaged in public intellectualism, confronting such crises must take on new urgency and primacy in our work. Fortunately, pedagogical space can be created and leveraged to critique unsustainable social systems while building social, cultural, political, and scientific alternatives, and public intellectuals can analyze and seize upon the existing and potential opportunities to do so.

Given the necessity of counter-hegemonic critique and the development of sustainable alternatives, how are contemporary struggles against and away from capitalism manifesting on the terrain of public education? How can we view public education as a space for meaningful resistance, political critique, and the building of counter-hegemonic forms of knowledge and community among students and educators?

Connections between the classroom and broader communities (from local streets to the international stage) as political terrains continue to reveal themselves, as struggles between teachers and the Mexican government play out in Oaxaca.[9] The intensity of the Oaxacan teachers' struggle demonstrates the relevance of public education as a political terrain, the counter-hegemonic potential for a critical pedagogy that extends the classroom as a material place and pedagogical space beyond the school walls into the streets, and grounds learning in the actual struggles and experiences of working people to thrive and survive. What might educators in the U.S. take from the Oaxacan example, and what opportunities for counter-hegemonic resistance and the building of alternatives exist in the schools, universities, and communities of the U.S.? Though different in their location within the global division of labor, and in not facing a contemporary narco-state, teachers and students in the U.S. also face the brutal implications of neoliberal austerity, evidenced in the struggles over closing schools (Chicago, IL), deplorable conditions in schools and neighborhoods (Flint and Detroit, MI), and the crushing effect on teachers and students by out-of-control costs of living reflecting concentrated wealth (California).

DEMOCRACY, CRITICAL PEDAGOGY, AND SOCIAL CHANGE

Early twentieth-century-American philosopher John Dewey conceptualized the classroom as a space and public education as a political terrain for building democratic societies.[10] Dewey joined other progressive liberals and members of the more libertarian left in seeing public education as a potential driver of political-economic alternatives through the active nurturing of freely associated, cooperative communities of students, rather than competitive hierarchical meritocracies aimed at producing and ranking dutiful wage workers for the private and public sectors. As Chomsky argues, Dewey's vision of democracy stood in stark contrast to the far more authoritarian political models of state socialism and neoliberal state capitalism.[11] Dewey's democratic classroom was an organic terrain of exploratory learning, where students would master traditional academic subjects (mathematics, composition, the sciences, and so forth) as they proved useful in asking and answering concrete and abstract questions of the world surrounding them. He believed that to the extent education is a productive activity, its aim was not to support the "production of goods, but the production of free human beings associated with one another on terms of equality."[12]

Dewey's classroom was a political terrain where students could experiment with democratic organizing and decision-making relative to their immediate communities of the classroom, family, and neighborhood. The classroom was conceptualized as a space of political creation and transformation, and as a unique place where the outside world is subject to reflection and change. For those striving toward alternatives to dominant political-economic models, the classroom as a political space has some utility in the creation and maintenance of horizontal democratic political systems:

> As even Max Weber warned in his work pointing out the fundamental differences between bureaucratic and democratic forms of human organization at the onset of industrial capitalism, democratic societies cannot flourish and reproduce themselves if people have no experience in or significant

exposure to democratic organizations and the doing of democracy ... [This] assumption is easily identifiable in the works of Dewey and Freire, who conceptualized pedagogical space as having the capacity for horizontal democratic organization, and for "students" and "teachers" (to the extent these should be exclusive categories at all) to develop together as active subjects and agents of social change.[13]

Both Dewey and Freire understood and developed practical approaches to build democratic society through classrooms conceptualized as places in and a part of students' broader communities, with pedagogies grounded in the real questions and challenges facing those communities and students.[14] The well-established body of literature on critical pedagogy that was considerably influenced by their work developed these approaches further in the late twentieth and early twenty-first centuries.[15]

Critical pedagogy should be understood as an educational approach and body of theory that draws on the works of progressive educators like Dewey and Freire and various elements of Marxist, neo-Marxist, (and later) anarchist, critical race, anti-colonial, queer, and feminist theories to imagine and reconstruct pedagogical spaces as counter-hegemonic, capable of critiquing and confronting capitalism and other oppressive social systems while developing their alternatives through the exploration of shared social problems and their potential solutions. Epistemologically, critical pedagogy operates as and seeks to produce reflexively grounded theory and forms of knowledge, where real social struggle informs the classroom (theory, philosophy, and various forms of analysis) and the classroom informs social struggle:

> Critical pedagogy is not about an a priori method that simply can be applied regardless of context. It is the outcome of particular struggles and is always related to the specificity of particular contexts, students, communities, and available resources. It draws attention to the ways in which knowledge, power, desire, and experience are produced under specific basic conditions of learning and illuminates the role that pedagogy plays as part of a struggle over assigned meanings, modes of expression, and directions of desire ...[16]

According to this epistemological perspective, knowledge is relevant to the extent it informs and connects to the actual needs of students, their families, and their communities to thrive and survive in real time and real contexts. This can be seen in clear contrast to what Freire described as the alienating "banking" forms of education employed to train and socialize workers as neoliberal economic restructuring forced agrarian communities off ancestral land and into wage labor in the mid- to late twentieth century.[17] The banking model, arguably still dominant due to its utility in socializing new generations of wage slaves, presented knowledge as only relevant to the extent it would be tested—that is, to the extent that owners (employers) and the state found it suitable for people to know, regardless of social, cultural, or historical context, let alone personal curiosity, creative desire, or material need. The dominant model is an alienating one, and it takes advantage of economic conditions to submit its subjects.

A majority of educators teach working class students who have little choice but to prepare for their lives in wage work—they, like the educator, have to "get a job" in order to survive. Reflecting its Marxist and Gramscian roots, critical pedagogy takes advantage of the need for capitalism to train and socialize new generations of workers, largely through institutions of schooling. As the argument goes, properly infiltrated, challenged, and/or displaced by other pedagogical spaces, these institutions become the counter-hegemonic tools of capitalism's critique and replacement. Education through the prism of critical pedagogy proves useful to students,

> not only for gainful employment but also for creating the formative culture of beliefs, practices, and social relations that enable individuals to wield power, learn how to govern, and nurture a democratic society that takes equality, justice, shared values, and freedom seriously … [Critical] pedagogy is central to politics in that it is involved in the construction of critical agents and provides the formative culture that is indispensable to a democratic society.[18]

In practice, critical pedagogy invites and facilitates the critique of oppressive or otherwise problematic social systems, practices, policies, or ideologies. Students study the world around them, not according to the direction of an outside curriculum that perhaps meets the needs of an exit exam, but according to their actual needs, desires, and curiosities. These needs, particularly among the working class and otherwise impoverished, inevitably connect to structural variables, policies, institutional arrangements, and social systems that become targets of critique, analysis, and re-imagination. Students don't find themselves in a critical analysis of, for instance, fiscal austerity's effects on educational resources because the teacher inserted it in the curriculum. It might become the subject of analysis because the students and teacher(s) are confronted by the implications of austerity in their daily lives together—perhaps as school closings or resource shortages—and democratically organize to investigate root causes and potential remedies.

Over the last decade, teachers and students in Mexico have sought to confront the more recent effects of neoliberal global economic restructuring, or economic globalization "from above," as indigenous and agrarian communities like the Zapatistas (Chiapas) have done since the inception of The North American Free Trade Agreement [NAFTA] in the 1990s. In its contemporary form, global neoliberal capitalism wields new or re-entrenched debt-driven austerity as a bludgeon to global working publics.[19] Teachers in Oaxaca are now joined by students, community members, and other segments of labor in direct conflict with the Mexican government over educational reforms couched in the neoliberal logic of austerity, and delivered through direct coercion. Their struggle illustrates the role and opportunity for public intellectuals to engage public education as a political terrain where, through critical pedagogy and other forms of political action/organizing, the dominance of capitalism as an economic system and neoliberalism as an organizing and legitimating logic might be challenged and replaced.

Resisting Neoliberal Austerity Across Contexts

The political-economic (re)organization of the world, manifested in the current global division of labor marked by extreme resource and wealth inequalities, and in the utter political and economic dominance of military state-backed financial and corporate firms, arrived through decades of "global economic restructuring," according to a specific, "neoliberal" economic logic.[20] Perhaps the most prolific scholar on neoliberalism and its connections to public education is Henry Giroux, also a founder of critical pedagogy as a concept. It is worth noting his definition of neoliberalism at length, given its complex ideological reach into so many aspects of policy, social structure, and social life:

> [Neoliberalism] promotes privatization, commodification, free trade, and deregulation. It privileges personal responsibility over larger social forces, reinforces the gap between the rich and the poor by redistributing wealth to the most powerful and wealthy individuals and groups, and it fosters a

mode of public pedagogy that privileges the entrepreneurial subject while encouraging a value system that promotes self interest, if not an unchecked selfishness. Since the 1970s, neoliberalism or free-market fundamentalism has become not only a much vaunted ideology that now shapes all aspects of life in the United States, but also a predatory global phenomenon "that drives the practices and principles of the International Monetary Fund, the World Bank, and World Trade Organization, trans-national institutions which largely determine the economic policies of developing countries and the rules of international trade." ... Another characteristic of this crushing form of economic Darwinism is that it thrives on a kind of social amnesia that erases critical thought, historical analysis, and any understanding of broader systemic relations. In this regard, it does the opposite of critical memory work by eliminating those public spheres where people learn to translate private troubles into public issues.[21]

In contrast, critical pedagogy seeks to provide such a space—across notions of *place*, connecting classrooms, workplaces, public squares, and so on—where C.W. Mills' "sociological imagination," subtly referenced in Giroux's definition above, might thrive.[22] In these spaces, students and educators cooperatively analyze social structure, public policy, and their relationship to the reproduction or replacement of existing institutional and resulting power relationships. Political speech and action in the critique and re-imagining of existing social systems are not a result of critical pedagogy, but a part of it. It invites students and educators to define and nourish their shared interests in the classrooms, beyond there in their communities, while critically locating their communities in larger political-economic and social contexts.

Critical pedagogy expands the democratic classroom as a material *place* and pedagogical space to the broader public arena. In this sense, critical pedagogy does not only operate in formal classroom settings, but also in public places and through our public interactions and political expressions. As an organic, public intellectual, the critical educator at all times creates and nurtures pedagogical space for critique and growth—particularly in grounded contexts of struggle.[23] The current Oaxacan teachers' struggle illustrates this aspect of critical pedagogy in action.

Mexican President Peña Nieto proposed and implemented 11 neoliberal fiscal austerity measures in his first 20 months in office, beginning in 2013. These measures included controversial changes to public education, such as high-stakes teacher testing (that critics claim are thinly veiled attempts to decimate the ranks of critical and indigenous educators), reducing local and union control over the hiring and firing of teachers, and weakening of union resources and protections.[24] It is worth noting that these reforms—particularly the standardized testing of teachers—were implemented with the threat of force in places like Oaxaca, where teachers and students of the nation's leftist "normal schools" retain a legacy of organized, militant resistance to capitalism and the violent Mexican narco-state:

> At the end of last year, teachers across Mexico sat down for new nationwide teacher evaluations. In Oaxaca, the scene outside the testing site resembled a military exercise. Ten thousand federal police were deployed to facilitate the administration of the evaluations, reflecting both the federal government's desire to see their reform implemented as well as the widespread opposition to the new law. Oaxaca is home to one of the most outspoken union locals in Mexico, Local 22, a member of the dissident CNTE movement — a movement that emerged in the late 1970s in opposition to the authoritarian, PRI-aligned SNTE.[25]

The Local 22 Union and Oaxacan community earned their reputation as a force to be reckoned with 10 years earlier, in standoffs with the Mexican government in 2006 over the violent removal of striking Oaxacan teachers from the main public plaza (the Zócalo). In response to this act of state violence, "over 300 organizations and existing social movements united to form a broad based social movement, which maintained grassroots control of the city for nearly six months."[26] Today, the Mexican government is again pursuing aggressive repression in Oaxaca, presumably to avoid similar strategic losses in the current teacher strike that began in May 2016.

In June 2016, as resistance mounted in Oaxaca against the austerity measures and union leaders called for talks with the presidential administration, two leaders of the Oaxacan Local 22 teachers' union (Francisco Manual Villalobos Ricardez and Ruben Nuñez) were arrested on highly questionable claims of corruption. This led to widespread protests in the streets of Oaxaca days later, where teachers, students, and family/community members constructed roadblocks along major freeways and material transport routes. In response to the occupation of major freeways, Mexican national security commissioner Renato Sales Heredia warned that protesters would be removed by force, but promised no live ammunition would be used. However, live ammunition was employed as Mexican

federal police and military authorities violently converged on the protesters on June 19, 2016, killing at least eight people, and injuring many
more.[27] Days later, the mayor of the Oaxacan municipality of San Juan
Mixtepec (Adolfo Gomez Hernandez), a member of the left leaning
Morena party and supporter of the Oaxacan teachers' movement, survived
an assassination attempt when a bomb hidden in a postal package
exploded.[28] Protesters also stepped up their resistance to state authorities,
taking two federal police hostage before releasing them on a freeway
without shoes, asking that their demands for dialog with the presidential
administration be met.[29]

The violent repression of teachers, students, and community members
in Oaxaca in June inspired an international statement of solidarity by
religious groups, universities, and NGOs,[30] and solidarity actions in the
streets by other segments of Mexican labor, namely medical professionals
also fed up with the President's austerity measures:

> The group #YoSoyMedico17, which is comprised of doctors, pediatricians,
> surgeons, anesthesiologists and nurses, has been joined by more than
> 200,000 physicians from 32 states in opposing the so-called Universal
> Health System reform by Peña Nieto. The medical professionals say the
> measure is a "disguised way of privatizing health in Mexico," and said doctors
> were not consulted on the reform, according to Animal Politico. The
> doctors' protest will join the ongoing national general strike by teachers.[31]

The teachers in Oaxaca were also joined by the parents of the now well-
known "disappeared 43" teacher trainee students from Ayotzinapa—also
of the left and indigenous leaning "normal school" movement, who had
for some time battled state repression for their stances on political economy,
indigenous rights, and narco-corruption.[32]

The coalition of students, community members, community organizations, and other segments of organized labor continue to pursue specific
demands in addition to open dialog with the Mexican Presidential
Administration. In an interview with *Jacobin* magazine, teacher and
Local 22 organizer René González Pizarro described their counter-
proposal to the Nieto Administration's austerity measures:

> First, it proposes a curriculum based in the local culture and context of
> Oaxaca, which is diverse, indigenous, and multicultural. *Secondly, it is based
> in the theories of critical pedagogy.* Of the most important changes it

proposes, in my view, regards the system of teacher evaluation. The union's proposal eliminates standardized testing (there will be exams but the use of standardized exams will be abolished) to evaluate either students or teachers. It focuses entirely on the qualitative aspect of education.[33]

Here we see that the conflict between educators and the Mexican government revolve around (1) teachers' rights to collective (union) action and organization as a community and profession and (2) teachers', students', and community members' ability to transform the public educational terrain from hegemonic institutions operating according to the logic of neoliberalism and the demands of capitalists, to counter-hegemonic centers for the building of locally grounded knowledge and power according to the logic and practice of critical pedagogy. One can be certain that if critical pedagogy and the re-articulation of public educational space and place to include the streets and public squares were of little consequence, they would not be part of teachers' explicit demands, and their work would not elicit such aggressive repression from the state and other powerful interests. *In short, the ongoing Oaxacan movement illustrates the real threat to neoliberal capitalism posed by critical pedagogy and a more radical engagement with public education as a political terrain.* However, the reach and importance of the Oaxacan movement clearly extends to the global community, where opportunities for solidarity and the development of similar resistance also exist for educators and public intellectuals in the U.S.

Along these lines, the Zapatista collective in Chiapas publicly announced their support of and solidarity with the Oaxacan protesters, connecting their acts of resistance to the broader struggle of everyday people for human survival against the terrors of neoliberal capitalism:

> The resistance movement against the education reform has become a mirror for more and more people-people (meaning, not social and political organizations, but ordinary people). It is as if the resistance has awoken a collective sense of urgency in the face of the coming tragedy. It is as if every swing of a police baton, every canister of tear gas, every rubber bullet, and every arrest warrant were eloquent slogans: "today I attack her, him; tomorrow I'm coming for you." Perhaps that is why, behind every teacher there are entire families that sympathize with their cause and their struggle.[34]

Since their emergence in the 1990s the Zapatista movement has gone to great lengths to demonstrate the global manifestations of neoliberal capitalism and the anti-capitalist and anti-colonial resistance, it necessitates for traditional cultures and communities throughout the world. Their communiqué in solidarity with the current Oaxacan grassroots movement eloquently points to the shared experiences and interests of the protesting teachers and their extended communities/families who suffer under the same conditions of economic exploitation and state coercion.

Similar opportunities exist for public intellectuals in the U.S. to resist neoliberal capitalism in solidarity with the Oaxacan movement. Even in wealthy states like California—representing the sixth largest economy in the world—with large, relatively well-resourced public university systems, educators and students face shared challenges in an economic environment increasingly defined by brutal wealth disparity and arguably unsustainable, skyrocketing housing costs.

For example, the California State University [CSU] system is the workhorse of public higher education in the state. The CSU is the largest public university system in the U.S., with nearly half a million students and approximately 25,000 faculty members across 23 campuses, serving a vast majority of the state's working and (shrinking) middle class. In the past academic year (2015–2016), the California Faculty Association [CFA] negotiated its first successful contract with the CSU since the "great recession" of 2008, and the brutal public austerity programs that followed the recession, where, for example, CSU faculty were largely manipulated into "accepting" across the board (10%) furloughs, supposedly to avoid layoffs that, in the end, were also employed. The new contract won long overdue raises and cost of living adjustments for permanent faculty, counselors, and adjunct instructors.[35] As now par for the course, the contract was secured only at the threat of all-out strike—and final negotiations were initiated only days before scheduled strikes that would have shut down major campuses in the state. As in Oaxaca, austerity measures couldn't be effectively countered absent the threat of organized direct action in resistance to the state. Unlike Oaxaca, the CFA did not (1) take a position that was explicitly anti-capitalist or in contrast to neoliberalism—instead reflecting the more common stance in U.S. professional unions of moderate reform and a discourse of "fairness" or (2) materialize in solidarity with students, family members, and other members of the university and neighboring communities, who also suffer from earnings well out of pace with the cost of living.

Even given a new contract, the average salary of a tenured Associate Professor in the CSU ($75,896)[36] amounts to approximately *half* of the annual income required (~$150K) to purchase a median priced home in the San Francisco Bay Area (~$750K),[37] also falling well short of the $100K required to purchase a median (~$500K) home in the Los Angeles Metro Area.[38] Californian rental markets are equally brutal, where the average two-bedroom apartment in the San Francisco Bay Area runs for ~$2,500/month, and continues to climb considerably each year. This poses an economic challenge for educators in the CSU system, and for the CSU campuses that now face considerable difficulty recruiting talent, thanks to the outrageous cost of living.

Simultaneously, the astronomical cost of living has been devastating for CSU students and their families. A recent study found that 8–12% (approximately 1 in 10) of CSU students report being homeless and nearly one in four (21–24%) CSU students are food insecure.[39] The study also reports the experiences of CSU professors and staff, who are often charged with counseling and at times, personally resourcing students in need, absent more effective structural responses to the problem of poverty, food insecurity, and homelessness among CSU and the broader working class in major cities and rural communities throughout the state.[40]

Here we find an enormous opportunity to learn from (for example) the Oaxacan teachers' movement in how more effectively to leverage critical pedagogy against neoliberal capitalism and its effects in the U.S. For instance, why not make and act upon meaningful connections between CFA demands for faculty and the suffering of our students and community members under similar conditions of wealth disparity and austerity? Educators, students, and community members in California collectively suffer under a housing market wildly out of step with the earnings of most community members, and state austerity measures that have undermined public resources (including but not limited to universities), and continue to exacerbate wealth inequalities that define life in the state and nation. Critical pedagogy provides a theory and applied practice for public intellectuals in the CSU to bring these shared social problems into the classroom for analysis and (reflexively) expand the classroom as a pedagogical space and material place into the streets and public (policy) forums. While unions like the CFA do typically organize in conjunction with more progressive student groups, it seems far more could be done to conceptualize and act upon the connected material interests of educators, students, and community members. If determined and equipped to do so, public intellectuals working in systems like the CSU could be working to develop shared critical analyses of political economy (neoliberal capitalism) in and outside of the classroom—remembering that critical pedagogical space is not limited to such restraints. From there, real, grounded community and knowledge can be created democratically among educators, students, and community members in efforts to address these shared experiences with (for instance) unsustainable housing costs or cuts to public education. Recent data bodes well for building in this way with our current "millennial" generation of students, who are better educated and more likely to identify as "working class" than any other generation in recent history.[41]

These changes in how we think about our teaching, classrooms, and political activities require us to reflect on the "point" of being an educator in the first place. Critical pedagogy, and the gargantuan tasks ahead of us to avoid the disastrous implications of neoliberal capitalism, requires that we judge our work by its impact on those with whom we share community, commitment, and experience. Perhaps we are only valuable as public intellectuals to the extent that our work builds these communities of resistance and empowerment: "Knowledge production as a liberatory act must include an *acto in proximis*, meaning that the epistemology in question must have a practical effect on the world . . . We judge the truth of our actions in their effects on the lives of the oppressed."[42]

NOTES

1. See McLaren, *Pedagogy of Insurrection*. Also see Apple, *Can Education Change Society?*; Giroux, *On Critical Pedagogy*.; Giroux, *Neoliberalism's War on Higher Education*.; Darder, Baltodano, and Torres, *The Critical Pedagogy Reader* for extended definitions discussions and critiques of critical pedagogy as an applied practice and body of theory.
2. Gruenwald, "The Best of Both Worlds," 10. Also see Johnson, "Place-based Learning and Knowing."
3. Klein, *This Changes Everything*.; Parenti, *Tropic of Chaos*.; Ehrlich and Ehrlich, "Can a Collapse of Civilization Be Avoided?"; Ehrlich and Ehrlich, "Future Collapse."
4. Intergovernmental Panel on Climate Change [IPCC], *Climate Change 2014*, 64.

5. Parenti, *Tropic of Chaos*.
6. OXFAM, "An Economy for the 1%."
7. *Economist*, "Towards the End of Poverty."
8. OXFAM, "An Economy for the 1%," 6.
9. Telesur, "Death Toll Rises in Oaxaca as Govt. Represses Teacher Protests.";
Telesur, "200,000 Doctors to Join Teachers in Mexico National Strike.";
Dillingham, "Mexico's Classroom Wars."
10. Dewey, *Experience and Education*.
11. Chomsky, *Chomsky on Democracy and Education*.
12. Dewey quoted in Chomsky, *Chomsky on Democracy and Education*, 25.
13. Also see Adreski, *Max Weber on Capitalism Bureaucracy and Religion*.
Quote from Armaline, "Building Democracy Through Education, 161.
14. Freire, *Pedagogy of the Oppressed*.
15. McLaren, *Pedagogy of Insurrection*.; Apple, *Can Education Change Society?*;
Giroux, *On Critical Pedagogy*.; Giroux, *Neoliberalism's War on Higher
Education*.; and Darder, Baltodano, and Torres, *The Critical Pedagogy
Reader*.
16. Giroux, *On Critical Pedagogy*, 1.
17. Friere, *Pedagogy of the Oppressed*.
18. Giroux, *On Critical Pedagogy*, 2–3.
19. Graeber, *Debt*.
20. Armaline and Glasberg, "What Will States Really Do for Us?"; Armaline,
Glasberg, and Purkayastha, *The Human Rights Enterprise*.
21. Giroux, *Neoliberalism's War on Higher Education*, 1–2.
22. Mills, *The Sociological Imagination*.
23. Gramsci, *Selections from Prison Notebooks*.
24. Telesur, "Death Toll Rises in Oaxaca as Govt. Represses Teacher Protests.";
Dillingham, "Mexico's Classroom Wars."
25. Dillingham, "Mexico's Classroom Wars."
26. Magaña, "Educational Reform and Repression in Mexico."
27. Telesur, "Death Toll Rises in Oaxaca as Govt. Represses Teacher Protests.";
Dillingham, "Mexico's Classroom Wars."
28. Telesur, "Mexican Mayor Who Supports Oaxaca Teachers Survives Bomb
Attack."
29. Mexico News Daily, "Oaxaca Protesters Detain Two Police."
30. Telesur, "World Organizations Condemn Repression Against Mexican
Teachers."
31. Telesur, "200,000 Doctors to Join Teachers in Mexico National Strike."
32. Telesur, "Ayotzinapa Parents Attacked as They Join Mexico Teacher
Protests."
33. Dillingham, "Mexico's Classroom Wars."
34. National Indigenous Congress and EZLN, "From Within the Storm."

35. For detailed information on the CFA negotiated contract (2014–2017), and the history of contract negotiation ("the contract archive"), please see the CFA website: http://www.calfac.org/contract.
36. See average salary calculations here: http://www.calstate.edu/hr/employee-profile/2011/faculty/salary.shtml.
37. Brekke, "$142,448.33."
38. Manni, "The Salary You Must Earn to Buy a Home in 27 Metros."
39. Crutchfield, "Serving Displaced and Food Insecure Students in the CSU."
40. Rosanna, "1 in 10 Cal State Students Is Homeless, Study Finds."
41. Guastella, "Class is in Session."
42. McLaren, *Pedagogy of Insurrection*, 61.

BIBLIOGRAPHY

Andreski, S. (Ed). *Max Weber on Capitalism, Bureaucracy and Religion*. New York, NY: Routledge, 2008.

Apple, Michael. *Can Education Change Society?*. New York, NY: Routledge, 2012.

Armaline, William T. "Building Democracy Through Education: Human Rights and the Re-Introduction of Radical Civic Engagement." In *Critical Theories, Radical Pedagogies, and Social Education*, edited by A. Deleon and E. W. Ross, 151–162. Amsterdam, NE: Sense Publishers, 2010.

Armaline, William, and Davita Silfen Glasberg. "What Will States Really Do for Us? The Human Rights Enterprise and Pressure From Below." *Societies Without Borders* 4(3) (2009): 430–451.

Armaline, William, Davita Silfen Glasberg, and Bandana Purkayastha. *The Human Rights Enterprise: Political Sociology, State Power and Social Movements*. London: Polity Press, 2015.

Brekke, Dan. "$142,448.33: What You Need to Earn to Buy a 'Median' Home in Bay Area." *KQED News*, March 9, 2015. Accessed on July 10, 2016. http://ww2.kqed.org/news/2015/03/09/you-need-to-earn-142000-dollars-to-buy-a-home-in-san-francisco/.

Chomsky, Noam. *Chomsky on Democracy and Education*. Edited by CP Otero. New York, NY: Routledge-Falmer, 2003.

Crutchfield, Rashida. "Serving Displaced and Food Insecure Students in the CSU." January 2016. Accessed June 28, 2016. https://presspage-production-content.s3.amazonaws.com/uploads/1487/cohomelessstudy.pdf?10000.

Darder, Antonia, Marta Baltodano, and Rodolfo Torres. *The Critical Pedagogy Reader*. New York, NY: Routledge, 2003.

Dewey, John. *Experience and Education*. New York, NY: Collier Books, 1938.

Dewey, John. *Democracy and Education*. New York, NY: Free Press, 1944.

Dillingham, A.S. "Mexico's Classroom Wars" (and interview of teacher and Local 22 member, René González Pizarro)." *Jacobin*, June 24, 2016. Accessed June 28, 2016. https://www.jacobinmag.com/2016/06/mexico-teachers-union-cnte-snte-oaxaca-nieto-zapatistas-strike/.

Economist (no author). "Towards the End of Poverty." *The Economist*, June 1, 2013. Accessed on July 10, 2016. http://www.economist.com/news/lea ders/21578665-nearly-1-billion-people-have-been-taken-out-extreme-pov erty-20-years-world-should-aim.

Ehrlich, Paul, and Anne Ehrilch. "Can a Collapse of Civilization Be Avoided?." *Proceedings of the Royal Society [Biological Sciences]*, January 2013. DOI: 10.1098/rspb.2012.2845.

Ehrlich, Paul, and Anne Ehrilch. "Future Collapse: How Optimistic Should We Be?." *Proceedings of the Royal Society [Biological Sciences]*, July 2013. DOI: 10.1098/rspb.2013.1373.

Freire, Paulo. *Pedagogy of the Oppressed*. New York, NY: Continuum, 1970.

Giroux, Henry. *On Critical Pedagogy*. New York, NY: Bloomsbury, 2011.

Giroux, Henry. *Neoliberalism's War on Higher Education*. Chicago, IL: Haymarket Books, 2014.

Graeber, David. *Debt: The First 5000 Years*. Brooklyn, NY: Melville House Printing, 2011.

Gramsci, Antonio. *Selections from Prison Notebooks*. New York, NY: International Publishers, 1971.

Gruenewald, David. "The Best of Both Worlds: A Critical Pedagogy of Place." *Educational Researcher* 32(4) (2003): 3–12.

Guastella, Dustin. "Class is in Session." *Jacobin*, July 9, 2016. Accessed July 12, 2016. https://www.jacobinmag.com/2016/07/millennials-bernie-sanders-working-class-college-education-precarity-wages-jobs/.

Intergovernmental Panel on Climate Change [IPCC]. *Climate Change* 2014: *Synthesis Report. Contribution of Working Groups I, II, and III to the Fifth Assessment Report of the* IPCC, Core Writing Team, R.K. Pachauri and L.A. Meyer (eds.), 2015. Accessed July 10, 2016. http://ipcc.ch/pdf/assessment-report/ar5/syr/SYR_AR5_FINAL_full_wcover.pdf.

Johnson, Jay. "Place-based Learning and Knowing: Critical Pedagogies Grounded in Indigeneity." *GeoJournal* 77 (2012): 829–836. Accessed July 10, 2016. Doi: 10.1007/s10708-010-9379-1.

Klein, Naomi. *This Changes Everything*. New York, NY: Simon and Schuster, 2014.

Magaña, Maurice. "Educational Reform and Repression in Mexico." *Social Justice* [BLOG], June 22, 2016. Accessed July 10, 2016. http://www.socialjustice journal.org/educational-reform-and-repression-in-mexico/.

Manni, Tim. "The Salary You Must Earn to Buy a Home in 27 Metros." *HSH. com*, May 23, 2016. Accessed July 10, 2016. http://www.hsh.com/finance/ mortgage/salary-home-buying-25-cities.html#los-angeles.

McLaren, Peter. *Pedagogy of Insurrection: From Resurrection to Revolution.* New York: Peter Lang, 2015.

Mexico News Daily (no author). "Oaxaca Protesters Detain Two Police." *Mexico News Daily,* June 28, 2016. Accessed June 28, 2016. http://mexiconewsdaily.com/news/oaxaca-protesters-detain-two-police/.

Mills, C.W. *The Sociological Imagination.* New York, NY: Oxford University, 2000.

National Indigenous Congress and EZLN. "From Within the Storm: National Indigenous Congress and Zapatista Communique on Oaxaca Teacher Protests." June 22, 2016. Accessed July 10, 2016. http://upsidedownworld.org/main/mexico-archives-79/5649-from-within-the-storm-national-indigenous-congress-and-zapatista-communique-on-oaxaca-teacher-protests.

OXFAM International. "An Economy for the 1%: How Privilege and Power in the Economy Drive Extreme Inequality and How This Can Be Stopped [Summary]." January 18, 2016. Accessed July 10, 2016. https://www.oxfam.org/sites/www.oxfam.org/files/file_attachments/bp210-economy-one-percent-tax-havens-180116-summ-en_0.pdf.

Parenti, Christian. *Tropic of Chaos: Climate Change and the New Geography of Violence.* New York, NY: Nation Books, 2011.

Telesur (no author). "World Organizations Condemn Repression Against Mexican Teachers." *Telesur,* June 18, 2016. Accessed July 10, 2016. http://www.telesurtv.net/english/news/World-Organizations-Condemn-Repression-Against-Mexican-Teachers-20160617-0024.html.

Telesur (no author). "Death Toll Rises in Oaxaca as Govt. Represses Teacher Protests." *Telesur,* June 20, 2016. Accessed June 28, 2016. http://www.telesurtv.net/english/news/Mexican-Police-Kill-3-in-Clashes-with-Striking-Oaxaca-Teachers-20160619-0024.html.

Telesur (no author). "200,000 Doctors to Join Teachers in Mexico National Strike." *Telesur,* June 21, 2016. Accessed on June 28, 2016. http://www.telesurtv.net/english/news/200000-Doctors-to-Join-Teachers-in-Mexico-National-Strike-20160621-0015.html.

Telesur (no author). "Mexican Mayor Who Supports Oaxaca Teachers Survives Bomb Attack." *Telesur,* June 24, 2016. Accessed July 10, 2016. http://www.telesurtv.net/english/news/Mexican-Mayor-Who-Supports-Oaxaca-Teachers-Survives-Bomb-Attack-20160624-0021.html.

Telesur (no author). "Ayotzinapa Parents Attacked as They Join Mexico Teacher Protests." *Telesur,* June 27, 2016. Accessed on June 28, 2016. http://www.telesurtv.net/english/news/Ayotzinapa-Parents-Attacked-as-They-Join-CNTE-Protests-20160627-0014.html.

Xia, Rosanna. "1 in 10 Cal State Students Is Homeless, Study Finds." *LA Times,* June 20, 2016. Accessed June 28, 2016, http://www.latimes.com/local/lanow/la-me-cal-state-homelessness-20160620-snap-story.html.

CHAPTER 10

Queering Place: Using the Classroom to Describe the World

Abbey S. Willis

"Place" is the central theme of this edited collection. As a concept within pedagogical theory, place often refers to settings such as a community or town in which a campus or classroom might be *located*. But place contains meaning beyond a physical space; we might also consider people and the social relations that connect them as *places*.[1] For students new to the social sciences, introductory sociology courses can provide an excellent space to investigate social relations and meaning-making processes *as place*.

In this chapter, I argue that we might consider ideas emerging from queer theory to make discussions of place within our pedagogical practice *strange*—to queer them. Beyond interrogations into the configuration of gender and sexuality, queer theory offers two broad and persistently useful concepts (even as it enters the stages of what some claim to be its own demise[2]): 1) the ruthless criticism of binary logic and 2) demonstrating the limits and assumed stability of identity. After years of organizing, participating, and writing on queer theory and practice, I have come to think of these two concepts as representing a consistent antiauthoritarianism in regard to all existing relations of inequality, not solely a queer theoretical thought experiment.

While many scholars stress places external to the classroom as sites for connecting to community and the larger world around us, I argue in this

A.S. Willis (✉)
Department of Sociology, University of Connecticut, Storrs, CT, USA

© The Author(s) 2017
D. Shannon, J. Galle (eds.), *Interdisciplinary Approaches to Pedagogy and Place-Based Education*, DOI 10.1007/978-3-319-50621-0_10

chapter that it is not necessary to leave the classroom to coherently discuss and respect place in a globalized world, particularly in the social sciences. Focusing on the desk (a rather mundane and common object in college classrooms), as well social relations inside the classroom, I argue that we can use both as departure points to discuss broader questions about disciplinary power in hierarchical learning spaces and the global political economy and social reproduction in which we all take part. This makes the class*room* a specific site, with cultural artifacts and symbolic values within it, worthy of investigation, which in turn allows us to refuse the binary separation of the "school" or "university" and the "community" and, finally, the "globe" of which they are a part.

David A. Gruenewald synthesizes ideas emerging from critical pedagogy and place-based education (PBE) to form what he terms a "critical pedagogy of place," which can be defined as a pedagogical theory and practice that "ultimately encourages teachers and students to reinhabit their places, that is, to pursue the kind of social action that improves the social and ecological life of places, near and far, now and in the future."[3] Gruenewald argues that, oftentimes, PBE is heavily (perhaps *overly*) concerned with the outdoors and nature (a discussion of defining those terms will take place later in this chapter) as places that students directly experience, and yet PBE often fails to likewise *politicize* those very places.[4] Politicizing place can take many forms—for instance, asking how particular places might be connected to social transformation rather than solely inquiring into individual students' connection to their outdoor environment. Gruenewald's project of a critical pedagogy of place seeks to combine both the awareness of place with the awareness of *how* those places are connected to the maintenance or transformation of the status quo.

QUEERING PLACE

Gruenewald's project of merging critical pedagogy and PBE by combining them into a "critical pedagogy of place" can be extended by further interrogating both PBE's goal of *reinhabitation* and critical pedagogy's goal of *decolonization*.[5] In PBE, reinhabitation refers to becoming connected to and cognizant of the place (location) in which one lives and learning to "live well" there[6]; in critical pedagogical theory, decolonization refers to a process of unlearning dominant and harmful ways of knowing. Gruenewald explains, "If reinhabitation involves learning to live well socially and ecologically in places that have been disrupted and injured, decolonization involves learning to recognize disruption and injury and to address their causes."[7] This means a critical pedagogy of place might help both students and teachers with developing an awareness of social ills embedded in particular places, and importantly, with recognizing them as harmful, and seeking ways to transform particular places so people have the ability to actually "live well" *in* them.

As such, Gruenewald argues that a critical pedagogy of place will recognize the usefulness of *combining* these perspectives and their interrelatedness; a *queer* critical pedagogy of place might argue that we can stretch the terms of reinhabitation and decolonization to uncover new uses and meanings. Just as feminist pedagogical theory can function as a lens for recognizing issues critical pedagogical theory may be overlooking,[8] this chapter suggests that a queer critical pedagogy of place might be used to widen or stretch some of the useful concepts found in a critical pedagogy of place.

To be specific, these literatures (queer theory and critical pedagogy of place) are related and I see them strengthening and interrogating each other in two very important ways: critical pedagogy of place allows for a distinct project of recognizing what it means to "live well" in our "total environments" and unlearn harmful and injurious ways of thinking,[9] while queer theory provides a theoretical space to recognize and complicate binary thinking and, most importantly, to *disrupt* it. Thus, this chapter is an investigation into this theoretical intersection.

The Classroom as a Place—Connected to Many, Reducible to None

The classroom is not a placeless place; it is filled with students and instructors, desks and learning technology, emptied recycle bins and swept floors, and other hints of people, the relationships among them and the things they have created, ordered, or obeyed (rules, identities, tracks, ideologies, etc.). Consider, then, that people and perhaps more importantly, social relations, too, are not placeless. Again, part of PBE's reinhabitation is learning to "live well" in places that have been mistreated, just as part of critical pedagogy is decolonization, which means unlearning harmful ways of knowing so we can recognize that harm and actively deploy restorative efforts toward social justice. How, in our roles of "teacher," might we foster the ability to recognize, for example, the labor (which, under capital, necessarily contains harmful exploitative practices) embedded in common classroom objects? How might we help students recognize non-physical items that are likewise harmful, such as some of the social relations and ideologies that connect the bodies, items, and organization of any classroom?

I argue that reinhabiting class consciousness as well as recognizing the labor and production embedded in classroom artifacts (the desk, for example) evokes a queer critical pedagogy of place, which is a pedagogy that can offer a method not just for identifying (and perhaps for reappropriation of) material spaces and places in order to "live well," but also for reinhabiting our own solidaritous consciousness, or in other words, our class consciousness (as Marx might say, becoming a class *for* itself rather than a class *in* itself[10]). Developing our class consciousness can aid in extending our empathy and connection to working people existing in the intersections of these social relations within the classroom, not just when we step into the "outdoors." This is potentially important for pedagogues who want to stress place in their teaching because place is more than a physical location, it is also what constitutes "us." Similarly, it encourages us to think about human relationships with each other (in addition to our land, air, water, etc.) as we consider ecology.[11]

Consider the desk's place within the classroom and its possible connections to human creation and production: Where are the raw materials grown and harvested? And by whom? Who controls the means of production? Where is the desk assembled? Which labor laws exist and which are actually followed? Where does demand come from? Are cheaply made desks in demand? Are they assembled in export-processing zones? How do trade liberalization policies such as the North American Free Trade Agreement or austerity measures in overdeveloped nations relate to how desks are produced and which desks are bought, and importantly, by whom? It doesn't necessarily have to be a desk that serves as the entry point to understanding the global labor practices that connect each and every one of us, but the desk is a particularly interesting one because it also serves as a disciplinary tool for both teacher and student. The desk is rife with structural limitations such as how it can be placed within a classroom, how the placement of desks affects a class's ability to have open dialogue, even perhaps how it reinforces the hierarchical roles of the expert teacher who fills the empty heads of the students, or how assumed "expertise" can confine a classroom to the authority of the teacher and the subordination of the students; these are all interesting questions about power that come up when we critically assess the role of the desk as a cultural artifact.

CLASS(ROOM) CONSCIOUSNESS

David Sobel[12] writes of PBE as engaging with local community issues and organizations to teach concepts within the social sciences and beyond. Much of "experiential" learning uses methods of "get up and see what's around you" and there is much one could read on how to do this. I agree that these methods are eye opening and important, but, again, it is also important to be cognizant of the fact that one does not necessarily need to leave the classroom, per se, to engage students with the place in which their classroom is embedded. That classroom—well beyond my brief example of a desk above—is itself filled with connections to places, social relations, human creation, and all of the other "things" necessary for a classroom to be filled with particular students, particular instructors, and so on. Again, the classroom and the connections inside it are *place*.

For instance, we might *reinhabit* class consciousness as *place*. By using a queer theoretical lens focused on deconstructing binaries, we can apply the concept of "reinhabitation" toward reinhabiting class consciousness (as *place*) by investigating the established binaries of student/worker, inside/outside (classroom/nature) and local/global. In fact, we might use the classroom as a place to recognize that the global is *in* the local (and vice versa) and problematize the very notion of a stable place that is not at once everywhere and also particular. This is especially true in our contemporary globalized political economy, as we have become intricately connected through processes of production, consumptions, exchange, and reproduction. This includes, of course, the billions of points of information along global internet cables throughout the world where information technology and a highly financialized economy create ever greater capacities for a certain kind of trade liberalization, increased and relatively unencumbered flows of capital, rooted in the reduction of the local and expansion of global market networks. Again, queer theory largely serves as a theoretical orientation aimed at breaking down assumed gender and sexuality binaries such as man/woman or heterosexual/homosexual, but it is also used as a theoretical lens to break down binaries in general (such as the ones pertaining to the classroom that I've noted above) and, importantly, to recognize the limits of binary logic, and in this particular case, the binary logic that is reproduced in some PBE and critical pedagogy literatures. Ultimately, where and by whom classroom objects are produced matters. How they are distributed matters. And how they are consumed and used matters. And it especially matters if we are serious and ruthless in our attempts to recognize harm in places so that we abolish (or at least diminish, in the short-term) those harms so the students, and also everyone to whom they are connected in their role as student, can also "live well."[13]

For example, the suicides (as a form of protest) at the Foxconn plant in China are connected to nearly every single classroom in the United States (especially those filled with students staring at their iPhones throughout class).[14] Ten minutes of research into the commodity supply chains that enable a technology-ready classroom will leave students with a feeling of connection to those "other workers" "out there" who play a major role in the function of their classroom, especially if the instructor is helping connect the political economic dots. A sociology class does not require a specific focus on labor to bring this to the fore of classroom discussion at some point throughout the semester, especially in an introductory sociology class in which helping students develop a sociological imagination is often an instructor's main goal of the semester.[15] Briefly, a sociological imagination is the ability to connect the micro to the macro,[16] or in other words, the ability to connect what seem like personal troubles to the complex matrix of social institutions.

A critical pedagogy of place aims to "balance" the twin goals of transforming oppressive social conditions (stemming from critical pedagogy) with "empathetic connection to others, human and non-human"[17] (stemming from PBE). From a queer critical pedagogy of place, one might argue that rather than a balancing act, an alternative goal could be recognizing that these are one in the same, overlapping, interrelated, and complex goals. Another way that a queer theoretical lens can aid in recognizing instability is in the perceived divide between urban (critical pedagogy) and rural (PBE). Again, a critical pedagogy of place recognizes the interrelatedness of these concepts, but maintains that they can be conceptually or materially "balanced" whereas a queer critical pedagogy of place might argue that "balancing" these places requires that we understand them first as separate and distinct, stable entities.

For example, we can queer the binaries (meaning collapse the form and recognize the complexity and always-already interrelatedness of both "sides") of inside/outside. This is an important binary to deconstruct. Think, for example, about the physical classroom: natural resources are needed to construct the objects, even the walls. This complicates the inside/outside binary and by doing so, allows us to further our inquiries about what it means to reinhabit or decolonize our ways of knowing in regard to the classroom and the people, objects, and social relations contained within. Or consider how "nature" is supposedly "outside," among other ways that it is typically conceived in popular discourse in (post)industrial societies. "Nature" as we know it in the United States is largely a term used to refer to state-run land. Is there any place that is fully human-made or fully "natural"? Is this a useful division in terms of categorization and thinking? A queer pedagogy of place provides space to find assumed binaries and dissolve the "slash" that tries to keep both sides separate from each other. Why dissolve binaries? Binary logic is quite often hierarchical logic, and if we are tasked with recognizing social ills and harmful practices and ways of knowing, then part of "living well" is interrogating assumed and established hierarchies (assuming we equate institutionalized hierarchies with "harm"—which I do). The inside/outside binary likewise maintains a distinction between "in the classroom" and "out there."

One thing I want to make clear about class consciousness is that it is not really something one can "teach." John Dewey asserted that you cannot directly teach an idea to someone; rather, you do what you *can* do, which is alter their conditions or their environment in such a way that learning is more or most likely to occur.[18] One cannot teach class consciousness or how to reinhabit class consciousness, but classrooms can be arranged in ways in which discussions that foster room for the growth of class consciousness can occur on a regular basis.[19]

"OUT THERE"

I have participated in both undergraduate and graduate courses in which board games were used to demonstrate how various aspects of society function; in effect these games were a simulation. For example, the board game Monopoly can be used in the classroom to demonstrate some aspects of the production and reproduction of class society. While games like Monopoly are enjoyed by students, I often wonder why we feel the need to rely on artificially "bringing in" the "outside world" to the classroom when, from my perspective, the same social relations are always already "here." I was left wondering how we could switch our gaze from "out there" to "in here" (or better yet, recognize them as different aspects of the same thing: place).

For example, one of the concepts students may learn in an introductory sociology class is that inequalities require maintenance and reproduction to continue existing as they are. Since students are already embedded in the educational system, using education as an institution that perpetuates and reproduces class society is an easy place to begin teaching and learning not only about how inequalities manifest in the U.S. educational system, but also to *politicize* (by which I mean develop an analysis of power relations) the very place in which we find ourselves crossing paths. The classroom (and classroom building, larger campus, and so on, however wide you desire to cast the net) becomes a site, location, and place that we can analyze sociologically. Why use a simulation when the very social relations the class is studying are already present in the classroom? Further, by not recognizing the power relations inside the classroom, the default effect is to invisibilize those relations, which in turn reproduces them.

Pedagogy of place literature often remarks on the connection of people to the environment. While that endeavor is absolutely important, part of thinking of place as "in here" rather than solely "out there" (again, "out there" matters, but expanding our understanding of place is central to this chapter) is examining not only students' connection to the environment and the "outdoors," but also their connection to human creation and the production of things.[20] This can take numerous forms in the classroom. Questions I pose to students might include: How did you get here (literally, how did you arrive in this classroom) today? Did you drive in a car on a road? Did you take a bus? Who built the stairs you climbed or installed the elevator you used? How did this desk come into existence and get placed in front of you (everything from the raw materials grown to make it, the workers who assembled it, the infrastructure used to transport it, the bureaucratic systems that organized and appointed certain people to make the decisions of which desk would appear in front of you, and so on)? The labor embedded in the items and objects we use in the classroom (or embedded in most everyday objects) is often invisibilized, but labor connects us all, especially in a world such as ours that functions on such an extremely high global division of labor.

One useful way I have found to incorporate these connections is to assign an autobiography the very first day of class. The only direction provided for the assignment is to answer the question: How did you end up here? Students often have questions about the assignment since it remains so open-ended and broad, but I tell them that is precisely the point—to see how they interpret the query. Students answer in various styles, some solely individualistic, some hilariously literal, and maybe a handful attempt to plug into a broader understanding of the agency/structure debate within the social sciences. Having spent the semester alongside students developing their sociological imaginations, I assign the exact same assignment the penultimate day of class and we end our semester discussing how their answers and orientation to the question have changed or developed.

This exercise has both created and refined my sense that there is merit looking at place, critical pedagogy, and queer theory as an important intersection of ideas. Gruenewald's project of developing a critical pedagogy of place offers much to both critical pedagogy and PBE, and deconstructing the residual binary logic buttressing some components of a critical pedagogy of place offers new ways of thinking about how we can foster pedagogical practices that can support a more egalitarian world. This chapter is my first attempt at weaving together this particular theoretical fabric. I end here with a quote from Peter Kropotkin that nicely displays how labor connects us all and troubles any stable notion of place:

> Every machine has had the same history—a long record of sleepless nights and of poverty, of disillusions and of joys, of partial improvements discovered by several generations of nameless workers, who have added to the original invention these little nothings, without which the most fertile idea would remain fruitless. More than that: every new invention is a synthesis, the resultant of innumerable inventions which have preceded it in the vast field of mechanics and industry.
>
> Science and industry, knowledge and application, discovery and practical realization leading to new discoveries, cunning of brain and of hand, toil of mind and muscle—all work together. Each discovery, each advance, each increase in the sum of human riches, owes its being to the physical and mental travail of the past and the present.
>
> By what right then can anyone whatever appropriate the least morsel of this immense whole and say—This is mine, not yours?[21]

NOTES

1. See Gruenewald, "The Best of Both Worlds."
2. See, for example, Penney, *After Queer Theory*.
3. Gruenewald, "The Best of Both Worlds," 7.

144 A.S. WILLIS

4. For an example that does not fail to connect PBE to social transformation, see Sobel, *Beyond Ecophobia*.
5. Gruenewald, "The Best of Both Worlds," 9.
6. Ibid.
7. Ibid.
8. For example, see hooks, *Teaching to Transgress*.
9. Gruenewald, "The Best of Both Worlds," 9.
10. See Marx, *The Poverty of Philosophy*.; or Marx and Engels, *The German Ideology*, 78.
11. See, for example, Bookchin, *The Ecology of Freedom*.
12. Sobel, *Beyond Ecophobia*.
13. What "living well" actually constitutes is another aspect that critical pedagogies of place can take up.
14. See, for example, http://www.telegraph.co.uk/news/worldnews/asia/china/9006988/Mass-suicide-protest-at-Apple-manufacturer-Foxconn-factory.html.
15. For example, see Mills, The Sociological Imagination.
16. Readers can see Deric Shannon's chapter about teaching on the farm (in this collection) for more info on the micro-macro link in sociology.
17. Gruenewald, "The Best of Both Worlds," 8.
18. Dewey, *Democracy and Education*, 10.
19. For more on class consciousness, readers can look into Lukacs, *History and Class Consciousness*.
20. Gruenewald, "The Best of Both Worlds."
21. Peter Kropotkin, *The Conquest of Bread* (Oakland, CA: AK Press, 1892/2007).

BIBLIOGRAPHY

Bookchin, Murray. *The Ecology of Freedom: The Emergence and Dissolution of Hierarchy*. Oakland, CA: AK Press, 2005.
Dewey, John. *Democracy and Education*. London: Echo Library, 1916/2007.
Gruenewald, David A. "The Best of Both Worlds: A Critical Pedagogy of Place." *Educational Researcher* 32.4 (2003): 3–12.
hooks, bell. Teaching to Transgress: *Education as the Practice of Freedom*. New York: Routledge, 1994.
Kropotkin, Peter. *The Conquest of Bread*. Oakland, CA: AK Press, 1892/2007.
Marx, Karl. *The Poverty of Philosophy: Answer to the Philosophy of Poverty by M. Proudhon*, 1847. Retrieved online at https://www.marxists.org/archive/marx/works/1847/poverty-philosophy/ (last accessed September 12, 2016).
Marx, Karl, and Friedrich Engels. *The German Ideology*. Amherst, NY: Prometheus Books, 1998.

Mills, C. Wright. *The Sociological Imagination*, 40th ed. Oxford, UK: Oxford University Press, 2000, orig. 1959.

Penney, James. *After Queer Theory: The Limits of Sexual Politics*. London, England: Pluto Press, 2013.

Sobel, David. *Beyond Ecophobia: Reclaiming the Heart in Nature Education*. Great Barrington, MA: The Orion Society and the Myrin Institute, 1996.

CHAPTER 11

Seeking Peace, Seeking Justice: Place-based Pedagogies and Global Connections

Jill Petersen Adams and Margaret Thomas McGehee

By serving only first- and second-year college students and by focusing on high-impact pedagogies, Oxford College of Emory University—a two-year liberal arts intensive division of a large research university—provides unique opportunities to be intentional about creating developmentally aware approaches to place-based education in the context of global learning. One such opportunity comes through the Global Connections program of the Pierce Institute for Leadership and Community Engagement. In existence since 2006 and co-sponsored by Oxford's Office of Religious and Spiritual Life, Global Connections offers "a travel experience designed to help students create meaning in their lives and connect their religious and spiritual convictions with justice issues, including peace, poverty, human rights, and the environment. Seminar activities and service experiences that offer reflection and meaningful dialogue with others aim also to help participants become agents of change for healthy living both here and abroad."[1]

J.P. Adams (✉)
Office of Academic Affairs and Division of Humanities,
Oxford College of Emory University, Oxford, Georgia, USA

M.T. McGehee
Humanities Division, Oxford College of Emory University,
Oxford, Georgia, USA

© The Author(s) 2017
D. Shannon, J. Galle (eds.), *Interdisciplinary Approaches to Pedagogy and Place-Based Education*, DOI 10.1007/978-3-319-50621-0_11

Faculty and staff may apply each year to curate and lead a Global Connections trip, and we recently had the good fortune to be selected to participate in the program.[2] What follows below is an analysis of the place-based pedagogies that we brought to our respective journeys. We offer here an examination of the ways by which we sought to design short-term, place-based travel experiences that would offer students much more than superficial, tourist-like visits to various domestic and international locations, experiences that would help students achieve benchmark and milestone outcomes as part of a developmental, incremental model of "global" learning. To achieve such goals, we implemented a place-based pedagogy of defamiliarization, described in greater detail later in this chapter.

In May 2015, we took nine students on a trip to various locations in Japan, focusing on the topic of "Seeking Peace: Embodying Peace and Justice in Postwar Japan"; then, in May 2016, Margaret McGehee and Susan Ashmore (Professor of History) took eight students on a trip to various locations throughout the U.S. South, focusing on the topic of "Civil Rights and Social Justice in the U.S. South." To ensure that each Global Connections journey was as enriching and meaningful as possible, we prepared students in several meetings during the spring semester prior to our departure. Furthermore, we curated full yet flexible itineraries that included significant museums, memorials, and historical sites, but in moving students and ourselves beyond the role of "tourist," we also arranged for numerous meetings with individuals who either experienced firsthand some of the critical moments under consideration or whose present-day work as scholars and/or activists has been greatly informed by such moments. Along the way, we incorporated time for informal and formal reflection and discussion.[3]

These trips represented, in part, the bridging of a divide often found within institutions of higher education between the curricular and co-curricular. In their article on the value of the term "study away," Neal Sobania and Larry A. Braskamp write: "Internationalization efforts are often located in the academic program, while multicultural programs are generally found in student life . . . All too often, points of intersection are noted, but there is little overlap."[4] It is true on our campus that the Office of Campus Life, and the Office of Religious and Spiritual Life that co-sponsors the Global Connections program, support multicultural organizations and their programming. However, internationalization efforts are coordinated across campus, as in our Office of International Student

Programs, and between the Oxford and Atlanta campuses, as with global learning initiatives of the Office of Global Strategy and Initiatives and International Student and Scholar services.

Mirroring these latter joint efforts, the faculty- and staff-led Global Connections trips are based on a collaborative model across academic and student life areas and thus are ideal venues for blurring the lines between curricular and co-curricular interests, perhaps even revealing in the process the occasional arbitrariness of such lines. Global Connections opens the students to a range of academic interests and avenues that might not be served by a single disciplinary course. And, as noted earlier, such programs need not always be international in scope to promote "global learning" as a place-based pedagogy. "Students today are often seeking courses and co-curricular activities that focus on issues ranging from social justice and conflict resolution to national identity and assimilation," state Sobania and Braskamp, echoing the very desires that bring students to the Global Connections program: "Why must we look only overseas for programs that can meet such needs?" Indeed, "local" concerns are "global" concerns,[5] which is not to collapse a distinction but rather to note that the two perspectives come together in place-based pedagogies.

DIRECTING, DESIGNING: SETTING THE GLOBAL/LOCAL STAGE

Building an effective program using this topical, or problem-based, orientation requires extensive and early collaborative work in planning not only the goals or outcomes but also the itineraries and activities. There is no syllabus mapping the direction of the program, and the program intentionally combines, blends, and challenges the faculty and staff's areas of presumed "expertise" in a way curricular programming may not. While the program leaders prepare a thorough itinerary and serve to provide historical context or framing throughout the trip itself, we mostly served in the capacity of "director[s]," as described by former director of international education at Concordia College, Peter Hovde, in his piece, "Opening Doors: Alternative Pedagogies for Short-Term Programs Abroad." "A director is seldom on stage," he writes. "Rather, a director is gathering the needed resources for the performance, assembling the cast, interpreting the script, and coordinating the efforts of all toward a common end."[6] The faculty and staff leading Global Connections programs rarely "lecture," but they often facilitate seminars and discussions on top of developing complex itineraries and outcomes. The "common ends" of the domestic and international programs discussed in this essay are both unique to the places that ground them—common ends shared by the participants on a single program based on the background of those leading it—but also "common" to Global Connections, with its emphasis on peace, social justice, and human rights.

Our program goals, then, seek "common ends" in both of these senses. "Seeking Peace: Embodying Peace and Justice in Postwar Japan" took place in Japan in 2015, marking the 17th anniversary of the Battle of Okinawa, the bombings of Hiroshima and Nagasaki, and the end of the Pacific War/World War II. The program built on this commemorative occasion to provide a focused opportunity to engage the legacies of war and catastrophic loss in religious and secular spheres. Students had the opportunity to confront how "peace" and "justice" are words employed in trying to understand and dialogue with, in trying to act and react to, myriad experiences of catastrophic suffering. In doing so, students also attended to the (political, historical, and religious) precursors to that suffering in Japan as well as its ongoing legacies. The students were not "teambuilding" in Tokyo, bonding at the clubs in the Roppongi nightlife district. They were in Hiroshima; they were connecting the atomic bombing of Hiroshima with the firebombing of Tokyo; they were wondering why they were not aware of these other histories.

As we described to the students, "peace" (*heiwa*) was a word employed early, and frequently, in reactions to the Battle of Okinawa and the atomic bombings at individual, local, national, and international levels—by poets and novelists, activists, and politicians—and the word took on a multitude of meanings. "Peace" became a rallying cry and site of resistance, a buzzword of nationalist propaganda, an organizing principle of city governance, the foundation of a tourist industry, and an expression of the desperate longing of survivors, a word of hope and despair. Through myriad means—engaging survivor accounts and meeting with people affected by the bombings; visiting religious, cultural, and memorial sites; talking to people who preserve loss or hasten for change; debating in seminars and orientation meetings; confronting material remains in museums; examining art and other cultural products; and meeting with Japan-based youth and religious groups—students confronted and questioned the nature and meanings of peace and justice but also the pull and the power of those words to inspire change. Students were urged, through their place-based experiences in Hiroshima, Osaka, Kyoto, and Tokyo, to consider the care and responsibility that any "agent of change" needs to cultivate if they are to promote the health of persons, environs, and nations.

The directors of our domestic program also worked carefully to coordinate a program that would connect our "change agents" to place. For the "Civil Rights and Social Justice in the U.S. South" trip, McGehee and cofacilitator Ashmore spent 10 days driving students throughout Alabama, Mississippi, Tennessee, and Arkansas. The goal of the civil rights-focused Global Connections trip was to introduce students to the broad reach of the southern struggle for racial equality. Our primary objective was to encourage students to think critically about and reflect on the following: why was it so difficult to dismantle the legalized white supremacy of Jim Crow laws and how were different approaches and tactics used to do so; how do issues of the civil rights era—as well as slavery—continue to inform our present-day race relations and social structures and shape the lives of those living and working in the U.S. South; and what strategies and tactics do activists use today to address ongoing racial and class conflicts.

To help facilitate such thinking, our itinerary included the following: visits to major civil rights museums and historical sites in Montgomery, Birmingham, Selma, Jackson, Money, Little Rock, and Memphis; guided walking tours in various cities; and meetings with various scholars, professionals, and civil right activists (past and present).[7] We took as our premise, best articulated by Sobania and Braskamp, that a domestic program can "influence students to think, reflect upon themselves, and interact with others, and thereby generate outcomes similar to those of a study abroad program." As they claim, "Diverse cultures within a local, regional, or national community should be recognized for providing learning opportunities and experiences that can also be transformative." Furthermore, the relatively low cost of the trip allowed some students to participate who could not afford the international travel experiences being simultaneously offered, thus confirming Sobania and Braskamp's claim that "[a] domestic program that costs a participant only a few hundred dollars for travel, room, and board becomes a more realistic option. Even given students' limited resources, such programs may also hold the potential for increasing the number of students who participate."[8]

Furthermore, as with the program in Japan in May 2015, this journey adopted the "extensive relocation (travel model)" versus the "one site (residential model)" approach, also as described by Peter Hovde. Because of the focus in both programs on a movement or issue that spanned multiple places and populations, program leaders wanted students to see as many sites of historical significance, movement activity, and present-day activism as possible within our limited time frame and budget. We wanted the students to understand how and why things happened with particular people in particular places—to understand that this bridge or that riverbed was integral to the unfolding of events—and that these places come together in the problem or movement we engage. If the problem or movement is a constellation, we want the students to see as many points as possible to understand what makes up the overall shape. As Hovde argues in his discussion of pedagogical approaches abroad, "disciplinary or interdisciplinary foci can more than justify the traveling study abroad model"—or "study away," in our case. For example, "A seminar on conflict needs to hit the road, visiting historical sites (battlegrounds or museums) as well as organizations involved in conflict resolution (be they military organizations or peace nongovernmental organizations [NGOs]."[9]

A travel course specifically focused on a set of concerns or issues—which in our case drives the relocation model—seeks to counter the idea of study abroad trips as becoming a kind of "playground" for students. When Ben Feinberg discusses "What Students Don't Learn Abroad" for the *Chronicle of Higher Education*, he forcefully argues against a model of globalization "where the outside world is no more than a fantasy play-ground whose only real inhabitants are obsessed with our commodities," and where thus "it is no surprise that students … fill their travel stories with images of personal growth or bad behavior." In his pointed critique of the experience-as-playground, Feinberg claims that students "return from study abroad programs having seen the world, but the world they return to tell tales about is more often than not the world they already knew." It is a potential danger to keep in mind and to design against. Feinberg asks of colleges and universities, "can our programs challenge that perception of the world, instead of allowing it to sink in more deeply? The answer is probably not."[10] Against this skepticism, we argue that intentional program design and putting pedagogy first certainly can challenge students' existing perceptions of the world. Place-based education, in which the place serves and is served by the teaching and learning rather than being incidental to it, is one of the most important sites of such challenge.

Furthermore, because Global Connections programs focus on issues of social justice and peacebuilding, we want students on our trips who are serious about such issues and who have a particular desire to explore those in an intensive travel course. Therefore, students first must submit an application that requires short essay responses. Once the trip leaders have reviewed the applications, they select a group of students to interview, which gives further insight into the seriousness of the students and helps leaders gauge a student's level of emotional preparedness and maturity.

When the intentional focus of the trip is combined with this screening process, we are able to avoid several pitfalls that Feinberg describes. Feinberg claims that many students go on study abroad trips heavily influenced by commercial depictions of the inhabitants of global cultures as "obsessed with our commodities" and as "prescient consumers with a quirky knowledge of luxury cars or Internet stock trading." Their post-travel reflections tend to be "first-person pronoun"-laden texts, focusing primarily on what they took away about themselves and about intra-group dynamics rather than about what they learned about another culture or country or the systems therein.[11]

Feinberg, offering a glimmer of hope for those self-centered study abroad students, writes that at the very least, "we should avoid ... orientation sessions that focus on group dynamics and individual growth. Instead, those sessions could be used as opportunities for students to learn how to question the way that we tell stories about our travels." Gaining self-knowledge is no doubt important, but only when that self-awareness does not reinforce dominance of one's own worldview. Global Connections, with its focus on place, people, and justice, intentionally tries to move beyond a facile "individual growth." We seek to inform students and let them be informed, attend to diversity and difference *in* places and between the students and the places, start thinking about the wide-ranging consequences of their own and others' actions, and seek equitable and collaborative solutions to problems. Such gains offer a corrective to the study abroad "playground" and its pitfalls.

For example, in Hiroshima, in an area that had been decimated by the atomic bombing, the students participated in a seminar. From the window we could see the Peace Memorial Park, where the students spent the day walking among its monuments, listening to testimony, and engaging its memorial practices. We did not ask the students, "What did you think about today's stuff?" We asked them how their ideas about peace had changed, if they understood peace differently; we asked them if it surprised them that bomb survivors were as critical of the Japanese government as of the American government, and if so why; we asked them if they were aware of discriminatory practices against Koreans living in Japan and if their engagement with testimony from Korean survivors helped them better understand present-day tensions in East Asia any better.

Hovde points out that the goal of global education (which we expand, with a place-based education framework, to include well-designed and focused domestic trips as well) is "gaining an understanding of ourselves and of our self," but in Global Connections, we were more concerned with helping students gain "an awareness that we have a perspective (or, more accurately, perspectives)"—in other words, "perspective conscious-ness."[12] "Perspective Taking" is one of the outcomes identified in the developmental (or building-block) model for global learning outlined in the "Global Learning VALUE Rubric" distributed by the Association of American Colleges and Universities in collaboration with NAFSA, the Association of International Educators. This incremental model serves as the pedagogical foundation for place-based education in both Global Connections experiences.

"Global learning," the authors argue in the published rubric, "is a critical analysis of and an engagement with complex, interdependent global systems and legacies" that are natural, social, cultural, economic, political, and material. Students engaged in global learning should "[b]ecome informed, open-minded, and responsible people who are attentive to diversity across the spectrum of differences"; "seek to under-stand how their actions affect both local and global communities"; and "address the world's most pressing and enduring issues collaboratively and equitably."[13] Again understanding the local as global and the global in the local, we argue that these outcomes are pertinent, even integral, to the Global Connections mission.

These global learning outcomes cannot be attained in one go. The rubric provides a helpful frame for understanding how these overall goals can be staged across the undergraduate (and graduate) learning experi-ence. The rubric features six areas of growth:

- Global self-awareness
- Perspective taking
- Cultural diversity
- Personal and social responsibility
- Understanding global systems
- Applying knowledge to contemporary global contexts

Each of these areas carries a four-tiered approach to evaluating gains, with a benchmark level, two levels of "milestones," and a capstone level for each.

The example from Hiroshima above helps connect "perspective consciousness" with this developmental model. Students did speak from the site of their own experiences, but they were not self-congratulatory: "My parents are Korean, and now I understand why they always said … " or "I'm Chinese, and we still struggle with…" or "I wondered why my parents don't talk much about the Japanese invasion in the Philippines," or "As an American, I was taught in school that we had to drop the bomb to end the war, and now I'm not so sure." The responses met the benchmark level on the rubric for "cultural diversity" (describing the experiences of others primarily through one cultural perspective, demonstrating openness to varied views), but many surpassed it. They met or even exceeded the first milestone level, in which each student "explains and connects two or more cultures historically or in contemporary contexts with some acknowledgement of power structures, demonstrating respectful interaction with varied cultures and worldviews." In fact, using the rubric throughout the travel experience can help us push the students to engage a little more with the place, to delve deeper, to ask more questions of the people and places they encounter, so that even over the course of the trip we can see them grow and lay the foundations for their next experiences.

Oxford's institutional character—with its intensive focus on first- and second-year students and emphasis on experiential learning opportunities—allows us to aim, in our global learning and place-based programs, for these benchmark or higher levels as early as the freshman year; many other institutions (de facto or de jure) leave students waiting until the third or fourth year to begin these hands-on experiences. While we are not at the assessment stage, these frameworks are vital to course- and program design and could also be of great utility for institutions considering first- and second-year-experience programs.

The program-design goal in our context was for students to have the possibility of reaching and fully embodying capstone levels by the latter stages of their undergraduate career by giving them multiple, staged opportunities to practice these skills starting at the earliest opportunity. The approach is incremental: We plant seeds the fruition of which we may not see and have not yet assessed formally, but we can design around, strive for, and see *gains*—for example, moving from the benchmark level of "understanding global systems" described above to the first milestone level, in which the student "examines the historical and contemporary roles, interconnections, and differential effects of human organizations and actions on global systems within the human and natural worlds." A student participating in Global Connections as a freshman might appropriately attain the benchmark level, but when she goes on to, say, a credit-bearing course with a place-based travel component in her sophomore year, she has a foundation on which to build, achieving higher levels of milestones as she hones her attention to place on a global stage.

The "Rubric" in Practice

But how do we achieve such outcomes? How does "perspective consciousness" come about, one might ask? Broadly speaking, students must become "defamiliarized" with what they assume they know. "Defamiliarization," to use J.Z. Smith's adaptation of the idea for religious studies, means making the familiar strange—helping students reflect on their "ways of looking" and ways of being in the world, their ways of being students and proto-scholars, in order to come to more complicated understandings of people, places, and processes (and first of all, their own). Defamiliarization is thus both process and outcome.

The process can entail a variety of means and methodologies; for us, on both trips, that process involved students' daily immersion in a set of carefully and thoughtfully curated experiences while also allowing them time for adequate reflection (and in some instances, emotional recovery or renewal). We also allowed ourselves the flexibility for serendipitous and unplanned moments to occur, either collectively or individually—taking some roads less traveled, as it were. Moreover, in organizing each day, we sought to incorporate a variety of sensory experiences—not only to keep our students' minds and bodies moving (especially in the face of jetlag and road weariness) but also as a pedagogical practice of *place saturation* (i.e., not full or long-term cultural immersion but nevertheless substantive engagement). That process of defamiliarization is in part an affective one, relying on a stimulation of senses and emotional reactions to make students aware of the new-ness of what they are hearing, seeing, or feeling and to push them toward a reflection that is more than just a better understanding of self. It is a combination of visual, aural, and tactile (and sometimes olfactory) experiences that can help bring about that defamiliarization.

For example, in the heart of the memorial museum dedicated to the fire bombings of the Japanese city of Osaka, we found full-size bombs, destroyed remains of the city, a three-dimensional topographical map of the city, and other exhibits. When we wandered around the corner from the bombs, rubble, and twisted rebar, we found a to-scale underground air raid shelter. As we peered in the opening, unsure if we could enter, an air raid siren sounded. The shelter grew dark. Then we became immersed in the sounds of the air raids as light, representing fire raging, flickered at the top of the shelter. The raid simulation was protracted and uncomfortable, and we were mesmerized by how fully the museum engaged the senses to convey the horror of the raids. When we emerged back into the light, we were a bit disoriented by the intact, sterile museum. Then we went back around the corner and found ourselves in yet another air raid, this time using light projection over the three-dimensional topographical map of Osaka we had passed earlier (it was in a static state then): now anyone standing in front of the wall on which the map was displayed found themselves immersed in the raid, the light of the fires playing on their bodies.

Similarly, for the civil rights trip, a goal was to move students beyond a textbook, classroom-based understanding of civil rights history—for students to gain a better "feel" for the places where such significant moments occurred, a "feel" that can only come from "being there," to borrow Hovde's phrase.[14] For example, in Montgomery, Alabama, Mr Randall Williams—owner of New South Press and one of the founders of Klanwatch at the Southern Poverty Law Center—took students on a walking tour of the city, beginning on Commerce Street where the buildings were once used as part of the slave trade. From there we were led to the base of Dexter Avenue, in front of the Court Square Fountain: to our left in the distance was the site of the former department store where Mrs Rosa Parks worked and, closer in, the site of where she stepped on the city bus on December 1, 1955; behind us in the distance, we could see the stop where the bus driver told her to move from her seat; in front of us, about a half mile up on the right, Dexter Avenue Baptist Church, Dr. Martin Luther King, Jr.'s first church, and further up and center, the Alabama State Capitol, site of Governor George Wallace's reign. Later, we would walk up the street radiating to our right to the Greyhound Bus Station, site of the 1961 Freedom Rider attacks.

What such a walking tour provided was a sense of connectedness between place and history that is impossible to convey in a typical classroom lecture. Students may have seen various buildings or bus stops in film clips or photographs from the era, but being on the ground, being in immediate proximity to those sites, seeing the close proximity of one site to the next, and also noting (60 years later) how those sites have been or have not been memorialized in some fashion make the historical narratives that much more real to students. Regardless of the presence of an official memorial, marker, or monument, the sense of what has happened on that ground becomes more palpable for students in a context where a local expert can help ground them.

Throughout both trips, we focused students' attention on history, historical transmission, representation, and memory. One aspect of defamiliarization is to destabilize the students' temporality, their experiences of the passage of time—or perhaps especially their sense of "progress" as privilege. From a place-based perspective, one might think of it as pausing "in place" to "cross time." The experiences on Global Connections allowed students to connect to other temporal spaces: they recognized the difference, the disjuncture, in their experiences *as well as* similarities, their connection, to those experiences. We wanted to highlight temporal difference—students in one time and place connecting with other times *in those places.* We were not presuming to give students an opportunity for vicarious experience that would make them think they "feel just what those people felt"; instead, we asked, what does their present-day experience in this place help them realize about the past, about assumptions about "progress?" Museums in the U.S. South and in Japan work hard to emphasize that the issues they present—about civil and human rights, about nuclear bombing and nuclear proliferation—are not "past" events that are over and done with but events that are still relevant in the present and raise grave concerns about the future. What does that experience make students hope for the future? What desires for change does the experience engender? The Global Connections experience uses *place* as a platform for students to be informed by the past and present and build a shared concern for the future.

One morning, for example, the Global Connections: Japan group set off for West Hiroshima to find the Peace Institute at Hiroshima City University. There we met with Drs. Bo Jacobs and Ran Zwigenberg to discuss the work of the institute, their research, and our questions. One of the key points in the discussion covered the notion of "Global Hibakusha." *Hibakusha* is a Japanese word used to denote those affected by the bombing (either the bomb explosion or the effects of radiation), and Dr Jacobs is part of an initiative that explores the ties that bind nuclear test-site communities globally, particularly in communities that are less globally recognized *as* affected by nuclear development. The students learned that the experience of Hiroshima *hibakusha*, something they thought was part of the past, has been echoed in other communities in other places across the last century and remains a threat today.

Adding to these deep opportunities for engagement when we stop at particular places, we also *moved* through places. We took our fingers off the "pause" button and pressed "play" again. Walking through particular areas can provide sensory experiences for students that leave particular imprints. On the one hand, guided tours can give context or grounding in a place as well as a narrative with which to engage. Particularly with the "benchmark" level of engagement and the co-curricular aspect of the trip that assumes no grounding in the places or materials visited, these guided narratives give students a platform for later faculty-led discussion that can help them question or critically engage this narrative.

For example, students touring the Peace Memorial Park in Hiroshima stood before a memorial to Koreans who were in Hiroshima at the time of the bombing because of Japanese forced-labor policies, and the students were told by their tour guide that the park honors the experiences of this Korean population with this memorial; in later discussions, we were able to ask why that memorial was first denied admission, then admitted late, then placed on the margins of the park in an outlying area. The established narrative the tour guide presents was not exactly "wrong" and not exactly "right"; but based on the experience of this particular place, assumed knowledge was made less familiar, was questioned, and perhaps was reconstructed differently. Without the layer of critical engagement, the playground model might mean one engaged student feels outrage before the memorial, one feels honor, and another feels tired or hungry. But with the additional layer of discussion and critique that *being in the place* allows, we hoped to get more students moving past their initial assumptions or placid acceptance, their feelings of superiority or desire for simple answers. At the benchmark level, students may not have all the tools to work *through* defamiliarization, but they can begin to practice dwelling in this state.

As part of this practice, however, we did not want simply to counter a "guided" experience of a place with "our" experience of the place. We wished to allow students an unscripted experience of a place as well, allowing students to become "guides," even stepping into the roles of "directors" when they wanted to linger and "excavate" a site more dee-ply.[15] For example, we allowed students to move through the streets of Hiroshima noticing the strange shapes on the sidewalks and wondering about them; they might have wondered what a statue of a bodhisattva is doing in a municipal playground. They might have followed the shapes down streets and through alleyways. They might have sat on the swings and stared at the statue's welcoming gesture. With their interest piqued, they could begin the process of "excavation," of trying to see things that were not immediately apparent to them, things that run the risk of being lost to history. And eventually, they might come across a plaque that notes that the shapes on the sidewalks signal the outlines of bombed buildings; the back of the playground statue might note that this particular Buddha protects and guides children through the underworld. Perhaps they would check Wikipedia or do Google image searches. Or they may never fully know what pulled them in; they may take a religion class years later, and the image of the bodhisattva, and all the horror and salvation of its presence in the playground, come upon them all at once.

Another example: In traveling from Jackson, Mississippi, to Memphis, Tennessee, we stopped in the small, sleepy town of Sumner, Mississippi, to visit the Emmett Till Interpretive Center. Students were very familiar with the story of Emmett Till's murder as a catalyst for the civil rights move-ment. But they were quite unfamiliar with the geography in which such an atrocity took place. The interpretive center is located across the street from the courthouse where Till's murderers were tried and acquitted. Recently, efforts led by the center in collaboration with the William Winter Center for Racial Reconciliation at the University of Mississippi resulted in the production of a resolution signed by many members of the Sumner com-munity to condemn that act of violence. As we sat in the courtroom, facilitators had us read the resolution aloud, one person per sentence, and then engaged us in a workshop about our racialized experiences. In a short amount of time, the narrative and legacy of Emmett Till's lynching became new to them.

Later that day we drove to the former site of Roy Bryant's Grocery Store in Money, Mississippi, where Till allegedly whistled at Bryant's wife, Carolyn.[16] The store is now a dilapidated building covered in kudzu; other visitors to the site actually had to point us to the correct spot as we completely missed the building right in front of our faces upon our initial arrival. The direct view from where the front doors once were is a pictur-esque Delta landscape. No one was around; there was no noise. The students took note of what can best be described, in Rudolf Otto's words, as the *numinous* quality of the moment.[17] Prior to our departure, we gathered in a circle to acknowledge that palpable sense of the sacred, the heaviness of that place, and the weightiness of its history, then took turns reading aloud Kevin Young's recently published poem entitled "Money Road." "There are things/that cannot be seen/but must be," writes Young. "Buried/barely, this place/no one can keep—/Yet how to kill a ghost?"[18]

The power of recitation, of putting another's witnessing in one's own voice, was echoed in Hiroshima, too. We started one day hosted by the Hiroshima Peace Culture Foundation and the remarkable Ms. Yasuko Okane for a recitation of bomb-related memoirs and poems at the Hall of Remembrance for Victims of the Atomic Bombing. Three volunteers and the students participated in the poetry recitation, and as poems were repeated multiple times by different voices, all of us were overwhelmed by the experience. The group recitation—active, not passive—disrupted our expectations, disrupted the "script," and required participation in a way the students had not yet experienced, "resetting" everyone for the day and using the unsettling time to open them to the encounter.

Later, we finished the day rather as we began—with testimony. Ms. Keiko Ogura generously offered her time to share directly with the students her thoughts and reflections from the time of the bombing. Ms. Ogura worked as a translator, so not only was she able to speak to the students directly in the language that was native for most of them, but she demonstrated many other facets of *translation* as an intentional act of communication, a transmission of something vitally important, across time and space. She was more than a storyteller, and she delivered her message with intention, aiming directly for the hearts and minds of the students.

Hovde claims that "something meaningful occurs in each of us when we stand in the exact spot" where something happened and we go to sites "just to be there."[19] This idea is, in some way, reminiscent of the notion of rememory within Toni Morrison's novel *Beloved*. The main character, Sethe, who escaped a life of enslavement in Kentucky for one of tenuous freedom in Ohio, tells her daughter Denver, "Some things go. Pass on. Some things just stay. I used to think it was my rememory ... but it's not. Places, places are still there. If a house burns down, it's gone, but the place—the picture of it—stays, and not just in my rememory, but out there, in the world."[20] Echoing, to some extent, William Faulkner's claim—"The past is never dead. It's not even past" (*Requiem for a Nun*)—Morrison's "rememory" offers a theoretical framework for what we want students to come to understand through both intellectual and affective engagement with the experiences to which we intentionally and, at times, unintentionally lead them.

These approaches, then, are a kind of pedagogical memorial practice, or perhaps a memorial pedagogical practice. Rather than a stable transmission of facts, this pedagogy fosters a critical engagement with the presentations and representations of history, a questioning of the things that get included or excluded from official narratives. The moments of unanticipated "numinosity," which contribute to a process and outcome of defamiliarization, are a serendipitous surprise within such travel experiences. But they are also an ideal result of intentional planning of a range of experiences that can provide on the ground, immediate historical-geographical saturation that in turn elicits students' personal, emotional, and visceral reactions.

Combined with the lectures, guided tours, or gatherings that we had with "pop-in" guests, we also visited a range of Pacific War- and civil rights-focused museums to get a sense of how these histories have been represented in various ways. Students were prompted not only to read the material within the exhibitions but to consider its presentation—from organization, to narrative, to signage. Similar to the experience with the memorial to Koreans who died in the Hiroshima bombing, described above, visiting particular memorials and monuments in the U.S. South, including the James Meredith statue on the University of Mississippi campus to the Jefferson Davis statue and Confederate monument on the grounds of the Alabama State Capitol to the Civil Rights Memorial at Southern Poverty Law Center (designed by Maya Lin), students examined what forms had been given to historical figures, moments, or "causes," and what such designs intimate or project to their visitors.

This deep engagement with places in brief spans of time—the fusion of depth and breadth[21]—is especially appropriate for first- and second-year students, who can start to ask questions without being totally overwhelmed, to "defamiliarize" without losing their senses of self and to compare unfamiliar places without language fluency. Recall that the faculty members on these collaborative, co-curricular travel experiences are, in line with Hovde, not the star[s] but the director[s] of the show—teaching not "what [they] know" but rather *more than* they know.[22] Faculty open up avenues for student experience but do not manage or frame every inquiry. They provide *tools* for this early level of engagement, footholds and handholds in the students' own explorations and critical engagements. As the examples above show, the experience of place becomes *more than* the sum of its parts; the knowledge gained is more than the cumulative total of stories told on guided tours. And the faculty learn from the students' questioning and from each other as both are pushed beyond the boundaries of their own "expertise."

While we have yet to fully engage in assessing the extent to which our intended outcomes were achieved, we can comment on how transformative these trips have been for each of us as scholar-teachers who want to link our work to social change. For one, leading such trips moves us beyond what we know—not only moving us beyond traditional classroom-based pedagogies but moving us beyond our scholarly knowledge base. Participating in both trips allowed McGehee to make connections between memorialization efforts within the U.S. South, as related to the Civil War and civil rights, and within postwar Japan. Traveling with McGehee in Japan also brought these issues to the fore for Adams, as a non-specialist scholar residing in the U.S. South; Adams sought input from Japanese scholars and scholars of Japan to supplement her own expertise as she designed the Japan itinerary, thereby realizing areas that might have been overlooked and learning more in the process. Such collaborative trips allow faculty directors to break down disciplinary lines and to learn from one another. They allow us to examine— in articles such as this, for example—what brings us together in our intellectual and pedagogical pursuits, not what divides us. In this way, place-based pedagogies involving short-term travel ultimately return us to our homes— our college, our classrooms, our daily lives—better than when we left.

NOTES

1. "Global Connections."
2. The authors wish to express their sincere thanks to the following individuals for helping make our Global Connections programs possible: Dr David Gowler, Dr Lovick Pierce and Bishop George F. Piece Chair of Religion at Oxford College; Rev. Lyn Pace, Oxford College Chaplain; Ms Regina Barrett, Senior Associate Director of Programs, Academic Affairs; and Ms Allison McKelvey, former administrative assistant to the Pierce Program, and our on-site collaborators for each travel experience. McGehee would also like to thank colleague Dr Susan Ashmore, Professor of History at Oxford College, for her outstanding co-leadership of the May 2016 Global Connections trip.

3. For student reflections from the 2015 Japan trip, please see the blog located at: https://scholarblogs.emory.edu/globalconnections2015/.
4. Sobania and Braskamp, "Study Abroad or Study Away."
5. Here we engage Hovland's "Global Learning: Defining, Designing, Demonstrating," when he notes, "It is a common habit to think of global learning as occurring elsewhere. What kinds of designs emphasize the local in the global and the global in the local?" Hovland, "Global Learning," 9.
6. Hovde, "Opening Doors," 7.
7. Those individuals included: Rev. Ed King, chaplain of Tougaloo College during the civil rights movement; Dr Susan M. Glisson, Director of the William Winter Institute for Racial Reconciliation at the University of Mississippi; Randall Williams, founding member of Klanwatch at the Southern Poverty Law Center; Ellen Mertins from the Alabama Historical Commission; Jim Baggett, archivist at the Birmingham Public Library; and Adrienne van der Valk, managing editor of *Teaching Tolerance* at the Southern Poverty Law Center.
8. Sobania and Braskamp, "Study Abroad or Study Away," n.p. "As both a concept and strategy," they write, "study away recognizes that students can have experiences that open their minds, hearts, and behaviors to difference and allows them to experience such difference firsthand, either internationally or domestically. Additionally, by expanding the concept of study abroad to study away, the range of experiences that can move students toward living effectively with difference is greatly expanded. These various options provide students with multiple entry points to such learning. For some students the entry point will be an on-campus course and an internship or volunteer activity; for others it will be a short- or long-term study away program. For some that program will be overseas; for others it will here in the United States." It is our belief that the use of the term "study away" allows not only for a more expansive under-standing of what activities can enrich students' educational experiences but also provides a more inclusive and democratic model for student learning.
9. Hovde, "Opening Doors," 5.
10. Feinberg, "What Students Don't Learn Abroad," B20.
11. Ibid.
12. Hovde, "Opening Doors," 4.
13. The Global Learning VALUE rubric is available at https://www.aacu.org/value/rubrics/global-learning.
14. Hovde, "Opening Doors," 6.
15. We draw here from critical theorist Walter Benjamin's paired ideas of flânuering and excavation. Flânuering, for Benjamin, is an activity actually learned in childhood. In an early essay on children's books, Benjamin notes that typically people fail to notice that "the world is full of the most unrivaled objects for children's attention and use ... For children are particularly fond of

haunting any site where things are being visibly worked on." Benjamin, "Old Forgotten Children's Books," 408. Flâneuring is a kind of "aimless" or unscripted wandering that results from the childish attention described here. One aimlessly strolls arcades or food stalls, for example, and allows the experience of material objects—their sights, smells, tastes, and feel—to permeate one's senses; one may or may not be struck by "something" as a result. If one *is* struck by this wandering through "things being worked on," one then begins a kind of "excavation" as a mode of memory: memory, Benjamin writes, "is the medium of past experience, just as the earth is the medium in which dead cities lie buried. He who seeks to approach his own buried past must conduct himself like a man digging. This determines the tone and bearing of genuine reminiscences. They must not be afraid to return again and again to the same matter; to scatter it as one scatters earth, to turn it over as one turns soil." Benjamin, "Old Forgotten Children's Books," 611. We urged students toward both this wandering and this "digging."

16. Recently, historian Tim Tyson revealed that Carolyn Bryant had fabricated her story about Till. https://www.nytimes.com/2017/01/27/us/emmett-till-lynching-carolyn-bryant-donham.html

17. See Rudolf Otto, *The Idea of the Holy*, Trans. John W. Harvey (London: Oxford UP, 1923, 1950, 1958).

18. Young, "Money Road."

19. Hovde, "Opening Doors," 6.

20. Morrison, *Beloved*, 43.

21. Hovde notes that the single-site residential model is held "by some as an inherently superior model." "Clearly, if immersion in a culture is the primary goal of the experience, a single-site residential program may be a better way," he concedes. But a single-culture travel seminar, in which the itinerary is confined to a single country or cultural area, "could be enriched by the many exposures to important sites (cultural breadth) at a modest cost to immersion (cultural depth)." Hovde, "Opening Doors," 5. Disciplinary or interdisciplinary foci, such as those shared by Global Connections offerings, often drive the need for the *traveling* model.

22. Hovde, "Opening Doors," 7.

Bibliography

Benjamin, Walter. *Gesammelte Schriften*, 7 volumes. Edited by Rolf Tiedemann and Hermann Schweppenhäuser (Frankfurt: Suhrkamp Verlag, 1972–1989), translated as *Selected Writings*, 5 Vols: Vol. 1 (1913–1926), edited by Marcus Bullock and Michael W. Jennings; Vol. 2, Pt. 2 (1931–1934), edited by Michael W. Jennings, Howard Eiland, and Gary Smith. Cambridge, MA and London: The Belknap Press of Harvard University Press, 1996–2003.

Feinberg, Ben. "What Students Don't Learn Abroad." *The Chronicle of Higher Education*, May 3, 2009.

"Global Connections." Oxford College of Emory University, accessed June 20, 2016, http://oxford.emory.edu/academics/centers-institutes-programs/pierce-institute/global-engagement/global-connections/.

"Global Learning VALUE Rubric." American Association of Colleges & Universities, accessed June 20, 2016, https://www.aacu.org/value/rubrics/global-learning.

Hovde, Peter. "Opening Doors: Alternative Pedagogies for Short-Term Programs Abroad." In *The Guide to Short-Term Programs Abroad*, edited by Sarah E. Spencer and Kathy Tuma, 1–7. NAFSA: Association of International Educators, 2002.

Hovland, Kevin. Global Learning: Defining, Designing, Demonstrating. NAFSA: Association of International Educators and the Association of American Colleges and Universities, 2014.

Morrison, Toni. *Beloved*. New York: Vintage Books, 1987.

Sobania, Neal, and Larry A. Braskamp. "Study Abroad or Study Away: It's Not Merely Semantics." *Peer Review* 11, no. 4 (2009): n.p. https://www.aacu.org/publications-research/periodicals/study-abroad-or-study-away-its-not-merely-semantics.

Young, Kevin. "Money Road." *The New Yorker*, February 22, 2016, http://www.newyorker.com/magazine/2016/02/22/money-road.

CHAPTER 12

Redefining Learning Places in the Emerging Digital Ecosystem

Rebecca Frost Davis

Advocates of place-based education have viewed place as a pedagogical tool to personalize education and as a source of experiential learning, a tool for helping students understand their identity (their place in the local community and the world) as an integrating element in students' education, a tool to develop active citizenship and as a force to sustain the importance of local communities in opposition to the forces of economic and technology-enabled globalization. Students today, however, can experience many of these pedagogies just as much in our emerging digital ecosystem as they do in the physical spaces that surround them, and tend to view identity and community as a continuum from the physical to the virtual rather than as discrete experiences. How then should instructors practice place-based education in a world increasingly shaped by digital tools, methods, and environments? How might we intentionally prepare students for that world, and how might the pedagogies developed by place-based education contribute to that project? What does place-based education look like in the online classroom? How do place-based pedagogies transfer to a digital context, and how might digital pedagogy inform place-based teaching? To answer these questions, I will examine three aspects of place-based education

R.F. Davis (✉)
Director of Instructional and Emerging Technology, Instructional Technology, St. Edward's University, Austin, TX, USA

© The Author(s) 2017
D. Shannon, J. Galle (eds.), *Interdisciplinary Approaches to Pedagogy and Place-Based Education*, DOI 10.1007/978-3-319-50621-0_12

167

that intersect with digital pedagogy —experience, identity, and engaged citizenship—and consider the implications of this transfer for faculty, students, and institutions.

LEARNING IN PHYSICAL AND DIGITAL COMMUNITIES

Before examining place-based pedagogies in digital environments, let me begin by highlighting an implicit tension between place-based education and digital pedagogy.[1] "Place" implies physical, geographic locations. Because technology in the form of digital networks, automation, and standardization has enabled global communication, markets, and transnational corporations pushing a globalized consumer culture, many practitioners of place-based education also implicitly oppose technology-enabled communities. For example, David Gruenewald and Gregory Smith in their introduction to *Place-Based Education: In the Global Age* tie place-based education to "the new localism" as a movement that opposes the effects of community disruption stemming from economic globalization by "reclaiming the significance of the local in the global age."[2] Their pedagogy of place, then, is a pedagogy that engages with a community primarily defined by geographical proximity. In the digital age, however, community may be defined by proximity in a social network just as much as in geography. For example, Henry Jenkins, while advocating for media education for the twenty-first century, points to affinity spaces in which digital communities are "sustained by common endeavors that bridge differences in age, class, race, gender, and educational level."[3] We might also add physical location to that list of differences. In these virtual spaces, affinities or common interests, rather than physical geography, define community. These two approaches—place-based education and digital pedagogy—present seemingly opposing views for technology. For Gruenewald and Smith, technology is a potentially homogenizing tool that enables globalization; for Jenkins, technology encourages heterogeneity by enabling a variety of affinity communities. This dichotomy echoes the seeming clash between place-based learning and learning in the emerging digital ecosystem, between the physical and the virtual.

Despite the tension in attitudes toward technology, place-based education and digital pedagogy share common goals. In his definition of place-based education, David Sobel identifies multiple pedagogies and goals:

> Place-based education is the process of using the local community and environment as a starting point to teach concepts in language arts,

mathematics, social studies, science and other subjects across the curriculum. Emphasizing hands-on, real-world learning experiences, this approach to education increases academic achievement, helps students develop stronger ties to their community, enhances students' appreciation for the natural world, and creates a heightened commitment to serving as active, contributing citizens. Community vitality and environmental quality are improved through the active engagement of local citizens, community organizations, and environmental resources in the life of the school.[4]

By applying their classroom learning in real-world contexts, students solidify that knowledge through practice and exercise problem-solving skills as they are faced with unstructured problems often requiring interdisciplinary approaches. These authentic, real-world experiences also develop students' identities as they lead to the development of stronger community ties, enhanced appreciation for nature, and a stronger commitment to citizenship.

In examining the informal learning found in participatory cultures enabled by digital media, Jenkins finds similar effects from engagement with digital communities. Jenkins defines participatory culture as a culture:

1. With relatively low barriers to artistic expression and civic engagement.
2. With strong support for creating and sharing one's creations with others.
3. With some type of informal mentorship whereby what is known by the most experienced is passed along to novices.
4. Where members believe that their contributions matter.
5. Where members feel some degree of social connection with one another (at the least they care what other people think about what they have created).[5]

As with place-based community-engaged learning, members of a participatory culture form community ties and develop an active citizenship in that community, which is expressed by creating, sharing, mentoring, and reviewing each other's creations. Members have agency to contribute because of the low barriers to entry and the belief that their contributions matter. Jenkins continues, "We are using participation as a term that cuts across educational practices, creative processes, community life, and democratic citizenship. Our goals should be to encourage youth to develop the skills, knowledge, ethical frameworks, and self-confidence needed to be full participants in contemporary culture."[6] Like Sobel, Jenkins believes that participation leads to democratic citizenship; the two scholars differ only in the context—local physical or digital community—for that participation. Further, Jenkins' call for participation is not just for those engaged in digital communities but rather for anyone participating in contemporary culture.

Place-based education and digital pedagogy, then, share common goals of engaged community participation but differ in their definition of that community. In the models below, I will examine similarities and differences in methods of these pedagogies, explore how they complement each other, demonstrate parallels in effective pedagogy between the two, and consider how these pedagogical approaches might inform each other.

PLACE AND EXPERIENCE

Authentic learning experiences provide one of the clearest overlaps between place-based education and digital pedagogy, though the location of that experience and consequently methods of teaching through it differ. Place-based education is so compelling because it provides a plethora of real-world experiences that invite students to practice their learning. For example, multiple chapters in *Place-based Education in the Global Age* share cases of students gathering data and advocating for local changes, whether for urban renewal, economic opportunity, or improved air quality.[7] A veteran place-based educator, Clifford Knapp, explains the teaching philosophy behind this authentic learning, "Teaching means extending the classroom beyond the four walls of the classroom and the two covers of books. It means immersing students in direct experiences with people and places in order to learn in the context of realistic community situations."[8] By breaking down the walls of the classroom and the textbook, Knapp challenges his students with unfamiliar situations that require them to transfer learning into new contexts and provide opportunities for active learning by students rather than content delivery by the instructor.

When understood as a vehicle for direct experience, place-based education falls under the rubric of authentic learning. Marilyn Lombardi identifies 10 instructional design elements as a checklist for instructors designing authentic learning experiences: real-world relevance, ill-defined problem, sustained investigation, multiple sources and perspectives, collaboration, reflection (metacognition), interdisciplinary perspective, integrated assessment, polished products, and multiple interpretations and outcomes.[9] The local community context found in place-based learning experiences offers both real-world relevance and ill-defined problems. With such unscripted, complex problems the instructor does not necessarily know the answer because there may not be one neat answer as there so often is with textbook exercises. Rather than trying to please the professor by supplying a predetermined right answer, the student is motivated to synthesize, discover, and create new knowledge and new answers through their own agency. Such problems lend themselves to a multiplicity of sources, perspectives, interpretations, and outcomes. Engaging students in local advocacy and community action means sustained investigation, collaboration, and polished productions. While the unscripted problems offered by place-based education hold great potential for learning, Lombardi's design principles also highlight the importance of intentional pedagogy to help students learn effectively. The length and complexity of the engagement along with multiple perspectives and disciplines may make it difficult for students to derive learning from the experience. Structured reflection and formative assessment help turn experience into learning.

At first blush, it may seem impossible to provide similar authentic learning experiences through digital pedagogy because of the virtual environments that form the context for much digital pedagogy. In particular, online courses with no synchronous interactions may make it impossible for students to meet in person much less interact with local communities. On the other hand, the low barriers to artistic expression and community engagement found in online participatory cultures, combined with the explosion of information and communities available online, make digital places ripe for this kind of authentic learning. In addition, simulations offer students opportunities for direct experience conditioned by the digital affordances of repeatability and automated immediate feedback.

Habitable Worlds, an inquiry-driven online science class, illustrates one approach to place-based experiential learning in virtual spaces. This course, developed at Arizona State University by Professor Ariel Anbar and Dr Lev Horodyskyj, fulfills a general education science requirement that is intended to expose students to a variety of scientific disciplines and engage them in scientific inquiry. To achieve this goal, the course is organized around the unscripted problem of the possibility of extraterrestrial life. Students approach this problem through the Drake Equation, which contains a list of variables that must be met for extraterrestrial life to exist.[10]

In each module of the course students explore a different variable—stars, planets, earth, life, intelligence, technology, and sustainability—and draw on a different scientific discipline.[11]

Simulations in each module provide opportunities for students to engage in scientific inquiry. For example, in the openly available demonstration module, students explore the question of which stars can support earthlike planets by hypothesizing the relative lifespans of different types of stars then running a simulator to test their hypothesis.[12] Students can run the simulation as often as they like to answer the accompanying questions. Habitable Worlds illustrates the multiple advantages of simulations noted by cognitive psychologist Michelle Miller including repeatability, user control, as well as that they are "less dangerous, less expensive, and not as time-consuming compared to their real-world counterparts."[13] The lifespan of the star offers an extreme case of using a simulation where real-world experiences might take too much time and the scale of the real place (the universe) is too big to be local. Individually these simulations do not equal the complex unscripted problems of place-based community-engaged learning, but combined into one course they model how to approach such a complex problem by breaking down the inquiry process and integrating multiple disciplines as perspectives. In effect, this structure scaffolds authentic learning by breaking down a complicated experience to focus on individual elements.

Simulations may also enable students to experience places in ways that they may not have access to real life, such as walking in the shoes of an individual with an identity somehow different than their own. As Samantha Allen explains, "By requiring my students to play *dys4ia*, *Lim* and *Mainichi*, I wanted to teach them about the difficulties faced by women (particularly transgender women) as they move through public space."[14] Such experiences can help students develop empathy through direct experience rather than through reading or hearing about it. Mattie Brice, the designer of the role-playing game *Mainichi* (which means "everyday" in Japanese) explains, "This is an experiment in sharing a personal experience through a game system. It helps communicate daily occurrences that happen in my life, exploring the difficulty in expressing these feelings in words."[15] Players experience the everyday life and interactions of Brice as she prepares to leave the house, walks down the street, and interacts with others in a coffee shop. The player's choices determine how others react to her transgender identity. Allen's lesson plan for transgender studies through video games incorporates design principles for authentic learning. Students played the games in a lab together followed by a live discussion, which allowed for instructor interventions to guide understanding, and blog posts to encourage reflection. Allen reports the effect of the collaborative game play revealed in later student reflections: "Commenting on the class's frustration as a whole, Alex recalled that the room was 'filled with exasperated sighs and cries' when several people were playing *Lim* simultaneously but also noted that this 'din in the room... seemed to verbalize what is usually a secret, inner dialogue' for transgender people."[16] This collaborative game play experience created a second layer of authentic experience that contributed to the development of understanding and empathy by Allen's students.

Simulations also offer a long-recognized path to authentic learning where places are no longer or not easily accessible in real life. From the early educational game, "Oregon Trail" to the Getty Museum's virtual reality exhibit of the Dunhuang Caves, simulations allow students to go to impossible places and enable disciplines like history to access places that might otherwise be unavailable.[17] Just as local place-based experiences can enhance student learning about the environment, experiencing such virtual places can help students gain insights into historical processes that they might otherwise not understand.

Historian Shawn Graham turned to digital games to solve such a problem of understanding in an online Roman History Course:

> As I discussed the period with them, I realized that part of the problem, aside from confusion of cause and effect, was a poor understanding of the realities of Mediterranean geography and the difficulties of communication in a preindustrial world, which requires factoring in the time it took for news to travel and how that time lag influenced the political dynamic. I wanted my students to understand that due to the contingency of history, Vespasian's eventual triumph was not foreordained, and that physical and political geography played a role in his success.[18]

Students needed to experience preindustrial Roman geography to understand better this political situation but could not go to that time and place. In response, Graham modded the game Civilization IV (that is, he altered the content so the game operates in a manner different from its original design) and offered students the opportunity to play the game and analyze their experience as an alternative assignment to their final essay.[19] Graham planned to assess his students by having them take screenshots and record narrative in the role of historians; they would compare history presented in the game versus available facts about the past.[20] Because this was an online class, the game, existing outside of the learning management system, broke down the walls of the virtual classroom just as field trips might do for a face-to-face class. That is, in online classes the location where course interaction regularly takes place—whether in a learning management system or on a course blog—becomes the equivalent of the physical classroom as the regular meeting place. By inviting students to engage with a different, unexpected technology, Graham broke down the walls of the virtual classroom and moved students outside of their comfort zone just as place-based learning does for a local class.

Ultimately, Graham decided that this experience was not a pedagogical success—although students played his scenario, none chose to complete the alternative gaming essay—but not because the simulation was not effective at recreating the experience of ancient Rome. Rather, "The strangeness of the assignment, when combined with the unnatural imposition of technology, created a barrier that the students did not try to, or could not, overcome."[21] Graham concluded that the students needed more preparation because the gaming assignment was not a form they understood in the same way they understood writing a traditional academic essay and gaming did not conform to their expectations of what a history class should be. Upon reflection, Graham considered that the fan forum community that helped him build his mod had a better learning experience, albeit informal, than his own students. This fan community understood how to read the text (the game) and had prior experience engaging in this kind of active learning experience because they regularly modded games and reflected on gameplay. In response, Graham concluded "The most important lesson learned is that we, the instructors, should not be building and directing mods for history education; it should be the students."[22]

Increasingly, historians are now engaging their students in just this type of creation as a way of connecting to and understanding history. For example, Amy Absher had her students recreate the 1939 World's Fair in Minecraft for an undergraduate "symbolic world" seminar focusing on the year 1939[23]; the University of Hull invited participants to build the work of architect Francis Johnson in Minecraft based on plans from their archives[24]; and students at Lake Forest College created 3D models and map layers in Google Earth based on the never-built 1909 Plan of Chicago by Daniel H. Burnham and Edward H. Bennett.[25]

In the Fall 2014, Graham followed his failed modding experiment with an upper-level history course dedicated to video games and simulations for historians.[26] Graham's course objectives included exploring key concepts in digital history, developing facility with interrogating the representation of history in digital media, and expressing history through the affordances of digital media.[27] Students built digital literacy by exploring how history is represented in digital media, then practiced creating such digital history themselves, first using the game engine, Twine, an open-source text-based tool for telling interactive stories, then by creating historical simulations in Minecraft. In other words, they moved from the passive literacy of "reading" digital media to the active literacy of "writing" it. Students worked in groups for the summative project to create "Minecrafted History" for one of three sites:

- History of the Ottawa Valley
- The Canadians of the Western Front (WWI)
- Colonization and Resistance in the Roman World[28]

Graham assigned written work, which he termed a paradata document, alongside the digital project to help students justify their historiographical choices and provide substantiating data and citations. Three exemplary Minecraft worlds and their accompanying paradata documents are available on Graham's github site for the course.[29]

Graham followed best practice for authentic learning design by graduating student engagement with the experience—in this case moving from reading to creating digital media—and by building three checkpoints into the final assignment to allow for formative assessment. The course's explicit focus on gaming and deliberate pacing helped Graham avoid previous challenges of student resistance to combining history and digital games. The use of reflective elements like weekly blogging, the paradata document, in-class discussions, and final presentations helped surface learning from these experiences. In writing about the pedagogy of teaching history through games, Kevin Kee and Graham share student concerns with how they will be assessed.[30] By focusing on the process and grading individual elements that build to the finished product, instructors can alleviate some of these concerns. Kee and Graham also recommend the use of rubrics to make the terms of grading explicit and share a sample rubric for a gaming project that evaluates elements ranging from historical research and analysis to project design, teamwork, and tool use.[31] Kee also uses anonymous peer grading for a portion of the project grade to alleviate concerns about team member performance.[32]

Graham reports a notable shift in student thinking reflected in their weekly blogs as they move through such a course focused on game-based creation: "In the earliest posts, 'accuracy' is conceived in terms of visual fidelity to the props of history such as proper uniforms, correctly rendered architecture, period-appropriate speech (that is, with the 'skin' of the game rather than its underlying rhetorics)."[33] Later in the course, students can move from this focus on details to larger systems—the rhetoric of the game. Notably, the use of text-based games or the basic graphics in Minecraft's 16-bit animation, help students move past the distraction of digital media graphics to the deeper structures underlying historical epistemologies.

The activity of creating virtual places deepens students' historical understanding and moves them into higher-order thinking skills. Kee and Graham compare this progression to that achieved through traditional history assignments: "The task is both creative—students are developing their own representation of history—and synthetic—they are drawing on the literature created by historians. In a sense, they are playing with the texts."[34] Building on Ian Bogost's term, "procedural rhetoric," Graham compares the historical interpretation created by the world-building in a game to the historical conception a historian creates by writing history (historiography).[35] In other words, effective creation of a game scenario in Civilization or a world in Minecraft *is* historiography. Absher similarly turned to game creation to help students improve their analytical thinking to "take the students away from simply knowing what happened and move them toward understanding why people made certain choices and how all the parts of human interaction and imagination (from architecture to sports to politics to slang to sexism to racism to movies to the hemline) fit together to compose a culture."[36] For both Graham and Absher, this synthetic creation leads to understanding of historical systems.[37]

How does this creation of virtual places compare with place-based pedagogies used in teaching history? We might compare travel to a historical site that can help students better visualize historical action. In effect, Graham sought such insight into Roman history by inviting his students into the modded Civilization game. Simulations then, parallel the direct experience of places. Likewise, interactions with virtual communities like the Civilization fan forum parallel community engagement in place-based learning. By moving into the creation of virtual places and systems, however, historians like Graham and Absher move students beyond the direct experience of authentic learning to synthetic creation that leads to understanding of systems. This type of learning parallels rather the insight that comes from reflection on an extended authentic learning experience. Furthermore, by creating such interactive systems themselves when they create scenarios, games, or worlds, students may improve their ability to discover and analyze them in other contexts, like the real world. Just as simulations can help student learning by breaking an experience into its constituent parts and allowing focus on specific aspects in isolation, the act of creating virtual places to be experienced can help students better understand how systems in the world around them interact to determine experiences.

PLACE AND IDENTITY

Identity is another key learning outcome for place-based education. As Deric Shannon and Jeffrey Galle note in the introduction to this collection, there is a clear link between place and identity-formation, especially for teens. danah boyd's research on teens and social media demonstrates the persistence of that connection into virtual places.[38] boyd argues that this use has created new kinds of virtual places, which she terms networked publics, that combine virtual places with an imagined community.[39] These places are not opposite of physical spaces, but rather a continuation of face-to-face interactions for teens. In other words, networked publics are the natural successors of malls, roller rinks, and drive-in movies.

In all of these publics, whether local or virtual, teens perform their identities by interacting with communities. While teens use public places to socialize, boyd explains that networked publics differ from physical publics because they are conditioned by the affordances—characteristics that the technology enables—of social media, especially by "persistence: the durability of online expressions and content; visibility: the potential audience who can bear witness; spreadability: the ease with which content can be shared; and searchability: the ability to find content,"[40] and the ability of social media to scale such effects. These affordances can present challenges for a teen's identity, such as the experience of context collapse, when their interactions among an intended audience of friends are viewed by parents, an unintended audience. At the same time, teens can take advantage of different social media communities to try out different aspects of their identities.[41] As instructors turn to social media and networked publics, they encounter some of these same effects with both positive and negative consequences. For example, just as teens resist the collapsed context of parents showing up in social media where they are hanging out with friends, they may also resist the intrusion of educators into that same space. At the same time, networked publics can offer opportunities for place-based learning similar to local publics. While much has been written about the educational potential of social media, I am interested here in its intersection with place and identity.[42]

The Looking for Whitman Project structured a pedagogical experiment that took advantage of social media to build a networked public for students at three colleges—New York City College of Technology, University of Mary Washington, and Rutgers University-Camden—that were located in places where Walt Whitman lived and wrote, as well as a fourth college, the University of Novi Sad in Serbia. Students at each of the first three institutions studied Whitman's work produced in their locale and shared their experiences with each other through social media in the Fall of 2009.[43] Students from each institution brought a unique perspective to Whitman, in part because they studied Whitman's work associated with their location, but also because they came from different types of institutions (public, private, university, liberal arts college, international) and were studying Whitman at different levels ranging from beginning to graduate.[44] Their location and their identity colored their interpretation of Whitman, but it was their shared network that highlighted this diversity.

Students and faculty involved in the project shared assignments, content, and a social network. The Looking for Whitman website connected the course by providing students with individual blogs that were then aggregated to support networked learning.[45] This website used the popular blogging system WordPress, with an extension known as Buddy Press, which added features typical of social media platforms, such as user profiles, the ability to friend other users, user groups, and forums. Essentially, the project website was something like the social media platform Facebook with a Whitman focus. A central page on the website aggregated blog posts, digital images, videos, news feeds, wiki entries, and post tags from each of the classes, so that students could follow the progress of each other and of the collective project.

This project highlights the tensions between place-based learning in physically proximate communities and in virtual communities. While technology offered the promise of linking students in a larger community, their loyalties tended to lie with their local rather than virtual community.

Matthew K. Gold, who taught one of the local courses and led the project, identified multiple "barriers to connection—such as differences between socio-economic [status,] differences between institutions and students, level of academic preparedness in the shared subject matter, and willingness to share material."[46] Paradoxically, while instructors may value student exposure to diverse perspectives, students tend to discount perspectives of those in other places, and this resistance should be explicitly addressed in instructional design. Asynchronous interaction via social media did not sufficiently build virtual community for the courses. Instead, students asked for more synchronous, face-to-face interaction, even if only via Skype. Course evaluations reflected the lack of collaboration between courses at separate institutions. 69% of students reported that they collaborated with students at their own institution, while only 46% reported collaboration with students at another institution.[47] These numbers tell us that there is a learning curve for networked collaboration; it is an iterative process that requires scaffolding as well as practice and repetition in more than one course. Although virtual interaction can sustain communities, face-to-face interaction or intense interaction—especially at the outset—is an important factor in successful collaboration. This focus on local over virtual social networks confirms boyd's findings that for teens social media tends to replicate and extend local networks rather than create new ones. Here the ties of local place to identity and community proved too strong for the virtual community to overcome.

Some teens and adults, however, do use social media to create new virtual communities based on shared interests, as Jenkins describes.[48] Elsewhere I have explored how the game, "Minecraft," along with its attendant YouTube videos, mods, and minigames, exemplifies the kind of participatory culture defined by Jenkins as players share creations based on the game.[49] For example, players like DanTDM and Mr. StampyCat upload daily videos to their YouTube Channels in which they share their personal game play ("Let's Play" videos) or review mods and minigames (game scenarios created within the gaming platform).[50] Others create Minecraft-themed parodies of popular music, like "Don't Mine At Night," a parody of Katy Perry's "Last Friday Night," or even write original Minecraft Songs like "I Found a Diamond."[51] Sobel includes one effect in his definition of place-based education that is perhaps not as obvious in digital places—an appreciation for the natural world. For Sobel this appreciation stems from experiences in the local environment. Perhaps there is a parallel appreciation of their digital environment in all of these creations of Minecraft's participatory culture and these too are expressions of a community's identity. While the Looking for Whitman project attempted to create a shared identity through shared study of Whitman, the design of the experiment, which focused on different aspects of Whitman's work at each location, may have paradoxically worked against a communal appreciation of Whitman as a whole. Moreover, while students did practice place-based learning by visiting local places where Whitman wrote, those experiences reinforced their local community affiliations rather than supported their shared community around Whitman. In the end, aggregation of content was not a strong enough interaction to create a participatory culture built around Whitman. Perhaps shared creation of a Whitman simulation would have been more effective.

PLACE AND ACTIVE CITIZENSHIP

While games such as Minecraft may seem trivial or unimportant when compared to real life, the skills of participation and the agency developed by practice in the virtual environment transfer to engaged citizenship in local communities. Games and simulations may also form an important step in preparing students for active citizenship by providing practice in civic interaction. The interactive video game Civic Seed, designed through cooperation between the Tufts University's Tisch College of Citizenship and Public Service and the Engagement Lab @ Emerson College, scaffolds real-life experience as it prepares students for community-based service learning, a common variety of place-based education.[52] In particular the game helps students learn in advance about the people and challenges of the communities where they will be serving and approach issues systematically. Community partners also benefit; as the game website explains: "For local organizations, it's difficult to know which students have the necessary knowledge and skills to make a positive impact, and whose personal goals align with the goals of the organization and the community."[53] By playing the game, students develop a profile that becomes their Civic Resume, which partner organizations can review. This game explicitly scaffolds the reflection that is so important in achieving the learning outcomes from authentic learning experiences by having students repeatedly reflect on the resources they gather and their experiences. Explicit learning outcomes articulated by Tisch College include:

1. The ways in which positive community change happens
2. Successful approaches to challenges in a community

3. How differences in race, culture, and socioeconomic status impact collaboration within communities and how to navigate these successfully
4. An asset-based approach; that every community has strengths
5. Approaching the campus/community relationship with mutual respect and reciprocity
6. The importance of sustainability in community work
7. The specific community in which a student will be engaged
8. One's own goals, values, and motivations for civic engagement
9. Connections between coursework, career goals, and with civic engagement work[54]

These learning outcomes prefigure the learning outcomes expected from the real-life service-learning experience, but let the students practice this type of learning in a safe environment where the consequences of failure are not as high. How well does such scaffolding work? A research study comparing introductory physics students who did simulated lab experiences versus those who did hands-on labs found that the students trained via simulations outperformed the other students on end-of-semester exams for both conceptual skills and in assembling and explaining a real circuit, in part due to the reduced complexity, removal of distractions, and the ability to make the invisible visible.[55] Notably, the simulation better prepared students for using the real equipment than actual practice with that same real equipment. These improved learning outcomes demonstrate the importance of scaffolding authentic experiences and the value of simulations paired with authentic learning. The complementarity between game and place-based authentic experience also suggests that digital pedagogy and place-based education can mutually benefit each other rather than constitute opposing forces.

The natural extension of this relationship comes in the integration of digital and local citizenship. Gavin Newsom, lieutenant governor of California, in his 2013 co-authored book *Citizenville: How to Take the Town Square Digital and Reinvent Government* argues for connection and collaboration between citizens and their government on the analogy of the popular social media game, Farmville. Rather than taking care of virtual farms, citizens would take care of their own neighborhoods. Newsom goes on to offer case studies that demonstrate the possibility of engaged digital citizenship, like Mike Migurski's creation of the Crimespotting tool.[56] A citizen of Oakland, California, in 2007 Migurski combined government data that were available online but not easily findable or standardized with his own data-scraping and development skills to create and make openly available an easy-to-use interactive website useful for both himself and his neighbors.[57]

In response to such civic hacking, many cities and other government entities are now making their data more readily available. For example, in 2011 the city of Austin, Texas launched an Open Data Initiative and now offers an open data portal to make such hacking easier for its citizens.[58] The portal website invites digital civic engagement: "This portal provides easy access to open data and information about your city government. We encourage the use of public data that the City of Austin has published to spark innovation, promote public collaboration, increase government transparency, and inform decision making."[59] Such efforts are not one-sided; they are driven by volunteer organizations and citizen groups like Open Austin, a brigade affiliated with the nonprofit "Code for America," which describes itself as "advocating for open government, open data, and civic application...which believes government can work for the people, by the people in the 21st century. Open Austin is focused on the needs of our own community and we use design, technology, and open data to improve the quality of life in our city."[60] Engaged digital citizenship requires digital skills like the ability to understand, manipulate, and apply data and then share it in ways that can be used by others in the local community. This citizenship combines the desired outcomes of place-based education and the digital pedagogy of Jenkins' participatory culture.

REDEFINING LEARNING SPACES

The preceding examples demonstrate that we must expand our understanding of place in place-based learning. Despite an apparent conflict between place-based education and digital pedagogy, these two approaches have much to offer each other. Place-based education in our emerging digital ecosystem combines the affordances of digital technologies applied in a local context. Skills developed in virtual communities reinforce local communities and lead to engaged citizenship. Digital tools may also improve the learning outcomes of direct authentic learning experiences by scaffolding that experience in preparation, breaking down its elements to make it easier to understand, or by allowing students to understand an entire system through synthetic creation rather than just reflection. Digital places can be both a continuation of local places, such as in the Looking for Whitman Project, and a preparation for local learning, such as in the Civic Seed game. Digital places also open up many more opportunities for place-based learning for accessing nonexistent or inaccessible places like ancient Rome or a nursery for star formation. These environments in our emerging digital ecosystem offer new opportunities for place-based education and prepare our students for engaged citizenship in both local and digital contexts. Rather than homogenizing culture, digital networks may also preserve heterogeneity by revealing diversity, such as with the Looking for Whitman Project, and enable affinity communities to develop despite geographic separation.

What will it take to expand the use of this hybrid pedagogy? Instructors will need development in both place-based pedagogy and the use of digital tools. They will also need technological support, as well as support in finding partners for creating learning networks. In other words, instructors themselves will need to build learning networks and collaborate with technologists and others. These digital learning places also rely on open networks to allow students to connect outside of the walls of the classroom and the log-in of the learning management system. Just as institutional policies must enable local community-engaged learning, they must also enable learning in digital places. For information technology, that may mean identity management that allows remote students, while for administrators it may mean rewarding those faculty members who build such networks. By engaging students in local, digital, and hybrid communities, we enable them to develop agency to engage in their personal, public, and professional lives.

NOTES

1. I use the term "digital pedagogy" to cover pedagogy that employs digital methods, tools, and platforms and is shaped by engagement in our emerging digital ecosystem. While the adjective, "emerging" points to the constant change in digital tools and environments that shape this ecosystem, it is also characterized by constants including networks, participatory creation, data, and algorithms. Bass and Eynon have defined the emerging digital ecosystem: "The emerging ecosystem is shaped by networks, which are fundamentally social; characterized by horizontal access to creation and production; and increasingly driven by data, algorithms, and artificial intelligence." (Bass and Eynon, "Open and Integrative," 13.) See Davis et al., *Digital Pedagogy in the Humanities* for models of this heterogeneous pedagogy as practiced in the humanities and curated by keyword. Much of digital pedagogy is shaped by learning in digital culture and communities, such as that described by Jenkins in "Confronting the Challenges of Participatory Culture."

184   R.F. DAVIS

 2. Gruenewald and Smith, *Place-Based Education in the Global Age*.
 3. Jenkins, "Confronting the Challenges of Participatory Culture," 8.
 4. Sobel, *Place-Based Education*.
 5. Jenkins, "Confronting the Challenges of Participatory Culture," 7.
 6. Jenkins, "Confronting the Challenges of Participatory Culture," 8.
 7. Gruenewald and Smith, *Place-Based Education in the Global Age*, "Introduction."
 8. Knapp, "Place-Based Curricular and Pedagogical Models."
 9. Lombardi, "Authentic Learning for the 21st Century," 3–4.
10. Anbar and Horodyskyj, "Habworlds Beyond."
11. Ibid.
12. "Which Star to Wish Upon."
13. Miller, *Minds Online*, ch. 7.
14. Allen, "Video Games as Feminist Pedagogy," 64.
15. Brice, "Mainichi." In her recent work, "Empathy Machine," while acknowledging the value of empathy, Brice critiques the "pattern of the wider industry and games audience only caring about what marginalized creators are doing if it involves them talking about their pain and trauma." (Brice, "Empathy Machine.")
16. Allen, "Video Games as Feminist Pedagogy," 66.
17. Rosenberg, "Sally Has Diphtheria."; Pressberg, "LA's Getty Center Blends Oculus-Ready VR with Ancient Chinese Art in Virtual Reality Museum Exhibit." The original Dunhuang Caves lie in the Gobi Desert of western China and the number of visitors is limited to avoid further damaging the site. Cf. Reede and Bailiff, "When Virtual Reality Meets Education."
18. Graham, "Rolling Your Own," 216.
19. "Mod (video Gaming)."
20. Graham, "Rolling Your Own," 218.
21. Ibid.
22. Ibid., 225.
23. Absher, "From Minecraft to Mindcraft."
24. "HullCraft | History Makers."
25. "VBI About the Initiative."
26. Graham, "Admin | #hist3812a Fall 2014 Video Games & Simulations for Historians." This page from the course blog includes information about course requirements and assignments.
27. Graham, "shawngraham/hist3812a."
28. Graham, "Evaluation | #hist3812a Fall 2014 Video Games & Simulations for Historians."
29. Graham, "shawngraham/hist3812a." Github is a platform used by software developers to collaboratively develop code while tracking submissions and changes.

30. "Students in our courses have three main concerns: (1) How will they receive regular feedback on their progress? (2) How will they know what is being marked? (3) In the case of group projects, how will the instructors ensure that students' grades reflect their participation in the group project?" Kee and Graham, "Teaching History in an Age of Pervasive Computing," 285.
31. Ibid., 287.
32. Ibid., 288.
33. Graham, "Pulling Back the Curtain."
34. Kee and Graham, "Teaching History in an Age of Pervasive Computing," 278.
35. Graham, "Pulling Back the Curtain"; Kee and Graham, "Teaching History in an Age of Pervasive Computing," 275; Bogost, *Persuasive Games.*
36. Absher, "From Minecraft to Mindcraft."
37. Allen finds similar insights into systems even from playing games. She explains her use of video games in a feminist classroom: "Because video games highlight the interactivity of systems, they can help students develop the critical thinking skills necessary to understand the operation of systems of oppression." Allen, "Video Games as Feminist Pedagogy," 62.
38. boyd's 2014 book, *It's Complicated* is based on more than seven years of research (including study of social media, semi-structured interviews, and hanging out with teens) into teen use of social media. danah boyd does not capitalize her name. For an explanation see her web page, "what's in a name."
39. boyd, *It's Complicated*, 8.
40. Ibid., 11.
41. Ibid., *It's Complicated*, chapter 2 on identity.
42. See for example, Rheingold, *Net Smart*, for an examination of the literacies required by social media and how to use them effectively.
43. "About Looking for Whitman—Looking for Whitman." New York University was intended to be the fourth institution, but the project participant from that institution received a Fulbright to teach in Serbia for a year, so the University of Novi Sad was substituted.
44. Gold, "Disrupting Institutional Barriers Through Digital Humanities Pedagogy."
45. See Ito et al., "Connected Learning"; Siemens, "Connectivism." For arguments in favor or connected or networked learning modeled after the learning in digital culture, for example, the participatory cultures described by Jenkins, "Confronting the Challenges of Participatory Culture."
46. Gold, "Disrupting Institutional Barriers Through Digital Humanities Pedagogy."
47. Gold, "Looking for Whitman."
48. Jenkins, "Confronting the Challenges of Participatory Culture."

49. Davis, "Pedagogy and Learning in a Digital Ecosystem." Minecraft, available for personal computers, gaming systems, and mobile devices, is one of the most popular games in the world with well over 100 million registered users. (Eddie Makuch, "Minecraft Passes 100 Million Registered Users, 14.3 Million Sales on PC.") The Minecraft game is available for download at https://minecraft.net/.
50. DanTDM, "The Diamond Minecart"; Mr. Stampy Cat, "Stampylonghead."
51. BebopVox YOGSCAST, *"Don't Mine at Night"—A Minecraft Parody of Katy Perry's Last Friday Night (Music Video)*; BebopVox YOGSCAST, *I Found A Diamond—An Original Minecraft Song*.
52. "{ ::: Civic Seed ::: }."
53. "About | Civic Seed."
54. "Civic Seed | Jonathan M. Tisch College of Civic Life."
55. Finkelstein et al., "When Learning about the Real World Is Better Done Virtually."
56. Newsom and Dickey, *Citizenville*, chapter 4.
57. "Oakland Crimespotting: About."
58. "About Austin's Open Data Initiative."
59. "Open Data | City of Austin Texas."
60. "About | Open Austin."

Bibliography

"About." *Open Austin*. Accessed July 5, 2016. http://www.open-austin.org/about/.
"About." *{ ::: Civic Seed ::: }*. Accessed July 6, 2016.http://civicseed.org/about.
"About Austin's Open Data Initiative." Accessed July 5, 2016. http://cityofaustin.github.io/open-data-manual/about/.
"About Looking for Whitman—Looking for Whitman." Accessed July 9, 2016. http://lookingforwhitman.org/about/.
Absher, Amy. "From Minecraft to Mindcraft: Integrating Digital Humanities into History Courses." *Process*, October 27, 2015. http://www.processhistory.org/from-minecraft-to-mindcraft-integrating-digital-humanities-into-history-courses/.
Allen, Samantha Leigh. "Video Games as Feminist Pedagogy." *Loading* 8, no. 13 (November 17, 2014). http://journals.sfu.ca/loading/index.php/loading/article/view/135.
Anbar, Ariel, and Lev Horodyskyj. "Habworlds Beyond." Accessed July 6, 2016. https://www.habworlds.org/.
Bass, Randy, and Bret Eynon. "Open and Integrative: Designing Liberal Education for the New Digital Ecosystem." Association of American Colleges and Universities, June 16, 2016. https://www.aacu.org/publications-

research/publications/open-and-integrative-designing-liberal-education-new-digital.

BebopVox YOGSCAST. *"Don't Mine At Night"—A Minecraft Parody of Katy Perry's Last Friday Night (Music Video)*. Accessed July 5, 2016. https://www.youtube.com/watch?v=X_XGxzMrq04&feature=youtu.be.

BebopVox YOGSCAST. *I Found A Diamond—An Original Minecraft Song*. Accessed July 5, 2016. https://www.youtube.com/watch?v=XaVDspBuEmM&feature=youtu.be.

Bogost, Ian. *Persuasive Games: The Expressive Power of Videogames*. Cambridge, MA: MIT Press, 2010.

Boyd, danah. *It's Complicated: The Social Lives of Networked Teens*. New Haven: Yale University Press, 2014.

Boyd, danah michele. "what's in a name." Accessed August 16, 2016. http://www.danah.org/name.html.

Brice, Mattie. "Mainichi." *Mattie Brice*, November 6, 2012. http://www.mattiebrice.com/mainichi/.

Cat, Stampy. "Stampylonghead." *YouTube*. Accessed July 5, 2016. https://www.youtube.com/user/stampylonghead.

"{ ::: Civic Seed ::: }." Accessed July 6, 2016. http://civicseed.org/.

"Civic Seed | Jonathan M. Tisch College of Civic Life." Accessed July 6, 2016. http://activecitizen.tufts.edu/civicseed/.

DanTDM. "The Diamond Minecart." *YouTube*, Accessed July 5, 2016. https://www.youtube.com/user/TheDiamondMinecart.

Davis, Rebecca Frost. "Pedagogy and Learning in a Digital Ecosystem." In *Understanding Writing Transfer and Its Implications for Higher Education*, edited by Jessie Moore and Randy Bass, 27–38. Sterling, VA: Stylus Publishing, 2017.

Davis, Rebecca Frost, Matthew K. Gold, Katherine D. Harris, and Jentery Sayers, eds. *Digital Pedagogy in the Humanities: Concepts, Models, and Experiments*, Accessed August 21, 2016. https://github.com/curateteaching/digitalpedagogy.

Finkelstein, N. D., W. K. Adams, C. J. Keller, P. B. Kohl, K. K. Perkins, N. S. Podolefsky, S. Reid, and R. LeMaster. "When Learning about the Real World Is Better Done Virtually: A Study of Substituting Computer Simulations for Laboratory Equipment." *Physical Review Special Topics—Physics Education Research* 1, no. 1 (2005). doi:10.1103/PhysRevSTPER.1.010103.

Gold, Matthew K. "Disrupting Institutional Barriers Through Digital Humanities Pedagogy." *Diversity & Democracy*, 2012. http://www.diversityweb.org/DiversityDemocracy/vol15no2/gold.cfm.

Gold, Matthew K. "Looking for Whitman: A Multi-Campus Experiment in Digital Pedagogy." In *Digital Humanities Pedagogy: Practices, Principles and Politics*, edited by Brett Hirsch, 151–176. Cambridge: Open Book Publishers, 2012. http://www.openbookpublishers.com/reader/161.

Graham, Shawn. "Pulling Back the Curtain: Writing History Through Video Games." In *Web Writing*, edited by Jack Dougherty and Tennyson O'Donnell. Ann Arbor, MI: University of Michigan Press, 2015. http://epress.trincoll.edu/webwriting/chapter/graham/.

Graham, Shawn. "Rolling Your Own: On Modding Commercial Games for Educational Goals." In *Pastplay: Teaching and Learning History with Technology*, edited by Kevin Kee, 214–254. Ann Arbor, MI: University of Michigan Press, 2014. http://hdl.handle.net/2027/spo.12544152.0001.001.

Graham, Shawn. "shawngraham/hist3812a." *GitHub*. Accessed July 8, 2016. https://github.com/shawngraham/hist3812a.

Graham, Shawn. "Admin |#hist3812a Fall 2014 Video Games & Simulations for Historians." August 20, 2016. http://hist3812a.dhcworks.ca/category/admin/.

Graham, Shawn. "Evaluation |#hist3812a Fall 2014 Video Games & Simulations for Historians." August 20, 2016. http://hist3812a.dhcworks.ca/2014/08/20/evaluation/.

Gruenewald, David A., and Gregory A. Smith. *Place-Based Education in the Global Age: Local Diversity*. New York: Lawrence Erlbaum Associates, 2008.

Ito, Mizuko., Kris Gutierrez, Sonia Livingstone, Bill Penuel, Jean Rhodes, Katie Salen, Juliet Schor, Julian Sefton-Green, and S. Craig Watkins. "Connected Learning: An Agenda for Research and Design." Connected Learning Research Network, December 31, 2012. http://dmlhub.net/publications/connected-learning-agenda-for-research-and-design/.

Jenkins, Henry. *Confronting the Challenges of Participatory Culture: Media Education for the 21st Century*. John D. and Catherine T. MacArthur Foundation Reports on Digital Media and Learning. Cambridge, MA: MIT Press, 2009. http://digitallearning.macfound.org/atf/cf/%7B7E45C7E0-A3E0-4B89-AC9C-E807E1B0AE4E%7D/JENKINS_WHITE_PAPER.PDF.

Kee, Kevin, and Shawn Graham. "Teaching History in an Age of Pervasive Computing: The Case for Games in the High School and Undergraduate Classroom." In *Pastplay: Teaching and Learning History with Technology*, 270–291. Ann Arbor, MI: University of Michigan Press, 2014. http://hdl.handle.net/2027/spo.12544152.0001.001.

Knapp, Clifford E. "Place-Based Curricular and Pedagogical Models: My Adventures in Teaching through Community Contexts." In *Place-Based Education in the Global Age: Local Diversity*, edited by David A. Gruenewald and Gregory A. Smith. New York: Lawrence Erlbaum Associates, 2008.

Lombardi, Marilyn M. "Authentic Learning for the 21st Century: An Overview." ELI White Papers. Educause Learning Initiative, January 1, 2007. http://www.educause.edu/library/resources/authentic-learning-21st-century-overview.

Miller, Michelle D. *Minds Online: Teaching Effectively with Technology*. Cambridge, MA: Harvard University Press, 2014. http://www.hup.harvard.edu/catalog.php?isbn=9780674368248.

"Mod (video Gaming)." *Wikipedia, the Free Encyclopedia*, July 27, 2016. https://en.wikipedia.org/w/index.php?title=Mod_(video_gaming)&oldid=731740938.

Newsom, Gavin Christopher, and Lisa Dickey. *Citizenville: How to Take the Town Square Digital and Reinvent Government*. New York: Penguin Press, 2013.

"Oakland Crimespotting: About." Accessed July 5, 2016. http://oakland.crimespotting.org/about.

"Open Data | City of Austin Texas." *Austin*. Accessed July 5, 2016. https://data.austintexas.gov/.

Pressberg, Matt. "LA's Getty Center Blends Oculus-Ready VR With Ancient Chinese Art In Virtual Reality Museum Exhibit." *International Business Times*, May 5, 2016. http://www.ibtimes.com/las-getty-center-blends-oculus-ready-vr-ancient-chinese-art-virtual-reality-museum-2364802.

Reede, Elizabeth, and Larissa Bailiff. "When Virtual Reality Meets Education." *TechCrunch*. Accessed July 6, 2016. http://social.techcrunch.com/2016/01/23/when-virtual-reality-meets-education/.

Rheingold, Howard. *Net Smart: How to Thrive Online*. Cambridge, MA: The MIT Press, 2012.

Rosenberg, Eli. "Sally Has Diphtheria: Is Oregon Trail the Greatest Video Game of All Time?" *The Wire*. Accessed July 6, 2016. http://www.theatlanticwire.com/entertainment/2011/01/sally-has-diphtheria-is-oregon-trail-the-greatest-video-game-of-all-time/21417/.

Sobel, David. *Place-Based Education: Connecting Classrooms & Communities*. Great Barrington, MA: Orion Society, 2005.

"Which Star to Wish Upon." *Habitable Worlds*. Accessed July 6, 2016. https://aelp.smartsparrow.com/v/open/fb7555c0da3c11e2a28f0800200c9a66.

CHAPTER 13

Teaching and Learning from Within: A Placed-Based Pedagogy for Heartfelt Hope

Jasmine Brown and Phoebe Godfrey

INTRODUCTION

There is a Zen saying that states, "There is no transference of secrets from master to disciple. Teaching is not difficult, listening is not difficult either, but what is truly difficult is to become conscious of what you have in yourself and to be able to use it as your own. This self-realization is known as 'seeing into one's own being' which is *satori*. *Satori* is an awakening from a dream. Awakening and self-realization and seeing into one's own being—these are synonymous."[1] Accepting this Zen insight that what remains difficult in teaching and listening is actually the practice of becoming conscious of what one has within oneself and to be able to use it as one's own and to use it to see into one's own being, this chapter explores–what we collectively have come to understand as "heartfelt hope" in

J. Brown (✉)
Department of Forest Ecosystems and Society, Oregon State University, Covallis, OR, USA

P. Godfrey
Department of Sociology, UCONN, Mansfield, USA

© The Author(s) 2017   191
D. Shannon, J. Galle (eds.), *Interdisciplinary Approaches to Pedagogy and Place-Based Education*, DOI 10.1007/978-3-319-50621-0_13

relation to teaching/learning about sustainability using place-based education. In *Pedagogy of Hope: Reliving Pedagogy of the Oppressed*, Paolo Freire
states, "Without hope, we are hopeless and cannot begin the struggle to
change. To attempt to do without hope, which is based on the need for truth
as an ethical quality of the struggle, is tantamount to denying that struggle
one of its mainstays".[2] Yet it can be argued that teachers and students who
are teaching/learning about global climate change and/or sustainability are
confronted with personal and political needs for hope in ways not previously
experienced. Therefore, we seek to build upon Freire's call for hope by
combining it with Joanna Macy's and Chris Johnson's conception of an
"active hope" and with Henry Giroux's call for an "educated hope".[3] In
addition, we are engaging with David Gruenewald's linking of critical and
place-based pedagogy in order to situate our conception of heartfelt hope
that incorporates a more intimate, aware and vital connection to our emotional and physical selves as places thereby enabling us to connect more
deeply to the place-based communities of life that sustain us.[4]

In bell hooks' *Teaching Community: A Pedagogy of Hope* she extends in
her chapter "Keepers of Hope" a dialogue with her colleague Ron Scapp, a
"white, heterosexual, male, tenured professor of relative financial security"
that they started in *Teaching to Transgress: Education as the Practice of
Freedom*. These two dialogues are, as she states in *Teaching Community* an
example of "border crossings, the process by which we make community", as
well as a way "we bear witness publicly to engender hope.[5] Taking our
inspiration from hooks and Scapp, we also chose to engage in and record
two dialogues on hope and sustainability that were also conceived as being
examples of border crossing, while being messier based on our process
constituting a form of "entanglement".[6] We are a former undergraduate
student and former professor who met in a sociology course, *Sustainable
Societies*, in the fall of 2014. This course engaged critical, place-based pedagogy that invited students to foster, as Goralnik, Dobson, and Nelson state,
" ...attentive relationships, critical engagement with concepts and place,
personal and community awareness, and responsibility for mindful participation in the world (built and natural)."[7] Hence, our dialogues were both a
testament to the effectiveness of this pedagogical practice in that we chose to
have them, and our opportunity to collectively reflect on how we each
experienced this pedagogical practice given our differing positionalities.[8]
Based on our differing positionalities we too crossed many borders; in relation
to the social positions of race (J is African-American, P is white/grew up
in Europe), class (J grew up lower middle-class, P upper middle-class), age

(J is 21, P is 51), education level (J has a B.S., P a Ph.D.) and area of expertise (J is a Natural Recourses major and P is a Sociologist) Additionally, we are sharing our dialogues for similar objectives as hooks', which is to "make community"[9] as a place through the evocation of heartfelt hope, firstly in ourselves from our actual class experience, leading to the experience of the dialogues, and secondly in our readers who can subsequently bear witness. However, unlike her approach that was not "altered",[10] we sought to create a layered effect that allowed for multiple engagements, hence entanglements, with our words in terms of listening to our first dialogue and using the second as a place to respond to and possibly reflect more deeply upon our own and each other's statements and to then edit them both during the writing process. As such we chose not to privilege what we first uttered, over what we later understood in terms of seeing our words and ideas as being on a relational continuum continually affected by context, hence place.

In preparing for our dialogues and in writing about them, we took time separately to reflect upon the class and the work/material (J read back over old journals while P looked at classroom notes), and we also engaged with works by critical educational theorists and other education practitioners[11] for whom conceptions of hope are a central tenet of their progressive pedagogies. Having primed ourselves we then used their works to further analyze the results of our dialogues, finding that the work of Macy and Johnson and Giroux were particularly salient in that they brought together the necessary ingredients for our conception of heartfelt hope, which we see as being specifically about the teaching/learning about sustainability in progressive, transformative and place-based ways within an educational setting.

Our dialogues focused on two main overlapping topics: our understandings of the relationship between sustainability and hope; and the critical, place-based pedagogy of the class and the ways in which it was practiced to engender hope despite the challenges in learning about climate change and sustainability. For Gruenewald, the linking of critical and place-based pedagogy "means challenging each other to read the texts of our own lives . . . [by] making place for the cultural, political, economic, and ecological dynamics of places whenever we talk about the purpose and practice of learning".[12] For us this "challenging each other to read the texts of our own lives" was done both within the place of the class and within the place of our dialogues that collectively led us to the embodied conception of heartfelt hope as will be explored.

OUR UNDERSTANDINGS OF THE RELATIONSHIP BETWEEN SUSTAINABILITY AND HOPE

In *Active Hope: How to Face the Mess We're in Without Going Crazy*, Joanna Macy and Chris Johnson begin by sharing the "high levels of alarm" people in their workshops feel about the "condition of our world".[13] They name this collective uncertainty "a pivotal psychological reality of our time" although due to the view that it is "too depressing to talk about, it tends to remain an unspoken presence at the back of our minds".[14] Yet for Macy and Johnson this is exactly where we must begin "by acknowledging that our times confront us with realities that are painful to face, difficult to take in and confusing to live with".[15] In so doing we can then embark on "an amazing journey that strengthens us and deepens our awareness" and that the " ... purpose of this journey is to find, offer and receive the gift of Active Hope".[16] For them "Active Hope is about becoming active participants in bringing about what we hope for".[17] It is a "practice ... something we *do* rather than *have* [emphasis in original]".[18] Their process of engaging in active hope "involves three key steps" that include: firstly seeing reality clearly, secondly deciding what it is "we hope for in terms of the direction we'd like to see things move in or the values we'd like to see expressed" and finally taking "steps to move ourselves or our situation in that direction".[19] For them no optimism is required given that it is about intention; "we choose what we aim to bring about, act for, or express".[20]

This view of active hope resonated with us when we began to talk about how we saw the connection between hope and sustainability. What we liked most was their identification of the vital combination of looking at reality in relation to climate change, finding changes we'd like to see and then actively working toward them and doing all in relation to specific places that we or others inhabit. Through our dialogues we came to recognize that ultimately concepts of sustainability and hope are inseparable, and most easily emerge from becoming conscious of our own physical bodies and our hope to sustain them. However, in J's case she was not looking for any such embodied awareness but rather came to P's class merely "looking for the dictionary, cut and dry definition of sustainability." The idea that sustainability "wasn't one thing, it wasn't a book definition, it transcended across so many issues" hadn't occurred to her but once it did, "it became a way of life ... ".[21] In this manner, once J was able to grasp that sustainability, when looked at realistically, was seen as transcending across so many issues, including the sustaining of her own body as her living place, she was able to apply changes to her life or even, as she said, to make it her way of life. For example, from our dialogues we discussed insights and activities from the class that were done to reveal the reality of the entanglement and inseparability between our bodies and the air, water, earth around us.

P: The reason I invited the class to recognize social justice on one end and self-care on the other as both being parts of sustainability was to help see the body as a place and as a metaphor of the planet... knowing that we need air, water,... then why would this be any different for all life on the planet... Seeing those connections I believe can expand the scope of our compassion and activism.

J: Yes, I remember realizing if I took this breath for myself today now what can I do for others... that on a smaller scale gives me the strength to not give up...

P: And to see I took this breath because the world gave it to me and now can I give back... it begins with a gift and so we can ask how we can pass it on...

J: One thing that just come to me is how you promoted self-care in relation to caring for the planet... I often wonder how the planet is still functioning, knowing that we are destroying it and yet that gives me hope... the plants are still growing, the soil is alive... I can get hope from that... that we have done so much damage and yet it is still a beautiful place.[22]

Along with discovering and simultaneously collectively creating for ourselves the insight into the inseparability of sustainability and hope, we also came to see halfway through our first dialogue that how we understand them, as individual concepts and as combined ones depend largely on our position-ality.[23] The issue of positionality, however, is not something discussed by Macy and Johnson, although whatever acts of active hope an individual or community are likely to *do* will, we realized, be directly linked to their positionality. For example, out of this topic emerged J's insight that, "For marginalized people like me, the American Dream has always been some-thing we can't actually or as easily attain so... we have a different under-standing of hope... for us the American Dream is something that we may want but that we also realize is something we may not actually attain".[24] This insight regarding the elusiveness of the American Dream in relation to issues of social inequality helped us to see that without the emphasis on sustain-ability being "just",[25] society could become merely a "green" version of the current one. These thoughts took us both further into a discussion on the connections between sustainability, social justice and hope.

P: So often mainstream definitions of sustainability exclude issues of equality. Like [our school] is supposedly the #1 sustainable campus because we've got Leadership in Energy and Environmental Design (LEED) certified buildings but if you look at racism or sexism or inequality on campus...

J: Or the price of tuition

P: Yes, that too...we are not doing so well...So why aren't those included in how we evaluate what is seen as sustainability...?

J: It is much easier to get a certification for a green building than to address racism and sexism on campus

P: yes, you're right.

J: That's something you can't get a certification for...

P: True. So it's really challenging to maintain hope when even the general definition of sustainability...doesn't include many of the things we hope for...even as we started off saying that sustainability and hope are inseparable,...yes, we hope for a reduction in CO2 but we should also hope for social justice, equality, an end to police brutality, violence against women...etc.

J: I just remembered in one of my forestry classes the professor gave us the book definition of sustainability, which was "managing something so it's there for the next generation". And that's all that I had to memorize.... Ok, got it, took a test, done, got an A. But then I took your class and found out that sustainability is a whole new way of looking at myself and at the world, which made me realize that the book definition that I was required to memorize, actually didn't cover much...sustainability is a way of life that encompasses everything, including hope...[26]

What becomes evident in this section of our dialogue is how our ideas built upon each other ending this section further emphasizing the inseparability of sustainability and hope. In fact, as Freire identifies when discussing the power of dialogue in *Pedagogy of the Oppressed*, "dialogue cannot exist without hope. Hope is rooted in men's incompletion, from which they move out in constant search—a search which can be carried out only in communion with others."[27] Our creation of "communion" through our dialogues adds to the recognition of hope as ultimately being about collective aspirations for the collective good, as opposed to a mere individual emotion. Additionally, the use of the term "communion" adds a deeper, more spiritual and intimate quality to the collective experience than that of community. And even though we didn't use the term "communion", our notion of heartfelt hope is about an intimate place-based communion with self and all life. Therefore, for us, hope in relationship to sustainability must include a sense of "communion"—with ourselves, other humans and with all life on Earth. In our discussion of widening the definition of sustainability to include the issues of social justice or what Agyeman refers to as "just sustainability"[28] we recognized that achieving it becomes all the more challenging. As J observes, "It is much easier to get a certification for a green building than to try and address racism, or sexism".[29] When concepts of sustainability are limited to, for example merely the book definition, as taught and memorized in J's first class, it does invite an attitude as described by her,—"Ok, got it, took a test, done, got an A" or the attitude we also discussed that if we have LEED certified buildings on campus then it becomes a "sustainable school". Such thinking links to what Freire calls in *Pedagogy of the Oppressed* "limit-situations", as opposed to what happens when, in this case, we widen the scope of sustainability, hence hope, to include the possibility and necessity of social justice. Yes, achieving it is more challenging but in its quality of being what Freire calls the "untested feasibility", as in "the future which we have yet to create by transforming today, the present reality", it can take on a more engrossing quality, especially *if* we " . . . feel the call to act, to mobilize".[30] We have added this "*if*" to recognize that for many students, teachers and others confronted with the present reality of climate change, the line between feeling "the call to act, to mobilize"[31] as in feeling hopeful, as opposed to feeling hopeless or despair is very thin,[32] especially if the class is not grounded in the physical realities of our bodies as places and the surrounding social and natural places that sustain them.

When teachers engage critical place-based pedagogy, that also involves a "pedagogy of care that attends to our relationships near and far"[33] the threat of despair is held back as students are constantly invited to both question the status quo while also "mak[ing] themselves available to others and to possibility",[34] beginning with the possibility of their own, and collective, transformation/s.

A Pedagogy of Hope Within Our Place-based Classroom Community

As mentioned above Gruenewald argues for the integration between critical and place-based pedagogy. To this end he states that "despite clear areas of overlap between critical pedagogy and place-based education (such as the importance of situated context and the goal of social trans-formation) significant strands exist within each tradition that do not always recognize the potential contributions of the other".[35] In his dis-cussion of critical pedagogy, Gruenewald highlights the work of Henry Giroux and notes a trend that overlooks "...the fact that human culture has been, is, and always will be nested in ecological systems".[36] We also recognize this deficit, however we found Giroux's conception of "edu-cated hope" influential in developing our place-based conception of heart-felt hope which, as Gruenewald terms it, seeks "the best of both worlds".

Giroux's educated hope is understood as "a subversive force when it pluralizes politics by opening up a space for dissent, making authority accountable, and becoming an activating presence in promoting social transformation."[37] Additionally, as a subversive force:

> Educated hope...should provide a link, however transient, provisional, and contextual, between vision and critique on the one hand, and engagement and transformation on the other. That is, for hope to be consequential it has to be grounded in a project that has some hold on the present. Hope becomes meaningful to the degree that it identifies agencies and processes, offers alternatives to an age of profound pessimism, reclaims an ethic of compassion and justice, and struggles for those institutions in which equal-ity, freedom, and justice flourish as part of the ongoing struggle for a global democracy.[38]

Educated hope in being "grounded in a project that has some hold on the present" links well with the place-based pedagogy practiced in our class. As stated, never before have educators needed to traverse this "link" between "vision and critique on the one hand and engagement and transformation on the other"[39] than those who attempt to address climate change. This drastic context certainly provides educators with ample opportunity to invite students to "tap" what Giroux refers to as their "hidden utopian desires", which invite a questioning of "human possibi-lities"[40] similar to Freire's "untested feasibility".[41]

However, Giroux and other critical theorists distinguish their "peda-gogy of critical hope" from that of Freire's in that they resist shaping such future human possibilities for students, whereas Freire asserts that at times "educators [should] have the courage to take responsibility for the job of showing the way'.[42] Thus, the distinction in approaches focuses on the extent that educators emphasize the journey by "creating spaces of possibility" (Webb, 2013, p. 403), as opposed to identifying and naming a destination. But what if when it comes to critically teaching in a place-based way about the possibilities for sustainability, an individual's intimate learning journey and their potential destination are inseparable, thereby dissolving this distinction? It is this proposed inseparability that is key to our notion of "heartfelt hope".

In reflecting back on our class and in discussing her experience of learning about the problems linked with climate change, J identified that at the same time "you also gave us tools to look within ourselves, and that was very necessary to invite us to ask 'what am I doing /what are we doing?'...and keeping that balance between problem and solution".[43] P then picked up on her use of the term "tool" and added that for her the tools she offered were about;

> finding out "who am I'"...it's not like the tools are separate but rather they are a means to look inward and find out "who am I" what do I care about...while also recognizing that as a physical being I need air, I need food, I need water...I care about my life, I care about my body, that my body is my primary place and therefore I must care about this topic...and as I care about myself then I find connection with the person next to me in the class, or in the rest of my life or around the world...or with all living beings.[44]

What is significant here is that for P the pathway for students to reclaim, as Giroux states, "an ethic of compassion and justice, and struggles for those institutions in which equality, freedom, and justice flourish as part of the ongoing struggle for a global democracy"[45] began by inviting them to go within, and to situate themselves within the place of their physical bodies and from there to initially experience, and to also share in, the classroom-based intimacy practices that could then be expanded upon into their larger lives if they so choose. These classroom-based intimacy place-based practices brought a critical lens to the macro and micro levels of self and society and included, but were not limited to meditation (individual and collective both inside the classroom and outside), journaling (individual shared with teacher and done both inside the classroom and outside), written work sharing in class, peer to peer deep listening, group activities (such as problem mapping, impromptu theater, poetry, in-depth text analysis, general assemblies,...etc.) all of which had the intention of inviting students to simultaneously experience the journey and the destination of self-awareness and from there to experience the possibilities of a *just* sustainable society. As J observes;

> I remember when you asked us "why is it ok that things are the way they are? [creating climate change and inequality]" and I remember thinking "that's just the way things are, that's life" and you proposed that this wasn't the case...and invited us to look at the timeline of the earth and how things haven't always been the way we see them. This got me questioning "why don't I want to connect with the person next to me?" and I remember you telling us to try and be present, to be here in the room...and I remember at first thinking "why do I need to be present?" but then I came to realize that that was at the center of a lot of my issues..of.me not actually caring what was going on in the moment where I was...so to ask "why things are the way they are"...you have to be conscious to even think of that question... I do that a lot more now that I have the tools.[46]

Here J provides an example of what we consider educated hope in practice, in that she makes connections from critically questioning the present, "the way things are", to seeing room for other possibilities by again questioning both, why society is the way it is, and, why she is the way she is, as well. Additionally, she offers feedback to P's affirmed attempt to get students to find "their tool box within" and to use it as a point of internal intimacy and as the site for expanding her scope of intimacy, hence compassion. As Giroux states "educated hope accentuates the notion that politics is played out not only on a terrain of imagination and desire, but is also grounded in relations of power mediated through the outcome of situated struggles dedicated to creating the conditions and capacities for people to become critically engaged political agents".[47] However, what we seek to add is that such a politics of "grounding", "struggles", "capacities", "engagement" and "agency" *must* be rooted within an individual's heart, hence body, *place* and not just their mind. In this manner we are recognizing the intimate overlap between love and hope in that as Jacobs observes, "Love helps renew hope and invites us to enter into communion"[48] including, as we observed above, a place-based communion with all life, hence the Earth, in mutually respectful and beneficial ways.

Our understanding of heartfelt hope begins with becoming aware of our bodies as places, hence *as* nature. Additionally, given that our bodies are the stages upon which our social identities have been constructed, as in such attributes as our race, sex, gender, ability...etc., then when we connect with them first and foremost as physical entities that are entirely dependent on air, potable water and edible food we can begin to become aware of these needs and how our access to these needs is affected positively and/or negatively by our positionalities within a given social and physical place. From recognizing how we and others have been socially constructed we can then begin the personal and social healing work that is needed to forge new engagements based on justice and equality. In other words, by critically and intimately recognizing the ongoing dance between our physical bodies and our social bodies, as well as recognizing that of other physical and social bodies, then we can create the shared space to genuinely feel hope; a hope rooted in our physical and socio-emotional hearts, hence heartfelt. In grounding our hope both in our physical bodies, as our first place of being and as in our need to breathe air as provided by the Earth, and in our needs for socio-emotional intimacy, as provided by communion with ourselves, other humans and other living beings, we propose that this is how the division between the journey and the destination, both on the part of students and teachers dissolves. Yes, an educator can attempt to create "spaces of possibility"[49] but the real "space of possibility" emerges within a student the moment it becomes *a place* felt within them and experienced as a new level of self-awareness that recognizes the journey and the destination as inseparable.

We observed the overlapping of the journey and the destination when J spoke about her experiences in P's class. She stated:

> I always remember telling myself to take in bits and pieces of knowledge so that I wouldn't' get overwhelmed or give up, but I definitely feel that I left your class with a stronger sense of self...I am now able to question whether or not I am living in the present moment, for example by waking up and breathing...which I usually don't do. I just wake up and go. I am usually stressed and anxious but now I am able to tap into the present moment and ask myself "why am I so stressed?", "why am I living my life this way?" I left your class with a more positive sense of self...yeah and feeling more hope.[50]

This observation of J's that she left class with a "more positive sense of self" and "more hope" illustrates the connection. Likewise, taking the positionality of J into account, P brought it back to her identification as a forester and to P's pre-existing awareness that through the class J had developed a deeper connection with trees. She stated "I think that this positive sense of self has enabled you to connect with trees in ways you have not done before".[51] To this J replied:

> It's weird that you say that because I always felt a connection to trees . . . and I've never really fit into my family because of that connection but once I realized that there is life all around us, it was hard for me to be so self-centered, and just focus on my little world . . . This allowed me to see the deeper meaning in my connection to trees . . . yeah, it was amazing for me to be alive for so long and not realize the depth in my connection to trees, and all life on Earth prior to this class.[52]

J's realization that she and all of us are connected to trees, regardless of how we have been socialized, is for us a perfect example of heartfelt hope. We say this because again our definition of heartfelt hope is not only about intimacy with ourselves, as in a more positive sense of self, nor is it just about hope as in her feeling more hopeful but rather it is a combination of both that incorporates a more intimate, aware and vital connection to the living being and places around us.

CONCLUSION—CREATING PLACE-BASED COMMUNITY THROUGH HEARTFELT HOPE

Through having shared a class together that then led to having and analyzing these dialogues, shaped by our differing positionalities we engaged in transitional border crossing. As a result of this shifting of positions both within ourselves and in relation to each other, we have inspired in ourselves, and potentially in others, a heartfelt hope. By this we mean that we have conceptualized a form of hope that opens up the visceral possibility for us to recognize how we are linked beyond our own perceived limitations into the very matter of life. In this way, returning to Barad's work, we see our heartfelt hope as being directly connected to her concept of "intra-action", which "recognizes that distinct agencies do not precede, but rather emerge through, their intra-action".[53] However, she goes on to qualify that "'distinct' agencies are only distinct in relation to their mutual entanglement: they don't exist as individual elements".[54] Likewise, in our individual and shared journeys we have not been able to make clear distinctions between where our ideas, insights, inspirations and feelings came from, in that we have been influenced by readings, by classroom exchanges and activities, by individual reflections and shared dialogues since in all the ultimate objective has been self-and-other discovery. This observation of our intra-action is apparent in our second dialogue, a section of which we quote in order to further show the "entanglement".

J: ...in most classes the teacher is not asking you to find yourself. So if I'm writing a journal, I'm finding myself, you're reading that journal which in itself is like a new connection that wasn't there before
P: a new form of intimacy...
J: For me, that helped with my learning. At times I really struggled in your class because it affected me so much...So learning in your class was a more holistic experience. I wasn't going through it by myself. Even opening myself up to that trust and friendship and that relationship with you, helped me in the end.[55]

In *Teaching Community* hook's speaks about how the topic of love in the classroom is taboo, even as our hearts understand, that love "is the foundation on which every learning community can be created....Love will always move us away from domination in all its forms. Love will always challenge and change us. This is the heart of the matter".[56] An example of love challenging and changing us is when J discussed how her intimacy with P "helped her in the end"[57] to stay with difficulties involved in further discovering her inner landscapes, including her love of trees. As J remarked, "you'd think that the thing that is within would be the easiest to discover".[58] But then P replied "it goes back to the Zen saying that talks about how teaching is easy, listening is easy, what's difficult is to find what's within yourself and to use that to create your life".[59] To which then J realized "That's probably connected to why I reacted to the class the way I did. Because I knew within me there was a connection to trees".[60] She just had to go within to find it and from there she also found the trees—where we, to quote Gruenewald again, "challeng[ed] each other to read the texts of our own lives" in relation to the cultural, political, economic and ecological places that we have and do inhabit.

Originally sustainability was just something she had to memorize, but then with a different pedagogical approach based on critical, place-based pedagogy it became a potential way of life that could be accessed through the inner tools of self-discovery. Another insight we had while listening to our first dialogue was that from the perspective of heartfelt hope, regardless of anyone's given positionality, we are all *always* in relationship with place, with the world, with nature, with our bodies and so this seems to be the grounding point from which we can continually return in order to reinvigorate and reinvent all that which is an "untested feasibility".[61] Freire's concept is more vital now than ever given that globally we are engaging in the "destruction of life in dimensions that confronted no previous generation in recorded history..."[62]. Still, as Macy urges, "We can choose life" knowing that "we can meet our needs without destroying our life-support system" [63] despite what the existing society continually tries to tell us.

By choosing life, those of us who teach/learn about climate change and sustainability must do so in the ways that allow all of us to discover ourselves through a connection to ourselves as a place. As P stated, "I try to offer students the real learning by saying, 'discover yourself. That's where you will find the most joy, the most value, the most connection and the most hope because that is unlimited. And that cannot ever be controlled by anybody else but yourself".[64] To this J replied, "That was the most interesting part...the fact that you were the first teacher that asked me to do that...I have never had a class that made me learn about myself".[65]

In teaching/learning about sustainability in ways that invite heartfelt hope not only must we see the "mess we are in without going crazy" (Macy and Johnson, 2012), but we must also see our own inner mess and use that as the material for our transformation, so that like us, we can move from critical, place-based pedagogy to living its tenants of practice in our everyday lives. For in continuing to share together in ever more intimate ways through our dialogues we had co-created a community of place for ourselves rooted in our heartfelt hope that was, and remains individually and collectively our journey and our destination.

NOTES

1. D.T Suzuki, *Zen and Japanese Culture* (Bolingen Foundation Series LXIV, New York: Pantheon Books, 1959).
2. Paulo Freire, *Pedagogy of the Oppressed* (20th edition, New York: Continuum International Publishing Group, 1996), 8.
3. Joanna Macy & Chris Johnson, *Active Hope: How to Face the Mess We're in without Going Crazy* (California: New World Library, 2012). Henry Giroux. "When Hope Is Subversive", *Tikkun*, 19.6 (2004): 38–39; Henry Giroux, "Utopian Thinking in Dangerous Times: Critical Pedagogy and the Project of Educated Hope." In *Utopian Pedagogy: Radical Experiments against*

Neoliberal Globalization edited by Mark Cote, Richard J.F. Day &, Greig de Peuter (Toronto: University of Toronto, 2007).

4. David A. Gruenewald, "The Best of Both Worlds: A Critical Pedagogy of Place," *EducationalResearcher*, 32.4 (2003).

5. bell hooks, *Teaching Community: A Pedagogy of Hope* (New York: Routledge, 2003), 106 & 111.

6. Karen Barad, *Meeting the Universe Halfway: Quantum Physics and the Entanglement of Matter and Meaning* (Durham: Duke University Press, 2007).

7. Goralnik, L., Tracy Dobson and Paul Nelson, "Place-Based Care Ethics: A Field Philosophy Pedagogy." *Canadian Journal of Environmental Education*, 19(2014): 187.

8. Alison Hope Alkon and Julian Agyeman, eds. *Cultivating Food Justice: Race, Class, and Sustainability*, (Cambridge, MA: The MIT Press, 2011).

9. hooks, *Teaching Community*, 106.

10. hooks, *Teaching Community*, 106.

11. Darren Webb, "Pedagogies of Hope", *Studies in Philosophy of Education*, 32.1 (2013): 397–414; Freire, *Pedagogy* 1996; Paola Freire, *Pedagogy of Hope: Reliving Pedagogy of the Oppressed* (New York: Continuum International Publishing Group, 2004); Henry Giroux, "Educated Hope in an Age of Privatized Visions", *Cultural Studies-Critical Methodologies*, 2.1 (2002): 93–112; Henry Giroux, *Stealing Innocence: Youth, Corporate Power, and the Politics of Culture* (New York: St. Martin's Press, 2000); Dale Jacobs, "What's Hope Got to do with It? Toward a Theory of Hope and Pedagogy". *Journal of Composition Theory*, 25.1 (2005): 783–802.

12. David A. Gruenewald, "The Best of Both Worlds: A Critical Pedagogy of Place," *Educational Researcher*, 32.4 (2003): 10.

13. Macy & Johnson, *Active*, 1.

14. Macy & Johnson, *Active*, 2.

15. Macy & Johnson, *Active*, 2.

16. Macy & Johnson, *Active*, 2.

17. Macy & Johnson, *Active*, 3.

18. Macy & Johnson, *Active*, 3.

19. Macy & Johnson, *Active*, 3.

20. Macy & Johnson, *Active*, 3.

21. J and P First Dialogue, 2015.

22. J and P First Dialogue, 2015.

23. Alkon & Agyeman, eds. *Cultivating Food Justice*, 2011.

24. J and P First Dialogue, 2015.

25. Julian Agyeman, Robert Doyle, & Bill Evans. *Just Sustainabilities: Development in an Unequal World* (Boston: MIT Press, 2003).

26. J and P First Dialogue, 2015.

27. Freire, *Pedagogy* 1996, 72.
28. Agyeman, *Just Sustainabilities,* 2003.
29. J and P First Dialogue, 2015.
30. Ira Shor & Paulo Freire, *Pedagogy for Liberation: Dialogues on Transforming Education* (New York: Bergin and Garvey, 1987), 153; Kate Ronald & Hephzibah Roskelly, "Untested Feasibility: Imagining the Pragmatic Possibility of Paulo Freire", *College English,* 63.5 (2001): 616.
31. Ronald & Roskelly. "Untested Feasibility", 616.
32. See Dale Jacobs, "What's Hope Got to do with It? Toward a Theory of Hope and Pedagogy". *Journal of Composition Theory,* 25.1, (2005).
33. Lizzy Goralnik, Tracy Dobson & Paul Nelson, "Place-Based Care Ethics: A Field Philosophy Pedagogy." *Canadian Journal of Environmental Education,* 19(2014): 193.
34. Jacobs, "What's Hope", 793.
35. Gruenewald, "The Best of Both Worlds", 4.
36. Gruenewald, "The Best of Both Worlds", 4.
37. Henry Giroux, "When Hope is Subversive", *Tikkun,* 19.6 (2004): 38–39.
38. Giroux, "When Hope", 39.
39. Giroux, "When Hope", 39.
40. Quoted in Webb "Pedagogies of Hope", 403.
41. Paulo Freire, *Pedagogy of the Oppressed* (New York: Continuum International Publishing Group, 1970): 83.
42. Freire quoted in Webb, "Pedagogies of Hope", 403.
43. J and P First Dialogue, 2015.
44. J and P First Dialogue, 2015.
45. Giroux, "When Hope", 39.
46. J and P First Dialogue, 2015.
47. Henry Giroux, "Educated Hope in an Age of Privatized Visions", *Cultural Studies-Critical Methodologies,* 2.1, (2002): 103.
48. Jacobs, "What's Hope", 796.
49. Webb "Pedagogies of Hope", 403.
50. J and P First Dialogue, 2015.
51. J and P First Dialogue, 2015.
52. J and P First Dialogue, 2015.
53. Karen Barad, *Meeting the Universe Halfway: Quantum Physics and the Entanglement of Matter and Meaning* (Durham: Duke University Press, 2007), 33.
54. Barad, *Meeting the Universe,* 33.
55. J and P First Dialogue, 2015.
56. hooks, *Teaching Community,* 137.
57. J and P Second Dialogue, 2015.
58. J and P Second Dialogue, 2015.

59. J and P Second Dialogue, 2015.
60. J and P Second Dialogue, 2015.
61. Freire, *Pedagogy of the Oppressed*, 1970, 83.
62. Macy, Joanna & Molly Y. Brown, *Coming Back to Life: Practices to Reconnect Our Lives, Our World*. (New York: New Society, 1998), 15.
63. Macy, *Coming Back, 16*.
64. J and P Second Dialogue, 2015.
65. J and P Second Dialogue, 2015.

DIALOGUES

Dialogue 1 of Jasmine Brown and Phoebe Godfrey Recorded June 10, 2015
Dialogue 2 of Jasmine Brown and Phoebe Godfrey, Recorded June 10, 2015

BIBLIOGRAPHY

Agyeman, Julian, Robert Doyle, and Bill Evans. *Just Sustainabilities: Development in an Unequal World*. Boston: MIT Press, 2003.
Alkon, Alison Hope, and Julian Agyeman (eds.). *Cultivating Food Justice: Race, Class, and Sustainability*. Cambridge, MA: The MIT Press, 2011.
Barad, Karen. *Meeting the Universe Halfway: Quantum Physics and the Entanglement of Matter and Meaning*. Durham: Duke University Press, 2007.
Freire, Paulo. *Pedagogy of the Oppressed*. New York: Continuum International Publishing Group, 1970.
Freire, Paulo. *Pedagogy of the Oppressed*. 20th edition. New York: Continuum International Publishing Group, 1996.
Freire, Paulo. *Pedagogy of Hope: Reliving Pedagogy of the Oppressed*. New York: Continuum International Publishing Group, 2004.
Giroux, Henry. *Stealing Innocence: Youth, Corporate Power, and the Politics of Culture*. New York: St. Martin's Press, 2000.
Giroux, Henry. "Educated Hope in an Age of Privatized Visions." *Cultural Studies-Critical Methodologies* 2.1 (2002): 93–112.
Giroux, Henry. "When Hope Is Subversive." *Tikkun* 19.6 (2004): 38–39.
Giroux, Henry. "Utopian Thinking in Dangerous Times: Critical Pedagogy and the Project of Educated Hope." In *Utopian Pedagogy: Radical Experiments against Neoliberal Globalization*, Mark Cote, Richard J.F. Day, and Greig De Peuter eds. Toronto: University of Toronto, 2007.
Godfrey, Phoebe.. "Teaching Society and Climate Change: Creating an 'Earth Community' in the College Classroom by Embodying Connectedness through Love." *Journal of Sustainability Education* 9.1 (2015). Accessed August 30,

2016. http://www.jsedimensions.org/wordpress/content/teaching-society-and-climate-change-creating-an-earth-community-in-the-college-classroom-byembodying-connectedness-through love_2015_03/#http://www.jsedimensions.org/wordpress/content/teaching-socie>).

Goralnik, Lizzy, Tracy Dobson, and Paul Nelson. "Place-Based Care Ethics: A Field Philosophy Pedagogy." *Canadian Journal of Environmental Education* 19 (2014): 180–196.

Gruenewald, David. "The Best of Both Worlds: A Critical Pedagogy of Place." *Educational Researcher* 32.4 (2003): 3–12.

hooks, bell. *Teaching to Transgress: Education as the Practice of Freedom*. New York: Routledge, 1994.

hooks, bell. *Teaching Community: A Pedagogy of Hope*. New York: Routledge, 2003.

Jacobs, Dale. "What's Hope Got to Do with It? Toward a Theory of Hope and Pedagogy." *Journal of Composition Theory* 25.1 (2005): 783–802.

Kate, Ronald, and Hephzibah Roskelly. "Untested Feasibility: Imagining the Pragmatic Possibility of Paulo Freire." *College English* 63.5 (2001): 612–632.

Macy, Joanna. *World as Lover, World as Self: Seeing the World as Oneself-or as a Lover Transforms Ordinary Reality and Provides a Greater Sense of Purpose*, (1993). Accessed August 10, 2016. http://www.context.org/iclib/ic34/macy/

Macy, Joanna, and Molly Y. Brown. *Coming Back to Life: Practices to Reconnect Our Lives, Our World*. New York: New Society, 1998.

Macy, Joanna, and Chris Johnson. *Active Hope: How to Face the Mess We're in without Going Crazy*. California: New World Library, 2012.

Shor, Ira, and Paulo Freire. *Pedagogy for Liberation: Dialogues on Transforming Education*. New York: Bergin and Garvey, 1987.

Suzuki, D.T. *Zen and Japanese Culture*, Bolingen Foundation Series LXIV. New York: Pantheon Books, 1959.

Webb, Darren.. "Pedagogies of Hope." *Studies in Philosophy of Education* 32.1 (2013): 397–414.

INDEX

© The Author(s) 2017   209
D. Shannon, J. Galle (eds.), *Interdisciplinary Approaches to Pedagogy and Place-Based Education*, DOI 10.1007/978-3-319-50621-0

CPI Antony Rowe
Eastbourne, UK
December 03, 2019